Richer Fare for the Christian People

Gail Ramshaw

RICHER FARE

FOR THE
CHRISTIAN PEOPLE

Reflections on the Sunday Readings
of Cycles A, B, C

PUEBLO PUBLISHING COMPANY

New York

Design: Frank Kacmarcik

The Editor and Publisher gratefully acknowledge permission to reprint portions of the copyrighted works listed in the Acknowledgments section.

ISBN: 0-925127-02-7

Printed in the United States of America

Contents

Introduction

"The riches of the Bible are to be opened up more lavishly, so that richer fare may be provided for the faithful at the table of God's word."

Constitution on the Sacred Liturgy II, 51

With this volume, Pueblo Publishing Company presents an anthology of reflections on the Sunday readings as appointed in the Roman Catholic, Episcopal, and Lutheran lectionaries, cycles A, B, and C. Like many other such collections past and present, this anthology enriches our weekly reception of God's word by keeping the great Christian tradition on the table.

Inspired by *The Sunday Sermons of the Great Fathers*, the fine but obsolete work of M. F. Toal, this volume has assembled reflections on the lectionaries' appointed gospels from sources throughout the church—from patristic homilies, early mystagogical catecheses, spiritual writings of the Middle Ages, mystical reveries, theologians of the Reformation traditions, and contemporary Christian meditations and sermons. Some meditations are selected from a homily on the gospel itself; others have a more oblique connection. This collection offers great diversity—we hear from fathers and feminists, from nuns and novelists, from treatises and diaries, from essays and prayers—because a feast is known for its variety of foods. It is hoped that these meditations from past and present will enlarge our understanding of the readings, supplement the sermons we hear, assist preachers in their preparation, and inspire all who teach in the church with biblical interpretations beyond their own imagination.

To keep the past spiritually nourishing in the present, we must judiciously select the best from much that is antiquated and even offensive. Thus these excerpts have been edited to delete that which has little contemporary relevance. Often, ellipses have not been used, in order to keep the selections visually clean. In some cases, translation, punctuation, and other stylistic matters have been modernized. The endnotes provide the source of the selections and a brief annotation on each author.

With gratitude to a host of editors and compilers whose work has made this anthology possible, we give *Richer Fare* to you, a banquet that is already yours, but one we too seldom partake of. May this wealth from Christians throughout the ages invite us to deeper truths about God and ourselves as we gather around the bread and wine.

Gail Ramshaw, editor
St. Ambrose Day, 1988

SUNDAYS AND MAJOR HOLY DAYS

CYCLE A

R E L FIRST SUNDAY OF ADVENT

Give me the grace, good Lord:

To set the world at naught, to set the mind firmly on you and not to hang upon the words of men's mouths; to be content to be solitary; not to long for worldly pleasures; little by little, utterly to cast off the world and rid my mind of all its business; not to long to hear of earthly things, but that the hearing of worldly fancies may be displeasing to me; gladly to be thinking of God, piteously to call for his help; to lean into the comfort of God; busily to labor to love him. To know my own vileness and wretchedness; to humble myself under the mighty hand of God; to bewail my sins and, for the purging of them, patiently to suffer adversity.

Gladly to bear my purgatory here; to be joyful in tribulations; to walk the narrow way that leads to life. To have the last thing in remembrance; to have ever before my eyes my death that is ever at hand; to make death no stranger to me; to foresee and consider the everlasting fire of hell; to pray for pardon before the judge comes.

To have continually in mind the passion that Christ suffered for me; for his benefits unceasingly to give him thanks. To buy the time again that I have lost. To abstain from vain conversations, to shun foolish mirth and gladness; to cut off unnecessary recreations. Of worldly substance, friends, liberty, life and all, to set the loss at naught, for the winning of Christ. To think my worst enemies my best friends, for the brethren of Joseph could never have done him so much good with their love and favor as they did him with their malice and hatred.

These minds are more to be desired of every person than all the treasures of all the princes and kings, Christian and heathen, were it gathered and laid together all in one heap. Amen.

Thomas More

R E L SECOND SUNDAY OF ADVENT

Already is there on you the savior of blessedness, O ye who are soon to be enlightened: already are you gathering spiritual flowers, to weave heavenly crowns withal: already hath the fragrance of the Holy Ghost refreshed you: already are you at the entrance-hall of the King's house: may you be brought into it by the King! For now the blossoms of the trees have budded; may but the fruit likewise be perfected! Thus far, your names have been given in, and the roll-call made for service; there are the torches of the bridal train, and the longings after heavenly citizenship, and a good purpose, and a hope attendant. Even now, I beseech you, lift up the eye of your understanding; imagine the angelic choirs, and God the Lord of all sitting, and his only-begotten Son sitting with him on his right hand, and the Spirit with them present, and thrones and dominions doing service, and each man and woman among you receiving salvation. Even now let your ears ring with the sound: long for that glorious sound, which after your salvation the angels shall chant over you, "Blessed are they whose iniquities have been forgiven, and whose sins have been covered"; when, like stars of the church, you shall enter in it, bright in the outward being and radiant in your souls.

Great indeed is the baptism which is offered you. It is a ransom to captives; the remission of offenses; the death of sin; the regeneration of the soul; the garment of light; the holy seal indissoluble; the chariot to heaven; the luxury of paradise; a procuring of the kingdom; the gift of adoption. But a serpent by the wayside is watching the passengers; beware lest he bite thee with unbelief; he sees so many receiving salvation, and seeks to devour some of them. Thou art going to the Father of Spirits, but thou art going past that serpent; how then must thou pass him? Have thy feet shod with the preparation of the gospel of peace; that even if he bite, he may not hurt thee. Have faith indwelling, strong hope, a sandal of power, wherewith to pass the enemy, and enter the presence of thy Lord. Prepare thine own heart to receive doctrine, to have fellowship in holy mysteries. Pray more often, that God may make thee worthy of the heavenly and immortal mysteries. Let neither day be without its work, nor night, but when sleep fails thine eyes, at once abandon thy thought to prayer. And shouldest thou find any shameful, any base imagination rising, reflect upon God's judgment, to remind thee of salvation; give up thy mind to sacred studies, that it may forget wicked things. If thou find anyone saying to thee, And art thou going to the water, to be baptized in it? what, hath not the city baths of late? Be sure that it is the dragon of the sea, who is plotting this against thee; give no heed to the lips of him who speaketh, but to God who worketh. Guard thine own soul, that thou mayest escape the snare, that abiding in hope, thou mayest become the heir of everlasting salvation.

Cyril of Jerusalen

R E L THIRD SUNDAY OF ADVENT

When the Lord had revealed himself in wonders, namely, in the blind seeing, the lame walking, in lepers being cleansed, the deaf hearing, the dumb speaking, in the dead rising again, and in the preaching of the gospel to the poor, he says: "Blessed are they who take no offense at me." Was there anything in what Christ had done which might scandalize John? Far from it. For in the whole course of his mission and teaching he had had nothing to say opposed to him. But the force and significance of the preceding sentence must be carefully dwelt on; on that, namely, which is preached to the poor; that is, they who have laid down their lives, who have taken up the cross and followed after, who have become humble in spirit, for these a kingdom is prepared in heaven. Therefore, because this universality of suffering was to be fulfilled in Christ himself, and because his cross would become a stumbling-block to many, he now declares that they are blessed to whom his cross, his death, and burial, will offer no trial of faith. So he makes clear that of which already, earlier, John has himself warned them, saying that blessed are they in whom there would be nothing of scandal concerning himself. For it was through fear of this that John had sent his disciples, so that they might see and hear Christ.

Hilary

R E L FOURTH SUNDAY OF ADVENT

The name that Joseph is to give the child is Jesus, "because he will save his people from their sins." The sequence in chapter 2 of Matthew will show how this New Testament Joseph, who receives revelation in dreams and goes to Egypt to save the infant, is reliving the great epic of the Old Testament figure named Joseph who interpreted dreams and went to Egypt, thereby saving Israel/Jacob. That Genesis epic is continued in Exodus by the story of Moses: he escaped as an infant from the wicked pharaoh who killed male children and then returned after those who sought his life were dead. Similarly, with Joseph's help, the infant Jesus escapes the wicked Herod who killed male children and is brought back to Palestine after those who sought his life are dead. The name Jesus fits into this parallelism between the Matthew story of Joseph and the Old Testament story of Joseph and Moses, for Moses' successor who completed his work by bringing Israel back to the Promised Land was also named Jesus (Joshua). Both Moses and Jesus are saviors of their people, but in Matthew's understanding the people of Jesus would be not only the Jewish descendants of Moses' Hebrews but all the nations. The bondage is no longer that of Egypt but of sin.

Matthew has now told us that the child in Mary's womb will through Joseph's naming be Son of David and the savior of his people. Yet there is a greater identity which Joseph must accept, but to which he cannot contribute: the child will be Emmanuel, "God with us," because Mary has conceived him through the Holy Spirit. Matthew has nothing of Luke's elaboration of this element in the annunciation to Mary. Yet the fact that the two different accounts mention conception through the Holy Spirit rather than through male generation suggests that this is a most ancient phrasing, antedating both evangelists and coming from Christian tradition. The New Testament indicates clearly that the awesome, creative, life-giving power of the Spirit was associated with the resurrection of Jesus: God's Son who was enabled to conquer death dispenses the Spirit enabling believers to become God's children. In the gospels the Spirit is primarily associated with the baptism of Jesus as he begins his public life of proclaiming the kingdom. But in the two infancy narratives it is related to the very beginning of Jesus' life: he is so much God's Son that God is his only Father, not through sexual intervention but through the same power of the Spirit that brought life into the world at the creation. If the genealogy of Matthew takes the story of Jesus back to Abraham, implicitly the virginal conception finds an analogy further back with Adam, the other human being whose life did not from human generation.

Raymond E. Brown

When now they were come to Bethlehem, the evangelist says that they were, of all, the lowest and the most despised, and must make way for everyone until they were shoved into a stable to make a common lodging and table with the cattle, while many cutthroats lounged like lords in the inn. They did not recognize what God was doing in the stable. With all their eating, drinking, and finery, God left them empty, and this comfort and treasure was hidden from them. Oh, what a dark night it was in Bethlehem that this light should not have been seen. Thus God shows that he has no regard for what the world is and has and does. And the world shows that it does not know or consider what God is and has and does.

There are many of you in this congregation who think to yourselves: "If only I had been there! How quick I would have been to help the Baby! I would have washed his linen. How happy I would have been to go with the shepherds to see the Lord lying in the manger!" Yes, you would! You say that because you know how great Christ is, but if you had been there at that time you would have done no better than the people of Bethlehem. Childish and silly thoughts are these! Why don't you do it now? You have Christ in your neighbor. You ought to serve him, for what you do to your neighbor in need you do to the Lord Christ himself.

The birth was still more pitiable. No one regarded this young wife bringing forth her first-born. No one took her condition to heart. No one noticed that in a strange place she had not the very least thing needful in childbirth. There she was without preparation: no light, no fire, in the dead of night, in thick darkness. No one came to give the customary assistance. The guests swarming in the inn were carousing, and no one attended to this woman. I think myself if Joseph and Mary had realized that her time was so close she might perhaps have been left in Nazareth. And now think what she could use for swaddling clothes—some garment she could spare, perhaps her veil—certainly not Joseph's breeches which are now on exhibition at Aachen.

Behold Christ lying in the lap of his young mother, still a virgin.
What can be sweeter than the Babe, what more lovely than the
mother! What fairer than her youth! What more gracious than her
virginity! Look at the Child, knowing nothing. Yet all that is belongs to him, that your conscience should not fear but take comfort
in him. Doubt nothing. Watch him springing in the lap of the
maiden. Laugh with him. Look upon this Lord of Peace and your
spirit will be at peace. See how God invites you in many ways. He
places before you a Babe with whom you may take refuge. You cannot fear him, for nothing is more appealing to us than a babe. Are
you affrighted? Then come to him, lying in the lap of the fairest and
sweetest maid. You will see how great is the divine goodness,
which seeks above all else that you should not despair. Trust him!
Trust him! Here is the Child in whom is salvation. To me there is no
greater consolation given to mankind than this, that Christ became
human, a child, a babe, playing in the lap and at the breasts of his
most gracious mother. Who is there whom this sight would not
comfort? Now is overcome the power of sin, death, hell, conscience,
and guilt, if you come to this gurgling Babe and believe that he is
come, not to judge you, but to save.

Martin Luther

R CHRISTMAS MASS DURING THE DAY
E CHRISTMAS DAY III
L THE NATIVITY OF OUR LORD, 2

The events of his life, and his own divine powers, teach those who
can learn that he is true God, and his sufferings openly proclaim
him true man. For if he were not flesh, for what reason did Mary
bring him forth? And if he was not God, who then did Gabriel call
Lord?

If he was not flesh, who then lay in the manger? If he was not God,
to whom did the angels coming on earth give glory? If he was not a
man, who was wrapped in swaddling clothes? If he was not God,
whom then did the shepherds adore? If he was not a man, whom
did Joseph circumcize? And if he was not God, in whose honor did
a new star appear in the heavens? If he was not a man, whom did

Mary nourish at the breast? And if he were not God, to whom did the magi offer gifts?

If he was not a man, whom did Simeon take in his arms? And if he was not God, to whom did Simeon say, "Dismiss me in peace"? If he was not a man, whom did Joseph take and fly with him into Egypt? And if he was not God, in whom was the prophecy fulfilled, "Out of Egypt have I called my son"?

If he was not a man, whom did John baptize? And if he was not God, of whom did the Father from heaven say, "This is my son, the beloved one, with whom I am well pleased"? If he was not a man, who fasted and hungered in the desert? And if he was not God, to whom did the descending angels minister? If he was not a man, who was invited to the wedding feast at Cana of Galilee? And if he was not God, who changed the water into wine? If he was not a man, in whose hands were the loaves of bread placed? And if he were not God, who fed and filled from five barley loaves and two fishes the multitude in the desert, five thousand men, not counting the women and children? If he was not a man, who slept in the boat? And if he were not God, who was it rebuked the winds and the sea? If he was not a man, who sat by the well weary from the journey? And if he was not God, who gave the Samaritan woman the water of life? If he was not a man, who spat upon the earth, and made mud from the clay? And if he were not God, who caused eyes to see because of the clay? If he was not a man, who wept at the tomb of Lazarus? And if he were not God, who by his command alone called forth the four days dead?

If he was not a man, who was it sat upon as ass's colt? And if he were not God, before whom did the crowd march to give him glory? If he was not a man, who was beaten with blows? And if he were not God, who healed the ear which Peter had cut off, and who restored it to its place? If he was not a man, whose face was spat upon? And if he were not God, who breathed the Holy Spirit upon the faces of the apostles? If he was not a man, upon whose garments did the soldiers cast lots, dividing them amongst them? And if he were not God, for what reason did the sun grow dark above the cross? If he was not a man, whose hands were pierced by the nails? And if he were not God, how was the veil of the temple rent in two, and the rocks split asunder, and the graves opened? If he was not a man, who cried out; "My God, why have you forsaken me"? And if he were not God, who then hath said "Father, forgive them; for they know not what they do"? If he was not a man, who hung with thieves upon a cross? And if he were not God, for what cause did he say "Today you will be with me in Paradise"? If he was not a man, whose side was opened by a lance, and there came out blood and water? And if he were not God, by whose command did the dead that slept in their graves come forth?

If he was not a man, whom did the apostles behold in the upper room? And if he was not God, in what manner did he enter, the doors being closed? If he was not a man, in whose hand did Thomas feel the wounds of the nails and the lance? And if he was not God, to whom did Thomas cry out saying, "My Lord and my God"? If he was not a man, who ate food by the sea of Tiberias? And if he were not God, by whose command was the net filled with fishes?

If he was not a man, whom did the apostles and the angels see received into the heavens? If he was not God, to whom were the heavens opened, whom did the powers adore in fear and trembling? If he were not both God and man, then is our salvation a false thing. For which reason the chaste John, who leaned upon that burning breath, confirming the voices of the prophets, and discoursing of the divinity, teaches us in his gospel, saying; "In the beginning was the Word, and the Word was with God, and the Word was God. And the Word became flesh, and dwelt among us," taking flesh from the virgin Mary, and from her made man, which he was not, remaining God, which he was, that he might redeem the world.

Ephraem

R HOLY FAMILY

E SECOND SUNDAY AFTER CHRISTMAS

L FIRST SUNDAY AFTER CHRISTMAS

The magi came and went during the forty days before the presentation. Foiled by them, Herod resolved to destroy the babe and worked on the supposition that he would still be in Bethlehem. To be sure of catching him, he killed all the children under two years. Such acts of bloodshed were not new to Herod.

He had two sons by a beloved wife, and yet executed both them and her, so that the Emperor Augustus said that he would rather be Herod's sow than his son. Yet the people did not rebel because they wanted a king of the seed of David and not a foreigner. When, then, the word came that such a king had been born, Herod was terror-stricken. "This bodes no good," thought he, and he called the magi and told them to seek out the young child so that he also might worship him. When he was mocked by them, he said, "I will get him yet." All the children under two years were to be killed, not only in Bethlehem, but in the region round about.

Thus we see how the little baby Jesus, while still in the manger, filled the world with fear. Herod decided to cover the whole territory, lest the child escape him. He could plausibly argue that it was better to bereave a few hundred fathers and mothers of their children than to ruin the whole land. The failure of the wise men to report only confirmed his suspicion that some plot was afoot. If the common people got wind of it, they might readily rise, whereas if they saw prompt action on the part of the government, they would be restrained. Thus Herod and his men took the sword, and became frightful murderers even though they put out such a persuasive defense that everyone thought they were keeping the peace.

What happened then to Christ happens now to the gospel. But Herod failed. The angel warned Joseph in a dream, and God had already provided that the wise men should have made presents which well supplied the costs of the journey. Matthew says they gave gold, frankincense, and myrrh. It would have been a very considerable contribution, out of which Joseph and Mary could support themselves for some time, and perhaps the poor besides. The devil, Herod, and the priest meant to destroy Christ, but God provided the escape.

Before daylight the holy family were well beyond the Bethlehem town line. I doubt whether it was more than three miles from the village center.

The mothers in Bethlehem that evening fed porridge to their children, rocked the cradles, and went to sleep themselves without a care. The next morning there was not a household in Bethlehem in which there was not one child dead, or two or three. Then was there weeping because of this bloodhound, Rachel weeping for her children and refusing to be comforted.

The children were taken straight to heaven as blessed martyrs, but what about the parents who would not be comforted? They did not understand that this was a spiritual testing because the Lord was come into the world in order that he might lay down his life.

Martin Luther

R L SECOND SUNDAY AFTER CHRISTMAS
E FIRST SUNDAY AFTER CHRISTMAS

O my God, who love to show mercy, my creator,
shine ever more on me your inaccessible light,
so as to fill my heart with joy!
For your light is you, O my God.
If indeed you are called by many and different names,
still you are a unique being.

For he is one who has created all things,
Jesus Christ with the Father who is without beginning
and with the Holy Spirit also without beginning.
The Trinity, therefore, is one, indivisible in all aspects.
In the one are the three and in the three are the one,
or rather, the three are as one to me and the one again as three.
Thus, think of this mystery, adore and believe now and forever.
For this unique being that appears, shines forth,
is radiantly splendid,
is participating in, is communicating, is everything good.
For this reason we do not call him by one name only but by several.
He is light and peace and joy,
life, food and drink, clothing, a robe, a tent and a divine dwelling.
He is the east, the resurrection, repose and a bath,
fire, water, river, source of life and a flowing stream,
bread and wine, the new delight of believers,
the banquet, the pleasure which we enjoy in a mystical way,

sun, indeed, without any setting, star always shining,
lamp that burns inside the dwelling of the soul.

Symeon

R E L THE EPIPHANY OF OUR LORD

Can anyone say that the Lord is made known to us by signs of little
import, when the magi come and adore him, the angels serve him,
and the martyrs confess him? He comes forth from a womb, but he
shines like lightning from above; he lies in an earthly resting place,
but round about him is the brightness of heaven. The espoused has
brought forth; but a virgin has conceived. A wife has conceived; but
a virgin has given birth.

There is here another mystery of no small significance, which the
holy Matthew makes known. Now to this little child, whom you, if
you believe not, will consider as an ordinary child, the magi from
the East, following on so long a journey, now come, and falling
down they adore him, and call him King, and profess that he shall
rise from the dead; and this they do by offering him from their treasures, gold, frankincense, and myrrh.

What are these gifts, offered in true faith? Gold, as to a king; incense, as to God; myrrh, for the dead. For one is the token of the
dignity of a king; the other the symbol of the divine majesty; the
third is a service of honor to a body that is to be buried, which does
not destroy the body of the dead, but preserves it. We also who
read and hear these things, let us offer similar gifts from our treasures. For we have treasures in earthen vessels. If you consider that
which you are as being, not from you but from Christ, how much
more ought you not to consider that which you own as being, not
yours, but Christ's?

The magi therefore offer him gifts from their treasures. Do you desire to know how precious was their reward? The star is seen by
them; where Herod is it is not seen; it is seen again where Christ is,
and shows them the way. Therefore this star is the way, and the
way is Christ: for in the mystery of the incarnation Christ is a star.
For he himself is the bright and morning star. He shows us himself
therefore by his own light.

Ambrose

R L BAPTISM OF OUR LORD
E FIRST SUNDAY AFTER EPIPHANY

In the next place the hand is laid on us, invoking and inviting the Holy Spirit through benediction. This is derived from the old sacramental rite in which Jacob blessed his grandsons, born of Joseph, Ephraim and Manassen; with his hands laid on them and interchanged, and indeed so transversely slanted one over the other, that, by delineating Christ, they even portended the future benediction into Christ. Then, over our cleansed and blessed bodies willingly descends from the Father that Holiest Spirit. Over the waters of baptism, the Spirit reposes, who glided down on the Lord in the shape of the dove, in order that the nature of the Holy Spirit might be declared by means of the emblem of simplicity and innocence, because even in its bodily structure the dove is without gall. And accordingly Jesus says, "Be innocent as doves."

Even this is not without the supporting evidence of a preceding figure. For just as, after the waters of the deluge, by which the old iniquity was purged—after the baptism, so to say, of the world—a dove was the herald which announced to the earth the assuagement of celestial wrath, when it had been sent its way out of the ark, and had returned with the olive-branch, a sign which even among the nations is the foretoken of peace; so by the selfsame law of heavenly effect, to earth-that is, to our flesh—as it emerges from the font, after its old sins, flies the dove of the Holy Spirit, bringing us the peace of God, sent out from the heavens, where is the church, the typified ark.

Tertullian

R SECOND SUNDAY IN ORDINARY TIME
E L SECOND SUNDAY AFTER EPIPHANY

Here a people of godly race are born for heaven;
the Spirit givest them life in the fertile waters.
The church-mother, in these waves, bears her children
like virginal fruit she has conceived by the Holy Spirit.

Hope for the kingdom of heaven, you who are reborn in this
spring,

for those who are born but once have no share in the life of blessedness.
Here is to be found the source of life, which washes the whole universe,
which gushed from the wound of Christ.

Sinner, plunge into the sacred fountain to wash away your sin.
The water receives the old man,
and in his place makes the new man to rise.
You wish to become innocent: cleanse yourself in this bath,
whatever your burden may be, Adam's sin or your own.

There is no difference between those who are reborn: they are one,
in a single baptism, a single Spirit, a single faith.
Let no one be afraid of the number or the weight of his sins:
He who is born of this stream will be made holy.

inscription of Lateran baptistry

R THIRD SUNDAY IN ORDINARY TIME

E L THIRD SUNDAY AFTER EPIPHANY

Not long ago she was in prayer after matins and she began to look at her book as was her custom. Just as she was looking attentively, it seemed to her that the book opened. She had only seen the outside of it earlier.

Inside this book there appeared a delightful place, so large that the whole world is only a little thing in comparison. In this place there appeared a very glorious light that was divided into three parts.

From there came all possible good things. From there came the true wisdom by which all things are made and created. There was the power to whose will all things submit. From there came such great charm and such strengthening that the angels and the souls were so satiated that they could desire nothing more. Such a delightful odor came forth from there that it drew to itself all the virtues of the heavens. Such a great kindling of love came from there that all the loves of this world are but sorrow and bitterness in comparison with this love. From there comes a joy so great that there is no human heart capable of imagining it.

When the angels and the saints look on the great beauty of our Lord and feel his kindness and his very great charm, they feel so much joy that they cannot keep themselves from singing, but they make a completely new song, so sweet that it is a great melody. This sweet song passes through all the orders of angels and saints, from the first to the last. And this song has not quite ended when they sing another, completely new. This song will last without end.

The saints will be within their creator just as the fish are in the sea; they will drink all they want, without becoming tired and without lessening the amount of water. The saints will be just like this, for they will drink and eat the great sweetness of God. And the more they receive of this sweetness, the more will be their hunger for it. This sweetness cannot be decreased any more or less than can the water of the sea. For just as the waves all go toward the sea and all come back, just so the beauty and the sweetness of our Lord, even though they are poured forth everywhere, always return to him. And for that reason they can never diminish.

Marguerite d'Oingt

R FOURTH SUNDAY IN ORDINARY TIME
E L FOURTH SUNDAY AFTER EPIPHANY

Evangelization announces Christ's liberation, a liberation which goes to the roots of all injustice and exploitation: the break with friendship and with love. However, this is not a liberation which is susceptible to a "spiritualist" interpretation which is still so tenaciously present in certain Christian spheres. Love and sin (that is, the negation of love) are historical realities. They live in concrete conditions. It is for this reason that the Bible speaks of justice and liberation as opposed to slavery and the humiliation of the poor.

The gift of being a child of God is lived in history. In making sisters and brothers of all others we receive this gift, not of word but of work. This is to live the Father's love and to give witness of him. The preaching of a God who loves all persons equally should become flesh in history. In a society marked by injustice and the exploitation of one social class by another, the proclamation of this liberating love will convert this "making self-history" into something questioning and conflictual. God becomes truth in the heart of the society when the social classes question themselves and take the part of the poor of the grass-roots classes, of the despised races, of the marginated cultures. From there we try to live and preach the gospel. This preaching to the exploited, workers, and farmers of our continent will make them perceive that their situation is contrary to God's will which is made known in liberating events. This will help them to become aware of the profound injustice of their situation.

Love is the very source of our existence, and therefore, only by loving can we realize ourselves. It is a matter of believing that God loves us in establishing justice and right in our conflictual history. To believe is to love God, to be united with the poor and exploited of this world from within the very heart of the social confrontations and "popular" struggles for liberation. To believe is to preach, as Christ did, the kingdom from within the struggle for justice which led him to his death. To evangelize is to communicate this faith in an irreducible God who demands an attitude of confidence and whom we recognize in his liberating works, in his Son.

Gustavo Gutierrez

R FIFTH SUNDAY IN ORDINARY TIME
E L FIFTH SUNDAY AFTER EPIPHANY

Moses received three decrees about food and uttered them in the spirit, but they in their fleshly desire received them as having to do with eating. Moses says, "Eat anything that has cloven hoofs and chews the cud." What does he mean? That when it is fed it knows who feeds it and, relying on him, seems to be glad. Well did he speak, regarding the command. What, then, does he mean? Associate with those who fear the Lord, with those who meditate in their hearts on the command they have received, with those who talk of the things ordained by the Lord and observe them, with those who know that meditation is a work of gladness and ruminate on the word of the Lord. But why does he speak of the cloven hoofed? The upright one both lives in this world and looks forward to the holy age. See how well Moses made laws. But how could they understand or grasp these things? But we, having an upright understanding of these commands, utter them as the Lord intended. This is why the Lord has circumcized our ears and hearts so that we may grasp these things.

Letter of Barnabas

R SIXTH SUNDAY IN ORDINARY TIME
E L SIXTH SUNDAY AFTER EPIPHANY,

Since then, brothers, we have asked of the Lord who is to inhabit his temple, we have heard his commands to those who are to dwell there: and if we fulfill those duties, we shall be heirs of the kingdom of heaven. Our hearts, therefore, and our bodies must be made ready to fight under the holy obedience of his commands; and let us ask God to supply by the help of his grace what by nature is not possible to us. And if we would arrive at eternal life, escaping the pains of hell, then—while there is yet time, while we are still in the flesh, and are able to fulfill all these things by the light which is given us—we must hasten to do now what will profit us for all eternity.

We have, therefore, to establish a school of the Lord's service, in the setting forth of which we hope to order nothing that is harsh or rigorous. But if anything be somewhat strictly laid down, according to the dictates of sound reason, for the amendment of vices or the preservation of charity, do not therefore fly in dismay from the way of salvation, whose beginning cannot but be strait and difficult. But as we go forward in our life and in faith, we shall with hearts enlarged and the unspeakable sweetness of love run in the way of God's commandments; so that never departing from God's guidance, but persevering in God's teaching in the monastery until death, we may by patience share in the sufferings of Christ, that we may deserve to be partakers of his kingdom.

Benedict

R SEVENTH SUNDAY IN ORDINARY TIME
E SEVENTH SUNDAY AFTER EPIPHANY, PROPER 2
L SEVENTH SUNDAY AFTER EPIPHANY

In these comments Jesus implies that God's behavior is intended as a model for human behavior. Because God gives sunshine and rain without discriminating between just and unjust people, those who wish to be known as God's children are instructed to love and pray for their acquaintances without discriminating between friends and enemies. Jesus even implies that it is precisely through loving our enemies and praying for those who persecute us that we become God's children! I do not see this as a contradiction of the concept of salvation by grace through faith. Instead, I read this as a gloss upon it, an explanation of the familiar resemblance that develops as the evidence of at-one-ment with God.

Here and elsewhere, Jesus implies that his disciples are expected to pattern their relationship after God's behavior in a mirroring process ("as in heaven, so on earth"), and that the mirroring of unconditional love is the sign of membership in the faith-family of God. This human embodiment of God's universal concern is surely one of the meanings of the prayer Jesus taught us to pray: "Your will be done on earth as it is in heaven." Apart from miracles, how would God's will be done on earth, if not through human agency?

What I am driving at is simple enough: that human responsibility, in its deepest and fullest dimension, entails *godding*, an embodiment or incarnation of God's love in human flesh, with the goal of concegating with God a just and loving human society.

Virginia Ramey Mollenkott

R EIGHTH SUNDAY IN ORDINARY TIME

E EIGHTH SUNDAY AFTER EPIPHANY, PROPER 3

L EIGHTH SUNDAY AFTER EPIPHANY

I now say again to you, what I am always saying: that Christ urges his hearers to obedience to his words, both by means of what is profitable to them, and by what is painful; like a good physician, pointing out the disease that comes through neglect, and the good health that will come through obedience to his directions.

See here then how he again points out what gain there is for us in this life; how he prepares for us things that are useful, and takes from us what is a danger to us. It is not for this only that wealth is harmful to you, he says: because it arms robbers against you, or because it can wholly darken your mind; but also because it drives you from the service of God, and makes you slaves of soulless riches; harming you as much by making you slaves of what you should rule, as by driving you from the service of God, whom before all others you must serve. Here he shows us that our loss is twofold: to be turned away from serving God, and to be made slaves of mammon.

We shudder to think of what we have compelled Christ to say, to place God side by side with mammon. And if this is a horrifying thing, it is still more horrifying to do this by our own acts: to prefer the tyranny of gold to the fear and love of God. But why not? Did not this happen among the ancients? Far from it. How then, you may say, was Abraham, was Job, so honored? I am not speaking of riches; I am speaking of those who are the slaves of riches. Job was indeed rich. But he was no slave of mammon. He possessed riches and ruled them, as a master, not as a slave. He held all he had as though he were the steward of another man's riches. And not only did he not rob others of what belonged to them, he gave what was his to those in need. And what was greater, he took no delight in present things. And so he did not grieve when he lost them. But the rich now are not like this, but rather in a state worse than any slave, and as though paying tribute to some tyrant. For such minds become a sort of stronghold, held by money; and from there each day money sends out its commands, commands that are fulfilled by the violation of justice, and decency; and there is no one who does not obey. There is no need here to philosophize.

For God once and for all has declared that it is not possible for the service of mammon to accord with the service of God. Therefore do not say it is possible. For when the one master commands you to plunder, the other to give away what is yours; the one commands you to be chaste, the other to commit fornication; the one invites you to drunkenness and gluttony, the other to restrain our appetites; again, when the one counsels you to think little of present things, the other to hold fast to them; the one tells you to adore rich marbles and gilded walls and panelled ceilings, the other not to esteem them, but to honor virtue only; how can there be concord between them?

John Chrysostom

E LAST SUNDAY AFTER EPIPHANY
L TRANSFIGURATION

He brought them up to the mountain that he might also show them, before his resurrection, the glory of his divinity, so that when he had risen from the dead they might then know that he had not received this glory as the reward of his labor, and as one who had it not, but that he had had it from all eternity, together with the Father and the Holy Spirit. It was therefore this glory of his divinity, which was hidden and veiled to humanity, that he revealed to the apostles on the mountain. For they beheld his face shining as the sun, and his garments white as snow.

The disciples upon the mountain beheld two suns: one, to which they were accustomed, shining in the sky; and another, to which they were unaccustomed, one which shone down on them, and from the firmament gave light to the whole world, and which then shone for them alone, which was the face of Jesus before them. And his garments appeared to them white as light, for the glory of his divinity poured forth from his whole body, and all his members radiated light. His face shone, not as the face of Moses, from without; from his face the glory of his divinity poured forth, yet remained with him. From himself came his own light, and was contained within him. For it did not spread out from elsewhere, and fall on him; it did not come slantwise to adorn him. Neither did he receive it, to use for a while, nor did he reveal to them the unfathomable depths of his glory, but only as much as the pupils of their eyes could take in and distinguish.

And there appeared to them Moses and Elijah talking with him. They gave thanks to him that their own words had been fulfilled, and together with them the words of all the prophets. They adored him for the salvation he had wrought in the world for humankind, and because he had in truth fulfilled the mystery which they had themselves foretold. The prophets therefore were filled with joy, and the apostles likewise, in their ascent of the mountain. The prophets rejoiced because they had seen his humanity, which they had not known. And the apostles rejoiced because they had seen the glory of the divinity, which they had not known.

Ephraem

R E L ASH WEDNESDAY

On the edge of the woods grows a larkspur. Its glorious blue blossom rising on its bending stalk from among the dark green curiously-shaped leaves fills the air with color. A passerby picks the flower, loses interest in it and throws it into the fire, and in a short moment all that is left of that splendid show is a thin streak of grey ash. What fire does in an instant, time is always doing to everything that lives. The delicate fern, the stout mullein, the rooted oak, butterflies, darting swallows, nimble squirrels, heavy oxen, all of them, equally, sooner or later, by accident, disease, hunger, cold, — all these clear-cut forms, all this flourishing life, turns to a little ash, a handful of dry dust, which every breeze scatters this way and that. All this brilliant color, all this sensitive, breathing life, falls into pale, feeble, dead earth, and less than earth, into ashes. It is the same with ourselves. We look into an opened grave and shiver: a few bones, a handful of ash-grey dust.

Remember man
that dust thou art
and unto dust shalt thou return.

Ashes signify man's overthrow by time. Our own swift passage, ours and not someone else's, ours, mine. When at the beginning of Lent the priest takes the burnt residue of the green branches of the last Palm Sunday and inscribes with it on my forehead the sign of the cross, it is to remind me of my death.

Memento homo
quia pulvis est
et in pulverem reverteris.

Everything turns to ashes, everything whatever. This house I live in, these clothes I am wearing, my household stuff, my money, my fields, meadows, woods, the dog that follows me, the clock in the hall, this hand I am writing with, these eyes that read what I write, all the rest of my body, people I have loved, people I have hated, or been afraid of, whatever was great in my eyes upon earth, whatever small and contemptible, all without exception will fall back into dust.

Romano Guardini

Since the gospel reading refers to these present days—for we who are now at the beginning of the season of Lent have just heard the gospel account of the forty days' fast—we must consider for ourselves, why it is this abstinence is observed for forty days? For Moses also fasted forty days, that he might receive the law. Elijah in the desert fasted for forty days. And he who is the author of all coming among humankind went entirely without food for forty days and forty nights. And we, as far as we are able, must also endeavor to mortify our bodies by abstinence during this yearly time of Lent.

Why is the number forty observed if not that the excellence of the decalogue is perfected by the four books of the gospel? For as ten multiplied by four make forty, so we perfectly fulfill the precepts of the decalogue when we faithfully observe the four books of the holy gospels. From this another thing may be learned. In this mortal body we are composed of four elements: and it is because of this same body we are made subject to God's commandments. The commands of the law are given to us in the decalogue. And since it is through the desires of the body we have despised the commandments of the decalogue, it is just that we chastise this same flesh four times ten times.

And if you wish there is yet another thing to be understood from this time of Lent. From this present day till the joyful solemnities of Easter there are six weeks; that is, two and forty days. From which if you subtract the six Sundays there remain six and thirty days of abstinence. And since a year continues throughout three hundred and sixty-five days, we, when we mortify ourselves for thirty-six days, give to the Lord a tithe as it were of our year; so that we who have lived for ourselves throughout the year we have received, may, during his tenth of it, die to our Maker through abstinence.

Gregory the Great

R SECOND SUNDAY IN LENT, *see page 21*

E SECOND SUNDAY IN LENT

Exult with joy in Christ. Borne on the wings of your every yearn-
ing, receive the gifts of heaven. For now the saving warmth of the
eternal font invites you. Now your mother adopts you to make you
her child. You are to be born not by the ordinary rules of childbirth—mothers groaning in the pains of labor and bringing you
into the miseries of this world, weeping, sullied, and wrapped in
sullied swaddling clothes—but exulting in joy, children of heaven,
children free from sin, to be bountifully nourished, not in the foul-
smelling cradles, but at the altar rails in the midst of sweet perfumes, through our Lord Jesus Christ.

Without delay and with more speed than words, enter the heavenly
gates. Do not believe that in immersing yourselves in the pool of regeneration, the source of eternal life, that a grace is conferred on
you that is an accepter of persons. With faith and fortitude, put off
that old man with his foul-smelling rags, all you who presently are
to take part in the procession, regenerated and clothed in white garments, having been enriched with the gifts of the Holy Spirit.

Why do you hesitate? Thanks to your faith, the wave of rebirth has
already begotten you. It is bringing you forth through the sacraments. Hasten with all speed to the center of your desire. Lo, a sol-
emn hymn is being chanted. Lo, the sweet wail of the newborn is
heard. Lo, the most illustrious brood of the begotten proceeds from
the one womb. A new thing, that each one is born spiritually. Run
then, forward to the mother who experiences no pains of labor although she cannot count the number of those to whom she gives
birth. Enter, then. Enter! Happily you are going to drink the new
milk together.

Why do you delay? Though differing in age, sex, and state in life,
you are soon going to be joined in unity. Fly to the fountain, to the
sweet womb of your virgin mother. It is where you belong, thanks
to your divine nobility and your faith. Realize that your future happiness will be proportioned to your faith. O admirable and most
holy benevolence of God, that birth takes place without maternal
labor, that our spiritual birth is free from tears. This regeneration,

this resurrection, this eternal life, our mother has given to all. She incorporates us in one body after assembling us from every race and from every nation.

Exult. Your own faith has given you birth. You have fled the snares of this world, its sin, its wounds, its death. You have invoked the assistance of your Father in majesty. Fly, then, not with swiftness of foot, but on wings of thought, to the water of the saving font. Immerse yourselves with confidence. Fortunately, by the death of your old man, you are destined to be victorious.

Hasten, hasten to the bath that will purify you thoroughly. The living water, tempered by the Holy Spirit and fire, most sweet, now invites you with its tender murmur. Already the attendant of the bath is girded, expecting your arrival, ready to give the necessary anointing and drying, and a golden denarius sealed with triple effigy. Therefore, rejoice. For you will plunge naked into the font, but you will soon emerge clothed with a heavenly garment, dressed in white.

You burn with thirst deep and ardent. The sweet murmur of the flowing nectar invites you. Fly without delay to the milk of this genital font. Drink with confidence while you may. Be bathed in the waves of the river flowing over you. Fill your vessels with all urgency and with much devotion, so that you will always have enough water, remembering this before all else that you can never spill a drop or come to fetch it again.

Zeno

R E THIRD SUNDAY IN LENT

L SECOND SUNDAY IN LENT

O celestial flood, be sanctified by the Word of God; O water that was trodden by the feet of Christ, be sanctified; thou upon whom the mountains weigh down, yet thou art not shut up; thou art dashed against the rocks yet thou art not destroyed; thou art spread abroad upon the earth and yet dost not fall. Thou art held up by the firmament on high; thou dost wash the whole universe about, cleansing all things, yet none cleanses thee. Thou when the people of the Hebrews took their flight was held back and hardened into ice. Thou melting upon the high peaks dost bring ruin upon the dwellers of the Nile, and with thy fierce ranging dost ever torment the world as it were thine enemy. Thou art one and the same: the salvation of the faithful, the avenger of the wicked. Moses smote the rock and the rock poured thee forth: the majesty of God commanded thee to come forth and thou couldest not hide among the boulders. Thou art borne upon the clouds and dost make fruitful the fields with joyful showers. Through thee a draught bringing grace and life is poured out upon bodies hot with summer heat. Thou dost move quietly upon thy tiny courses bringing life and fruitful sap, lest the dry lifeless earth deny their proper victuals to our bodies. The beginning of all things and their end exult in thee, yet God has provided that by thee we might know no end.

Yet thou, O Lord, almighty God, whose power we do not forget while we proclaim the merits of water and declare its marvelous works, look with favor upon sinners and of thy wonted goodness loose the captive. Restore the innocence which Adam lost in paradise. Give a healthful draught to all who are upset by the bitterness of the apple; purge the disorders of mortals and with a divine antidote cure their age-long distemper. Wash away the filth and squalor of the world: make a way through the wall of fire which protects the garden of paradise and open a flower-strewn path unto them that return. May they receive the likeness of God, which once was lost by malice of the serpent: may the iniquities which follow upon their disobedience be carried away in this pure stream. May they rise up unto rest: may they be brought forward unto pardon: that being renewed in the mystic waters they may know themselves to be redeemed and reborn.

blessing of the water

R E FOURTH SUNDAY IN LENT
L THIRD SUNDAY IN LENT

One thing I see in your light:
this will, which you have given us as free,
seems to receive its strength
from the light of faith,
for by this light

we come in your light to know your eternal will,
and we see that your will wants nothing else
but that we be made holy.

So the light strengthens the will
and makes it grow,
and the will,
nourished by the light of holy faith,
gives life to our human actions.

So there can be neither a true will
nor a living faith
without action.

This light of faith nourishes the fire within the soul
and makes it grow,
for we cannot feel the fire of your charity
unless the light shows us
your love and affection for us.

You, light,
are also the fuel for the fire,
since it is you
that make the fire grow in the soul.

Just as wood makes a material fire grow
and become more intense,
you, light, are the fuel
that makes charity grow in the soul,
for you show the soul the divine goodness.

And charity in turn nourishes you,
for charity desires to know its God
and you want to satisfy it.

Catherine of Siena

L FOURTH SUNDAY IN LENT

There was in front of my cell window in the Dachau concentration camp a gallows, and I often had to pray for those who were hanged on it, poor souls. This gallows put a question to me: What will happen when one day they will put you to this test and lay the rope around your neck? Will you then with your last breath cry out, "You criminals, you think you are right in executing me as a criminal, but there is a living God in heaven, and he will show you!"? And then the second question followed: What do you think would have happened if Jesus had died that way, cursing his enemies and murderers? You know the answer: Then you would be rid of him; for there then would be no gospel, no good things of great joy, no salvation, no hope! Not for anyone, not for you! But — thank God — he, Jesus, died otherwise, differently, not cursing his murderers, but praying on their behalf: "Father, forgive them; they know not what they do!" They could not get rid of him, for he held on and kept them in his forgiving love; and his Father heard his prayer and was well pleased with his Son. So there was no escape. This death worked too well—and there is no escape—this death marks his final victory: "I have overcome the world!" How? By overcoming hatred with love, evil with doing good! We want to save our life by fighting our enemies, but Jesus says, "Those who will save their life shall lose it." Therefore we want to get rid of him; but now we cannot, for he prayed for us, he died for us, for us, his enemies: and so he has overcome our enmity, thereby setting his example for us in an undeniable way. Our way does not work, and we know it; everybody knows it.

According to our old man we all want to get rid of Jesus, because he does not allow us to live as we want to live. We all want him to die, to get out of our way. We are willing to worship him; we are not willing to obey him. We are willing to pay him our reverence; we are not willing to follow him as our Master and Lord. Yet he wants us to be his servants, followers, and friends, and his is the last and decisive argument, for in dying he speaks his final word: "Even my death is meant for you. You may accept me, you may reject me; but one thing you cannot, you cannot get rid of me; for I am either your Savior or your Judge. This is the alternative, for I am he that liveth, and was dead, and behold, I am alive forevermore I, Jesus, I am the Christ!"

Martin Niemoeller

The Lord then comes to whom all things were of course easy. But here he reveals a certain difficulty. He groans in the spirit and makes plain that we need to cry out with a loud voice in rebuke, to raise those who have grown hard in evil habit. Nevertheless, at the voice of the Lord, crying with a loud voice, the bonds that seemed inescapable are burst asunder. The dominion of hell trembled; and Lazarus is restored to the living. And the Lord also delivers from evil habit those who are four days dead. For even one who is four days dead, to Christ, whose desire is to raise the dead, that one is but sleeping.

What then did Christ say? Consider well this raising to life. Lazarus came forth living from the tomb, yet could not walk. To his disciples the Lord says, "Unbind him, and let him go." He raises the dead; they loose those bound. Observe well that here there is something which belongs to the majesty of God alone: raising the dead to life. Someone buried in evil habit is rebuked, by the word of truth. How many are rebuked, but pay no heed! Who breathes life into the dead? Who drives out the hidden death, and give back the hidden life? Left to themselves after rebukes and after corrections, is it not true that people will begin to think within themselves of how evil is the life they are leading, how evil the habit they are buried under? Then, grieved with themselves, they resolve to change their lives. Such as these have risen again; they who grieved over what they were have returned to life. But, returning to life, they are unable to walk. The bonds of their former guilt remain. Those who have returned to life have need to be loosed and let go. And this task the Lord has given to his disciples.

Let us, dearly beloved, so receive this teaching, that they who are alive may live, and that they who are dead may return to life. If a man's sin is but conceived in the heart, and not yet come forth in deed, let him repent of his thought; let him correct it; let the death rise up within the house of his conscience. Or if he has already committed what he thought of, even he must not despair. The man dead within his house did not rise; let him arise when borne forth. Let him repent of what he has done, and let him return to life at once. Let him not go down to the dark of the grave; let him not become buried under the great weight of habit.

It may be that even now I am speaking to such folk, buried under the unyielding stone of habit and who now dead four days stink. Yet not even they must despair: they are dead, in the depths; but Christ is on high. He knows, by crying out with a loud voice, how to destroy these heavy loads; he knows how, through himself, to raise the soul within to life, giving it to his disciples to loose. But let such sinners also do penance. When Lazarus was raised to life, after four days in the grave, no evil odor remained in the living man. And so let those who are living, live; and those who are dead, in whichever of these three deaths they find themselves, let them act at once, to rise here and now from the dead.

Augustine

R L SUNDAY OF THE PASSION
E PALM SUNDAY

We were created for happiness: we were made happy when we were first made. We were given paradise, to enjoy its delight. We received a commandment, that obeying it we might win merit, not that God knew not what was to be, but as laying down the law of free will. Through envy we were deceived. We were cast forth, because we had broken the law. We hungered, because we did not deny ourselves, being defeated and overcome by the Tree of Knowledge. For the commandment was with us from our beginning, being in a manner an unvarying guide to our soul, and a restraint upon pleasure; and to it we were reasonably made subject, so that we might regain by keeping it what we had lost by not keeping it. That we might live we needed a God Incarnate, and dying for us. We died with him, that we might be cleansed of our sin. We rose with him, because we died with him. And with him shall we be glorified, because we have risen with him.

Many indeed are the wondrous happenings of that time: God hanging from a cross, the sun made dark, and again flaming out; for it was fitting that creation should mourn with its Creator. The temple veil rent, blood and water flowing from his side: the one as from a man, the other as from what was above a man; the earth shaken, the rocks shattered because of the Rock; the dead risen to bear witness to the final and universal resurrection of the dead. The happenings at the sepulcher, and after the sepulcher, who can fittingly recount them? Yet no one of them can be compared to the miracle of my salvation. A few drops of blood renew the whole world, and do for all what the rennet does for the milk: joining us and binding us together.

But, O Pasch, great and holy, purifier of all the world!— For I shall speak to you as to one living—O Word of God and Light and Life and Wisdom and Power! I rejoice in all your names.

Gregory of Nazianzus

R   HOLY THURSDAY

E   L MAUNDY THURSDAY

And what did the all-wise dispenser of the sacred mysteries say to this? What I am doing you do not now understand, Peter; but afterwards you will know. Let me then do this holy service for you also. If you do not, you shall have no part with me. When he heard this the chief of the apostles began instead to listen and did not know what answer to make. Alas, Lord, he says, I am straightened on every side. To be stubborn would grieve me. To contradict you would cause me pain. To refuse would bring punishment on me. And to consent would be the worst of all. So let the word of God prevail, not the arrogance of a slave. Let divine wisdom prevail, not the stupidity of a servant. But I beg pardon for my presumption. Do you bear with me, and bid me to receive this service from you. Do as you will, Lord. Fulfill what is in your mind, Lord. And that I may attain to this inheritance with you, wash not alone my feet, but also my hands and my head. I now implore you, I most earnestly entreat you, that I may receive this divine washing, so that I may not be deprived of your divine favor. May it be given to me to obtain the request of your adorable will, lest I be deprived of your great joy. I shall spread out my feet to you, I shall stretch out my hands to you, I shall bow my head, that I may not be cut off from the inheritance of my Lord. That I may not lose joy beyond all telling, I shall not hold to my own will, resisting God. Let every creature know that by a washing I, Peter, this day gain a heavenly kingdom.

After he had washed their feet, the Lord sat down again, and he said to them: "If then, your Lord and Teacher, have washed your feet, you also ought wash one another's feet." Imitate me, your Lord, so that through this sacred action of mine you may become partakers of the divine nature. I lay upon you this perfect way of exaltation. In time past I came down to this earth, when I was preparing for your race that first state of happiness. And taking the slime of the earth I formed a human being, and created spirit also upon the earth. And now it is my will to bend down again among you, that I may strengthen the foundations, the bases of my creation that have fallen.

Therefore, my beloved, and sharers with me of the heavenly vocation, imitate in this respect the author and the perfecter of our salvation, Jesus. Let us long for the uplifting of our lowliness, for the love that unites us to God, and for a pure sincere faith in the divine mysteries.

Cyril of Alexandria

R E L GOOD FRIDAY

O new and unheard-of happening! He is stretched out upon a cross who by his word stretched out the heavens. He is held fast in bonds who has set the sand a bound for the sea. He is given gall to drink who has given us wells of honey. He is crowned with thorns who has crowned the earth with flowers. With a reed they struck his head who of old struck Egypt with ten plagues, and submerged the head of Pharaoh in the waves. That countenance was spat upon at which the cherubim dared not gaze. Yet, while suffering these things he prayed for his tormentors, saying, "Father, forgive them, for they know not what they do."

He overcame evil by goodness. Christ undertook the defense of those who put him to death, eager to gather them into his net, annulling the charge, and pleading their ignorance. Made the sport of their drunken frenzy, he submitted without bitterness. He suffered their drunkenness, and in his love for humankind called them to repentance. What more could he do?

Profiting nothing from that goodness, they enclose him in a tomb whom creation cannot contain. They seal the tomb, safe-guarding our deliverance; and fearing he would rise again, they station soldiers to watch the sepulcher. Who has ever seen the dead placed under watch? If he was a mere man, then death will keep him. If he was a mere man, what need to seal his tomb? Is it not useless?

Cease to rage against the truth. Cease offering insults to the Sun of justice, thinking you can put out its light. Cease, I say, and do not try to seal up the fountain of life.

Amphilochius

R E L EASTER VIGIL

Dayeinu!

How many gifts God had bestowed upon us!

Had God brought us out of Egypt and not divided the sea for us,
it would have been enough!

Had God divided the sea and not permitted us to cross on dry land,
it would have been enough!

Had God permitted us to cross the sea on dry land and not sustained us for forty years in the desert,
it would have been enough!

Had God sustained us for forty years in the desert and not fed us with manna,
it would have been enough!

Had God fed us with manna and not given us the sabbath,
it would have been enough!

Had God given us the sabbath and not brought us to Mount Sinai,
it would have been enough!

Had God brought us to Mount Sinai and not given us the Torah,
it would have been enough!

Had God given us the Torah and not led us into the land of Israel,
it would have been enough!

Had God led us into the land of Israel and not built

for us the temple,
it would have been enough!

Had God built for us the temple and not sent us prophets of truth,
it would have been enough!

Had God sent us prophets of truth and not made us a holy people,
it would have been enough!

the Passover Haggadah

R E EASTER DAY

L THE RESURRECTION OF OUR LORD

It is he who, coming from heaven to the earth
because of the suffering one,
and clothing himself in that same one through a virgin's womb,
and coming forth a man,
accepted the passions of the suffering one
through the body which was able to suffer,
and dissolved the passions of the flesh;
and by the Spirit which could not die
he killed death, the killer of all.

For, himself led as a lamb
and slain as a sheep,
he ransomed us from the world's service
as from the land of Egypt,
and freed us from the devil's slavery
as from the hand of Pharaoh;

and he marked our souls with his own Spirit
and the members of our body with his own blood.

It is he that clothed death with shame
and stood the devil in grief
as Moses did Pharaoh.

It is he that struck down crime
and made injustice childless
as Moses did Egypt.

It is he that delivered us from slavery to liberty,

from darkness to light,
from death to life,
from tyranny to eternal royalty,
and made us a new priesthood
and an eternal people personal to him.

He is the Pascha of our salvation.

It is he who in many endured many things:
it is he that was in Abel murdered,
and in Isaac bound,
and in Jacob exiled,
and in Joseph sold,
and in Moses exposed,
and in the lamb slain,
and in David persecuted,
and in the prophets dishonored.

It is he that was enfleshed in a virgin,
that was hanged on a tree,
that was buried in the earth,
that was raised from the dead,
that was taken up to the heights of the heavens.

He is the lamb being slain;
he is the lamb that is speechless;
he is the one born from Mary, the lovely ewe-lamb;
he is the one taken from the flock,
and dragged to slaughter,

and sacrificed at evening,
and buried at night;
who on the tree was not broken,
in the earth was not dissolved,
arose from the dead,
and raised up a man from the grave below.

Melito

R E L SECOND SUNDAY OF EASTER

O Lord, bent over as I am I can only look downwards; straighten
me so that I can look upwards. Having mounted above my head,

my iniquities cover me over; and as a heavy burden they weigh me down. Deliver me from them, unburden me, so that the abyss of iniquities does not engulf me. Permit me, at least from afar or from the deep, to look upwards toward your light. Teach me to seek you, and reveal yourself to me as I seek; for unless you instruct me I cannot seek you, and unless you reveal yourself I cannot find you. Let me seek you in desiring you; let me desire you in seeking you. Let me find you in loving you; let me love you in finding you.

O Lord, I acknowledge and give thanks that you created in me your image so that I may remember, contemplate, and love you. But this image has been so effaced by the abrasion of transgressions, so hidden from sight by the dark billows of sin, that unless you renew and refashion it, it cannot do what it was created to do. Lord, I do not attempt to comprehend your sublimity, because my intellect is not at all equal to such a task. But I yearn to understand some measure of your truth, which my heart believes and loves. For I do not seek to understand in order to believe but I believe in order to understand. For I believe even this: that I shall not understand unless I believe.

Anselm

R E L THIRD SUNDAY OF EASTER

Lord! Open our eyes that we may behold thee! Open our ears that they may recognize thy voice. Not in some special religious experience, some great moment or wonderful service or perfect setting, but just as we go along the common road.

Teach us to recognize and welcome you in ordinary, homely events, for it is there that we shall surely find you.

Emmanuel—God with us! I am with thee, saith the Lord. Help me to remember that, up hill and down dale, in fog and rain and storm.

Teach us to stop arguing and listen to your voice: to be simple and quiet, to accept even when we do not understand, or when your deep and gentle teaching comes into conflict with our deepest prejudice, our longing for comfort, our hard and fast beliefs.

Come to us with your living touch on events; your sacred hand opening the scriptures. You have the words of eternal life.

Lord! Give me courage and love to open the door and constrain you to enter, offer all my resources, whatever the disguise you come in, even before I fully recognize my guest.

Come in! Enter my small life! Lay your sacred hands on all the common things and small interests of that life and bless and change them. Transfigure my small resources, make them sacred. And in them give me your very self.

When out of the heart of my own homely circumstances, you feed me—then my eyes are open to the presence I long for and can never understand.

Lord! Going out from this silence, teach me to be more alert, humble, expectant, than I have been in the past: ever ready to encounter you in quiet, homely ways: In every appeal to my compassion, every act of unselfish love which shows up and humbles my imperfect love, may I recognize you: still walking through the world. Give me that grace of simplicity which alone can receive your mystery.

Come and abide with me!
Meet me, walk with me!
Enlighten my mind!

And then, come in! Enter my humble life with its poverty and its limitations as you entered the stable of Bethlehem, the workshop of Nazareth, the cottage of Emmaus. Bless and consecrate the material of that small and ordinary life. Feed and possess my soul.

Evelyn Underhill

R E L FOURTH SUNDAY OF EASTER

"First of all, sir," said I, "show me this: the rock and the gateway—who is it?"

"This rock and gateway," said he, "are the son of God."

"How is it, sir," said I, "that the rock is old, but the gateway is new?"

"Listen," said he, "and understand, foolish man. The son of God is far older than all his creation, so that he was the Father's counselor in his creation. That is why the rock is old."

"But why is the gateway new, sir?" said I.

"Because," said he, "he was revealed in the last days of the consummation; that is why the gateway is new, so that those who are going to be saved may enter the kingdom of God through it. Did you see," said he, "that the stones that came in through the gateway were put into the building of the tower, but the ones that had not come in were put back in the place they came from?"

"I did, sir," said I,

"So," said he, "no one will enter the kingdom of God unless taking this holy name. For if you want to enter a city, and that city is walled around, and has a single gateway, can you enter that city except by the gateway that it has?"

"Why, sir," said I, "how can it be done in any other way?"

"Then if you cannot enter the city except by the gateway that it has, so," said he, "one cannot enter the kingdom of God in any other way than through the name of God's Son, the one beloved by God. "Did you see," said he, "the crowd that was building the tower?"

"I did, sir," said I.

"They are all glorious angels," said he, "so by them the Lord is walled about. But the gateway is the Son of God; this is the only entrance to the Lord. So no one can go in to God in any other way than through the Son. Did you see," said he, "the six men, and in the midst of them the tall, splendid man who was walking about the tower and rejecting the stones from the building?"

"I did, sir," said I.

"The splendid man," said he, "is the Son of God, and the six are the glorious angels attending him on his right and left. None of these glorious angels," said he, "can enter God's presence without him. Whoever does not take his name cannot enter the kingdom of God."

The Shepherd of Hermas

R E L FIFTH SUNDAY OF EASTER

He is the Way.
Follow Him through the Land of Unlikeness;
You will see rare beasts, and have unique adventures.

He is the Truth.
Seek Him in the Kingdom of Anxiety;
You will come to a great city that has expected your return for years.

He is the Life.
Love Him in the World of the Flesh;
And at your marriage all its occasions shall dance for joy.

W. H. Auden

R L SIXTH SUNDAY OF EASTER

Let us here consider what are common expressions for the Holy
Spirit, both those we have gathered from sacred scripture and those
we have received from the unwritten tradition of the Fathers. The
Holy Spirit called the Spirit of God, and the Spirit of Truth, who
proceeds from the Father, the Spirit of virtue a commanding Spirit.
The true and proper name however is the Holy Spirit, a name
which above all others declares that the Spirit is wholly incorporeal, free of matter, indivisible. For this reason the Lord, teaching
the woman who believed God must be adored in a given place that
the mind cannot know the incorporeal, said, "God is spirit."

When we hear of the Spirit the mind may not imagine to itself an
image of some limited circumscribed nature, liable to change, or al-
teration, or at all like a created thing, but must go on in its conception to the very highest notions, and form to itself an idea of an
intelligent Being, infinite in power, of greatness without measure,
bounded neither by time nor by ages, bountiful of its own goodness, to whom all turn who need sanctification, to whom all aspire
who live in holiness, as though watered and assisted by its breath
to arrive at their due perfection. A Being who perfects others, itself
needing nothing; existing as not needing to be renewed, yet giving
life abundantly; enlarging through no addition, but at once complete; at rest within itself, yet in all places; the source of holiness,
the light of the mind, and providing light from itself to every fac-

ulty of the soul that searches for truth; by nature inaccessible, yet yielding to goodness; filling every need by its power, but given only to those who are worthy of it, to whom it is not given in the same measure, but in the measure of each one's faith.

Simple in nature, manifold in powers, wholly present in each single one, and whole and entire in all places. Impassively divided, yet wholly bestowed, like the rays of the sun whose favor all enjoy as though it shone for them alone; yet it shines on land and sea and fills the air. So the Spirit, to each one who receives it, as though given to that believer alone, pours forth sufficient and perfect grace to each one, is enjoyed by each one, not in the measure of its power, but of their capacity.

Basil

E SIXTH SUNDAY OF EASTER

Why do you rush on to deed and achievement? I am the vine; it is I who achieve. What is your deed if it is not to ripen? Let my sap rise up within you that you may hang heavy and golden. Then will the chaotic dream of deeds dreamt by the shoots in the springtime, then will the leaves' proud summer craze, then will all earth's work become ripe within your little taut spheres. You can bear in yourselves the meaning of the earth, but only through me. And when in the bowers of heaven this wine is served up at the Lamb's marriage-feast, then the whole world will be borne within it—as spirit. Then one will be able to taste on which hillside and in what year of salvation it grew, will be able to savor in it the whole landscape of its origin, and not the least of your joys will be lost. But everything about it has invisibly turned within, and the dividing borderlines between being and being are dissolved in the unifying tide, and all bubbling eagerness has ceased fermenting, and all sadness has resurrected into brightness.

I am the resurrection and the life, but not as the world knows them: that decaying cycle of springs and autumns, that millstone of melancholy, that aping of eternal life. All the world's living and dying, taken together, are one great death, and it is this death that I awaken to life. Once I entered the world, a new and unknown sap began to circulate in the veins and branches of nature. The powers of destiny, the might of the planets, the demons of the blood, the rulers of the air, the spirit of the earth, and whatever other dark things still cower in the secret folds of creation: all of this has now been subdued and is ordered about and must obey the higher law. All the world's form is to me but matter that I inspirit. My action is not grafted from without to the old life, to the old pleasure-gardens of Pan; being the very life of life, I transform the marrow from within. All that dies becomes the property of my life. All that passes over into autumn runs ashore on my spring. All that turns to mold fertilizes my blossoms. All that denies has already been convicted; all that covets has already been dispossessed; all that stiffens has already been broken.

I am not one of the resurrected; I am the resurrection itself. Whoever lives in me, whoever is taken up into me, is taken up in resurrection. I am the transformation. As bread and wine are transformed, so the world is transformed into me. The grain of mustard is tiny, and yet its inner might does not rest until it overshadows all the world's plants. Neither does my resurrection rest until the grave of the last soul has burst, and my powers have reached even to the furthest branch of creation.

Hans Urs von Balthasar

R E L ASCENSION DAY

Let us partake of the Pasch, which even now is a figure, though more clear than that of old (for the Pasch of the law was, I venture to say, an obscurer figure of the figure); later it shall be still more perfect, purer, when, namely, the Word shall drink it with us new in the kingdom of his Father, making plain to us what he now teaches us less clearly. For that is always new which but now is becoming known. What that drink is, and what that enjoyment, it is for us to learn, and for him to teach, sharing his doctrine with his disciples. For teaching is food and the food of him who teaches. Come then, and let us also be partakers of the law, but not according to its letter, but according to the gospel; not imperfectly, but perfectly; not for a time, but for eternity.

Celebrate the Feast of the Resurrection. Help Eve: the first to fall; the first to greet Christ, and to tell of him to the disciples. Be like

Peter, or John; hasten to the sepulcher, running one against the other, striving in worthy rivalry. And if overtaken, then win by zeal: not stooped down, looking into the sepulcher, but going in. And if like Thomas you were not among the disciples to whom Jesus appeared, when you do see him be not faithless. Or if faithless, at least believe others who tell you of him; and if you do not believe them either, then at least trust the print of the nails. Should he descend into hell, go with him. Learn there also of the mysteries of Christ; what is the purpose of this second descent, what is the plan of it: appearing there did he save all, or, there also, those only who believed?

And if he ascend to heaven, ascend with him; be among the angels who accompany him upwards, or among those who receive him. Bid the gates be lifted up and become higher, that he may enter in who through his passion has become greater. Answer those who doubt because his body now bears the marks of his passion, which he had not coming down; and to those who ask, "Who is this king of glory," let you answer, "The Lord who is strong and mighty," both in all that he has ever done and does, and now also in this present battle and triumph for us. To the twofold doubt of the questioner, give a twofold answer.

And if they wonder, saying, how are his garments who is without body or blood red like a winepresser who has trodden the filled winepress, tell of the loveliness of the garment of his body that suffered, made beautiful by his passion, made glorious by his divinity, than which nothing can be more lovely, nothing more loved.

Gregory of Nazianzus

R E L SEVENTH SUNDAY OF EASTER

The halcyon is a sea bird which nests by the shore, laying its eggs in the sand, and bringing forth its young in the middle of winter, when the sea beats against the land in violent and frequent storms. But during the seven days while the halcyon broods, for it takes but seven days to hatch its young, all winds sink to rest, and the sea grows calm. And as it then is in need of food for its young ones, the most bountiful God grants this little creature another seven days of calm, that it may feed its young. Since all sailors know of this, they give this time the name of the halcyon days.

These things are ordered by the providence of God for the creatures that are without reason, that you may be led to seek of God the things you need for your salvation. And when for this small bird God holds back the great and fearful sea, and bids it be calm in winter, what will God not do for you made in the divine image? And if God should so tenderly cherish the halcyon, how much more will God not give you, when you call with all your heart?

Let us then be resolved that as in our other needs so also in time of temptations, not to count on human expectations or seek help there, but let us send upwards our entreaties, and with sighs and tears, with earnest prayer, with long watching. And in this manner shall we obtain deliverance from our affliction, rejecting human help as vain, and keeping a firm hope in the one who alone has power to save us.

Basil

R PENTECOST SUNDAY
E L DAY OF PENTECOST

The Spirit that is co-eternal with the Father and the Son is shown under the form of fire because God is invisible, ineffable, and incorporeal fire, as Paul testifies, "For our God is a consuming fire." God is called fire because by God the rust of sin is consumed. The Lord sends fire on earth when, by the breath of his Holy Spirit, he sets fire to the hearts of the unspiritual. And the earth catches fire when the heart of flesh, indifferent to its own evil pleasures, puts away the lusts of the present life, and becomes inflamed with the love of God. Fittingly then did the Spirit appear in fire; because in every heart entered the Spirit drives out the torpor of coldness and kindles there the desire of God's own eternity.

At the hearing of a sermon the soul is enkindled, the cold of mental listlessness departs from the heart, the mind becomes anxious with longing for heavenly things, and a stranger to earthly desires. The true love that fills it torments it with tears; yet tormented by this flame it is nourished by its very sufferings. It delights in hearing heavenly things; and the precepts that instruct it are like so many torches to inflame it; and where before it was chilled by its natural desires, hearing the words it presently grows warm. In the right hand of God, therefore, there is a fiery law; for the elect never hear the words of God with a cold heart, but loving with all their hearts they burn like torches at hearing them. As the word reaches their ear, their mind, angry with itself, is consumed by the flame of its own inner affection.

Gregory the Great

R E L TRINITY SUNDAY

Godhead!
Godhead!
Ineffable Godhead!
O supreme goodness
that for love alone made us in your image and likeness!
For when you created humankind
you did not say (as when you created the other creatures),
"Let it be made."
No, you said—O unutterable love!—
"Let us make humankind in our image and likeness,"
so that in this the whole Trinity might give assent together,
and in the powers of our soul
you fashioned us after the very Trinity,
Godhead eternal.
To fashion us after yourself, eternal Father—
you who as Father hold and keep all things within yourself—
you gave us memory
to hold and keep what our understanding perceives and knows
of you, infinite goodness.
And in knowing,
our understanding shares in the wisdom
of your only-begotten Son.
You gave us our will, gentle mercy, Holy Spirit,
which like a hand reaches up
filled with your love
to take whatever our understanding knows
of your unutterable goodness;

and then this will,
this strong hand of love,
fills our memory and affection with you.

Thanks, thanks be to you, high eternal Godhead,
that you have shown us such great love.

Catherine of Siena

R BODY AND BLOOD OF CHRIST

Because the Word has assumed manhood, i.e., the body and soul of
a man, he has become human while remaining God. For this reason
and also because he has left us in this sacrament his own body and
blood, he has made us the same as himself. For we have also become his body and through his mercy we are what we have received.

Recall what this creation of bread once was: how the earth begot it,
the rain nourished it, and ripened it; then human labor brought it
through various stages—transporting it to the threshing floor, ,
threshing and winnowing it, storing it, bringing it out, grinding,
kneading and baking it until at long last bread is produced.

Think too of your own progress: you were brought into existence
from non-existence; you were brought to the Lord's threshing floor
by the toil of oxen, i.e., by those preaching the gospel; you were
threshed. When you were on probation as catechumens you were
in storage in the granary. You enrolled your names, thereby beginning to be ground by fastings and exorcisms. Afterwards you were
brought to the water as in the kneading process, and thus became
unified. You were baked by the heat of the Holy Spirit and you became the bread of the Lord.

See what you have received. Just as you see that what was made is
a unity, let you also be one by retaining one faith, one hope, undivided charity. When the heretics receive the eucharist they admit
testimony against themselves, because they are pursuing division,
whereas this bread is a pointer to unity.

Likewise the wine existed in many grapes but is now reduced to
unity. It is one in the sweetness of the chalice after the bitter process
of squeezing in the winepress. Similarly, you, after your fastings, la-

bors, humility and contrition, have already come in the name of the
Lord to his chalice: you are there on the Lord's table, you are actually present in the chalice. You form this mystery with us: we are
united in one, we drink together because we live together.

Augustine

R NINTH SUNDAY IN ORDINARY TIME

E PROPER 4

L SECOND SUNDAY AFTER PENTECOST

For who that has been rightly taught and has become devoted to
the word does not seek to learn definitely the things that were
clearly shown by word to disciples, to whom the Word appeared
and revealed them, speaking plainly, unperceived by unbelievers,
but relating them to disciples, who being deemed faithful by him
learned the Father's secrets? That is why the Father sent the Word
to appear to the world, who was dishonored by the people,
preached through apostles, and believed by heathen. It is he who
was from the beginning, who appeared new and proved to be old,
and is ever born young in the hearts of saints. He is the eternal,
today counted a son, through whom the church is enriched and
grace unfolding is multiplied in the saints, affording understanding, revealing secrets, announcing dates, rejoicing over the faithful,
given to those who seek for it, that is, to those whose pledges of
faith are not broken and the boundaries set by the fathers have not
been passed over. Then the fear of the law is praised in song, and
the grace of the prophets is learned, and the faith of the gospels is
established, and what has been handed down from the apostles is
guarded, and the grace of the church exults. If you do not offend
this grace, you will learn what the Word talks about through those
through whom he wishes to talk, when he pleases. For whatever
we have been moved painstakingly to utter by the will of the word
that commands us, it is out of love of the things revealed to us that
we come to share them with you.

When you have faced these things and listened earnestly to them,
you will know what God bestows on those who become a paradise
of delight, causing to grow in themselves a thriving tree bearing all
kinds of fruit, and being themselves adorned with various fruits.

For in this place are planted the tree of knowledge and the tree of life. But the tree of knowledge does not kill; it is disobedience that kills. For the things that are written leave no doubt that God from the beginning planted a tree of knowledge and a tree of life in the midst of paradise, pointing to life through knowledge, and when those first created failed through the serpent's deceit to use it purely, they were made naked. For there is neither life without knowledge, nor sound knowledge without true life; therefore they were planted near each other.

Let your mind be knowledge, and your life the true message, fully comprehended. If you carry its tree and pick its fruit, you will always gather the vintage of the things desired by God, which the serpent cannot touch nor deceit defile by contact. Eve is not corrupted but trusted as a virgin, salvation is set forth, and apostles are given understanding, and the Passover of the Lord proceeds, and the seasons are brought together and are harmonized with the world, and the Word rejoices in teaching the saints; through him the Father is glorified.

Address to Diognetus

R TENTH SUNDAY IN ORDINARY TIME

E PROPER 5

L THIRD SUNDAY AFTER PENTECOST

Christ does not call us to an immediate possession of glory without doing anything in between. Our glorification was in his intention as soon as our election. In God who sees all things at once, both entered at once. But in the execution of his decrees here God carries us by steps; he calls us to repentance. In one word (one word will not do it, but in two words), it is aversion and conversion; it is a turning from our sins, and a returning to our God. It is both: for in our age, in our sickness, in any impotency toward a sin, in any satiety of a sin, we turn from our sin, but we turn not to God; we turn to a sinful delight in the memory of our sins and a sinful desire that we might continue in them. So also in a storm at sea, in any imminent calamity at land, we turn to God, to a "Lord, Lord"; but at the next calm, and at the next deliverance, we turn to our sin again. To sin and think God sees it not because we confess it not; to confess it as sin and yet continue the practice of it; to discontinue the practice of it and continue the possession of that which was got by that sin; all this is deceit and destroys, evacuates, annihilates all repentance.

To recollect all and to end all: Christ justifies feasting; he feasts you with himself. And feasting in an apostle's house, in his own house, he feasts you often here. And he admits publicans to this feast, men whose full and open life, in court, must necessarily expose them to many hazards of sin.

This Christ, with joy and thanksgiving, we acknowledge to be come; to be come actually; we expect no other after him, we join no other to him. And come freely, without any necessity imposed by any above him, and without any invitation from us here. Come, not to meet us, who were not able to rise without him, but yet not to force us, to save us against our wills, but come to call us by his ordinances in his church. Us, not as we pretend any righteousness of our own, but as we confess ourselves to be sinners, and sinners led by this call to repentance; which repentance is an everlasting divorce from our beloved sin, and an everlasting marriage and superinduction of our everliving God.

John Donne

R ELEVENTH SUNDAY IN ORDINARY TIME

E PROPER 6

L FOURTH SUNDAY AFTER PENTECOST

I have learned that some people have visited you from outside, and brought you an evil teaching, though you did not allow them to scatter it among you, but closed your ears, so that you might not receive what they scattered, since you are like stones of a temple of the Father, prepared for the building of God the Father, hoisted up on high by the crane of Jesus Christ, that is, the cross, using the Holy Spirit for a rope. Your faith is your windlass and love is the road that leads up to God. So you are all traveling companions, carrying God and temple, and Christ and your sacred things, and being fully arrayed in the commands of Jesus Christ. In this I rejoice that I have been thought worthy through what I write to converse with you and congratulate you that following another way of life you love nothing but God alone.

Pray constantly for others also, for in their case there is a hope of repentance, that they may find God. Permit them to be instructed by you, at least through your deeds. To their anger, be meek; to their boasts, be humble; to their abuse, utter your prayers; to their error, be steadfast in faith; to their savagery, be gentle; not zealous to imitate them. Let us be zealous to imitate the Lord, to see who can be more wronged, defrauded, set at naught, so that no plant of the devil may be found in you, but with all purity and sobriety you may remain in union with Jesus Christ, in both flesh and spirit.

Ignatius

R TWELFTH SUNDAY IN ORDINARY TIME

E PROPER 7

L FIFTH SUNDAY AFTER PENTECOST

Most High, all-powerful, good Lord,
yours are the praises, the glory, the honor, and all blessing.
To you alone, Most High, do they belong,
and no one is worthy to mention your name.
Praised be you, my Lord, with all your creatures,
especially Sir Brother Sun,
who is the day and through whom you give us light.
And he is beautiful and radiant with great splendor;
and bears a likeness of you, Most High One.
Praised be you, my Lord, through Sister Moon and the stars,
in heaven you formed them clear and precious and beautiful.
Praised be you, my Lord, through Brother Wind,
and through the air, cloudy and serene, and every kind of weather
through which you give sustenance to your creatures.
Praised be you, my Lord, through Sister Water,
which is very useful and humble and precious and chaste.
Praised be you, my Lord, through Brother Fire,
through whom you light the night
and he is beautiful and playful and robust and strong.
Praised be you, my Lord, through our Sister Mother Earth,
who sustains and governs us,

and who produces varied fruits with colored flowers and herbs.
Praised be you, my Lord, through those who give pardon
for your love
and bear infirmity and tribulation.
Blessed are those who endure in peace
for by you, Most High, they shall be crowned.
Praised be you, my Lord, through our Sister bodily Death,
from whom no one living can escape.
Woe to those who die in mortal sin.
Blessed are those whom death will find in your most holy will,
for the second death shall do them no harm.
Praised and bless my Lord and give him thanks
and serve him with great humility.

Francis of Assisi

R THIRTEENTH SUNDAY IN ORDINARY TIME

E PROPER 8

L SIXTH SUNDAY AFTER PENTECOST

Christ told Peter to put aside his nets and follow him. He told the
rich young man to sell what he had and give to the poor and follow
him. He said that those who lost their lives for his sake should find
them. He told his followers that if anyone begged for their coats to
give up their cloaks, too. He spoke of feeding the poor, sheltering
the homeless, of visiting those in prison and the sick, and also of in-
structing the ignorant. He said: "Be ye therefore perfect."

But too long have we had moderation and prudence. Today is a
time of crisis and struggle. Within our generation, Russia has rejected Christianity, Germany has rejected it, Mexico fights to exter-
minate it, in Spain there has been a war against religion, in Italy
Fascism has exalted the idea of the state and, rejecting the kingship
of Christ, has now a perverted idea of authority.

In this present situation when people are starving to death because
there is an overabundance of food, when religion is being warred
upon throughout the world, our Catholic young people still come
from schools and colleges and talk about looking for security, a
weekly wage.

They ignore the counsels of the gospels as though they had never heard of them, and those who are troubled in conscience regarding them speak of them as being impractical.

Why they think a weekly wage is going to give them security is a mystery. Do they have security on any job nowadays? If they try to save, the bank fails; if they invest their money, the bottom of the market drops out. If they trust to worldly practicality, in other words, they are out of luck.

If they sell their labor, they are prostituting the talents God gave them. College girls who work at Macy's—is this what their expensive training was for?—boys who go into business looking for profits—is this what their Catholic principles taught them?—are hovering on the brink of a precipice. They have no security and they know it. The only security comes in the following of the precepts and counsels of the gospels.

If each unemployed nurse went to her pastor and got a list of the sick and gave up the idea of working for wages and gave her services to the poor of the parish, is there not security in the faith that God will provide? This is but one instance of using the talents and abilities that God has given to each one of us.

What right has any one of us to security when God's poor are suffering? What right have I to sleep in a comfortable bed when so many are sleeping in the shadows of buildings here in this neighborhood of the Catholic Worker office? What right have we to food when many are hungry, or to liberty when the Scottsboro boys and so many labor organizers are in jail?

Dorothy Day

R FOURTEENTH SUNDAY IN ORDINARY TIME

E PROPER 9

L SEVENTH SUNDAY AFTER PENTECOST

Come to me, all you that labor and are burdened, and I will refresh you, where there is immortal life and the fount of every mercy. Come to me, all of you, and I will refresh you, where there is love alone, perennial joy, and everlasting happiness, where the light does not fade, nor the sun go down. Come to me, all you that labor and are burdened, and I will refresh you, where there is perfect life, and the fount of every good. Take my yoke upon you, and learn of me, because I am meek and humble of heart, and you shall find rest for your souls, where there is ever the sound of festival days, and where the hidden treasures of wisdom and knowledge shall be revealed.

Come to me, all of you, and I will refresh you, where there are wondrous gifts, and joy without compare, rest unchanging, happiness without end, unceasing melody, perpetual glory, unwearied giving of thanks, loving absorption in divine things, infinite riches, a kingdom without end, through all ages and ages, deeps of compassion, an ocean of mercy and kindness, which the human tongue cannot describe but makes known only through figures. There shall be the myriads of the angels, the multitudes of the firstborn, the thrones of the apostles, the dignities of the prophets, the crowns of the martyrs, the praises of the just. And there is laid up the reward of every order, of every power and principality.

Come to me, all you that hunger and thirst after justice, and I will fill you with all that you desire, and which the eye has not seen, nor the ear heard, nor has it entered into the human heart to conceive. These things have I prepared for those who love me. I have prepared them for the peacemakers. I have prepared them for those who suffer persecution, hate, reproaches, for my name's sake.

Come to me, all you that labor, and shake off and cast from you the burden of your sins. For no one who comes to me remains burdened, but casts off the evil way of life and learns of me a new way of life. The thief, putting an end to killing, putting away his life of robbery, received a true faith and became a dweller in paradise.

Come therefore to me; for whoever comes to me I shall not cast forth. You have heard the perfect hope, the sweet promises, the words of the Savior of our souls. Glory to his goodness! Glory to his loving kindness! Glory to his longanimity! Glory to his care for us, to his tenderness! Glory to his words of pity! Glory to his kingdom! Glory, honor, adoration to his holy name for ever and ever!

Ephraem

R FIFTEENTH SUNDAY IN ORDINARY TIME

E PROPER 10

L EIGHTH SUNDAY AFTER PENTECOST

Beginners in prayer are those who draw the water from the well; this is very hard work, for it will fatigue them to keep their senses recollected, which is extremely difficult because they have been accustomed to a life of distraction. At first beginners are not always sure that they have repented of their sins (though clearly they have, since they have determined to serve God so faithfully). Then they have to endeavor to meditate upon the life of Christ, which fatigues their minds. Thus far we can make progress by ourselves—with the help of God, of course, for without that, as is well known, we cannot think a single good thought.

That is what is meant by beginning to draw water from the well— and God grant there may be water in it! But that, at least, does not depend on us: our task is to draw it and to do what we can to water the flowers. And God is so good that when, for reasons known to the divine majesty, perhaps to our great advantage, God is pleased that the well should be dry, we, like good gardeners, do all that in us lies, and God keeps the flowers alive without water and makes the virtues grow. By water here I mean tears—or at least, if there are no tears, tenderness and an interior feeling of devotion.

What, then, will a person do here who finds for many days nothing but aridity, dislike and distaste? It will often happen that such a person is unable to think a single good thought, for working with the understanding is of course the same as drawing water from the well.

What then will the gardener do here? The gardener will rejoice and take new heart and consider it the greatest of favors to work in the garden of so great an Emperor, and will render Christ great praise. Let the gardener help him to bear the cross and remember how he lived with it all his life long. Let not the gardener wish to have God's kingdom on earth or ever cease from prayer, but rather resolve, even if this aridity should persist a whole life long, not to let Christ fall with his cross.

Teresa of Avila

Today the Lord relates another parable, again relating to the sower, who sowed good seed in his field. The Lord Christ explained this parable, saying that he was the sower of the good seed, that the devil was the enemy, the sower of tares, the harvest was the end of time and his field the world.

But hear what he says. See you not that the tares stand in the midst of the good growth, and you wish to uproot the bad? Remain quiet, it is not yet the time of harvest. Let it come, and let it reveal to you the true wheat. Why need you be angry? Why are you impatient that the bad should now be mixed with the good? They may be among you in the field, but in my barn they shall not be with you.

Recall the three places that were spoken of yesterday, where the seed grew not, the wayside, the stony ground, the thorny ground. The tares are the same as these. In another similitude they receive but another name. Because when one speaks in parables it is not an attempt to describe the properties of a thing, or some truth, but to convey a likeness of a truth.

In parables and figures one thing can be called by many names. And so it is not out of place for me to say to you that the wayside, the stony places, the thorny places, are weak Christians; and that they are likewise tares. For is not Christ a lamb? And is he not also a lion? Among wild animals and domestic that which is a lamb is a lamb, and a lion is a lion. Christ is both. They are what they are by nature. He is both in figure.

It happens also in similitude that things widely dissimilar are called by the same name. What is so widely dissimilar as Christ and the devil? Yet Christ is called a lion and so also is the devil. The one is a lion in strength, the other a lion in ferocity.

Augustine

R SEVENTEENTH SUNDAY IN ORDINARY TIME

E PROPER 12

L TENTH SUNDAY AFTER PENTECOST

As the leaven, when it is to be mixed in a heap of dough, is broken up and crushed into little pieces, and sprinkled through the mass until it is itself lost, so that it may bind together the scattered multitude of the grains of flour by its vigor, reducing to a solid mass what was inert and powerless when it was but powder, making this unity a potent whole of what had before seemed unprofitable, so the Lord Jesus Christ, since he is the leaven of the whole world, was broken by manifold torments, was wounded and pierced, and his sap, which is his precious blood, poured out for our salvation, so that mingling with him all humankind would be made into one body, they who before his passion were prostrate and divided.

So as to a leaven we cling to him, we who before were but dust of the Gentiles. We, I repeat, who before lay wholly scattered and broken in pieces, have by the power of his passion been kneaded into the body of Christ. We therefore who were cast away like dust among the nations, by the sprinkling of the blood of the Lord, are joined into the body of his oneness.

The woman who is said to hide the leaven in three measures of meal, who is she but the holy church, which each day strives to hide the doctrine of Christ in our hearts? She, I repeat, is the woman who in another place is said to be grinding at a mill. For the holy church grinds at the mill through her law, through the apostles, through the prophets, when she makes catechumens, and when she breaks down the hardness of paganism, and grinds it into little pieces, and being ground, as flour. She makes them ready to be joined together by the blood of the Lord.

The whole passion of Christ is a leaven. And the leaven is the symbol of our salvation, without which symbol or leaven no one can merit the substance of life eternal.

Maximus

Of our Lord, how many now say, I would wish to see his form, his face, his clothes, his shoes? Lo! you see him. And you indeed desire to see his clothes, but he gives himself to you not to see only, but also to touch and eat and receive within you.

Let then no one approach it with indifference, no one fainthearted, but all with burning hearts, all fervent, all aroused. For if Jews standing, and having on their shoes and their staves in their hands, ate with haste, much more ought you to be watchful. For they indeed were to go forth to Palestine, wherefore also they had the garb of pilgrims, but you are about to go to heaven.

With each one of the faithful does he mingle himself in the mysteries, and whom he begot, he nourishes by himself, and puts not out to another; by this also persuading you again, that he had taken your flesh. Let us not then be remiss, having been counted worthy of so much both of love and honor. See you not the infants with how much eagerness they lay hold of the breast? With what earnest desire they fix their lips upon the nipple? With the like let us also approach this table, and the nipple of the spiritual cup. Or rather, with much more eagerness let us, as infants at the breast, draw out the grace of the spirit; let it be our one sorrow not to partake of this food.

The works set before us are not of human power. He that then did these things at that supper, this same now also works them. We occupy the place of servants. He who sanctifies and changes them is the same. Let then no Judas be present, no one covetous person. Let anyone who is not a disciple, withdraw, the table receives not such. For I keep the passover, he says, with my disciples.

This table is the same as that, and has nothing less. For it is not so that Christ wrought that, and some person this, but he does this too. This is that upper chamber, where they were then; and hence they went forth unto the Mount of Olives.

Let us also go out unto the hands of the poor, for this spot is the

Mount of Olives. For the multitude of the poor are olive-trees planted in the house of God, dropping the oil, which is profitable for us there, which the five virgins had, and the others that had not received perished thereby. Having received this, let us enter in, that with bright lamps we may meet the bridegroom; having received this, let us go forth hence.

John Chrysostom

R NINETEENTH SUNDAY IN ORDINARY TIME

E PROPER 14

L TWELFTH SUNDAY AFTER PENTECOST

O Jesus, gentle love, you who are the true and complete peace in every discord, bring peace and concord to every conflict. When you are with me and I feel your power, my heart is merry and leaps with joy, my mind adorns itself with flowers of great beauty, and my soul dreams in the sweetness of blessed love. Let my enemies come, who in the world are so numerous, but if I feel myself to be with you, I overthrow them all, and the world itself I overthrow, along with all its speeches. I am like a fish that rests in the sea; when the waves sweep over it and the great tempests assail it, the fish enjoys swimming, because it cannot be captured, and it leaps more nimbly. Thus do I in this world that is a troubled sea: the great currents arrive, and I sail below them, and I take shelter in your bosom, and let them pass by. Then my soul arms itself with two wings so noble and flying so high that no one can see me: I rush then into your arms, O Jesus, up, into your heavenly realms. Still I offer invocations to you, so that you may be always near me. Feeling myself with you I have no fear of the currents. I even conquer them in navigating, and I come forth from them unharmed. But if I do not possess you, I am like the whale that when the tide goes out sits on the sand and is condemned to death, because without the tide it no longer has the chance to escape.

Umilta of Faenza

R TWENTIETH SUNDAY IN ORDINARY TIME

E PROPER 15

L THIRTEENTH SUNDAY AFTER PENTECOST

Be faithful to prayer, and, in the fulfillment of this duty, you will find all the rest sustained and rendered easy. If a sinner, pray: it was through prayer alone that the publican and the sinful woman of the gospel obtained feelings of compunction and the grace of a thorough penitence; and prayer is the only source and the only path of righteousness. If righteous, still pray: perseverance in faith and in piety is promised only to prayer; and by that it was that Job, that David, that Tobias, persevered to the end. If you live amid sinners, and your duty does not permit you to withdraw yourself from the sight of their irregularities and examples, pray: the greater the dangers, the more necessary does prayer become; and the three children in the flames, and Jonah in the belly of a monster, found safety only through prayer. If the engagements of your birth, or of your station, attach you to the court of kings, pray: Esther, in the court of Ahasuerus, Daniel in that of Darius, the prophets in the palaces of the kings of Israel, were solely indebted to prayer for their life and salvation. If you live in retirement, pray: solitude itself becomes a rock, if a continual intercourse with God does not defend us against ourselves; and Judith, in the secrecy of her house, and the widow Anna in the temple, and the Anthonies in the desert, found the fruit and the security of their retreat in prayer alone. If established in the church for the instruction of the people, pray: all the power and all the success of your ministry must depend upon your prayers; and the apostles converted the universe solely because they had appropriated nothing to themselves but prayer and the preaching of the gospel. Lastly, be whom you may, I again repeat it, in prosperity or in indigence, in joy or in affliction, in trouble or in peace, in fervency or in despondency, in lust or in the ways of righteousness, advanced in virtue, or still in the first steps of penitence, pray. Prayer is the safety of all stations, the consolation of all sorrows, the duty of all conditions, the soul of piety, the support of faith, the grand foundation of religion, and all religion itself. O my God! shed, then, upon us that spirit of grace and of prayer which was to be the distinguishing mark of your church, and the portion of a new people;

and purify their hearts and our lips, that we may be enabled to offer up to you pure homages, fervent sighs, and prayers worthy of the eternal riches which you have so often promised to those who shall have well entreated them.

Jean Massillon

R TWENTY-FIRST SUNDAY IN ORDINARY TIME

E PROPER 16

L FOURTEENTH SUNDAY AFTER PENTECOST

The Lord Christ is the Son of God by nature; Peter, and with him the other elect, is a son of God through grace. Christ is the Son of the living God, being born of God; Peter the son of the Holy Spirit, being re-born of the Spirit. Christ is the Son of God before all time, for he is the power of God, and the wisdom of God. Peter is the son of the Holy Spirit from that moment in which, enlightened by God, he received the grace of the knowledge of the divinity.

Peter, who before was called Simon, receives from the Lord the name of Peter, because of the strength and constancy of his faith; for with a firm and tenacious soul he clung to him of whom it was written, "And the rock was Christ." And this Rock, that is, the Lord Savior, who gave to him who knew him, loved him, and confessed him, the privilege of sharing his name, said that he would be called Peter from Petra (the rock), upon which the church is built. For only through the faith and the love of Christ, through receiving the sacraments of Christ, through keeping the commandments of Christ, can we come to share in the lot of the elect and to eternal life.

Bede

R TWENTY-SECOND SUNDAY IN ORDINARY TIME

E PROPER 17

L FIFTEENTH SUNDAY AFTER PENTECOST

The cross is laid on every Christian. The first Christ-suffering which every man must experience is the call to abandon the attachments of this world. It is that dying of "the old man" which is the result of his encounter with Christ. As we embark upon discipleship we sur-

render ourselves to Christ in union with his death—we give over
our lives to death. Thus it begins: the cross is not the terrible end to
an otherwise godfearing and happy life, but it meets us at the beginning of our communion with Christ. When Christ calls a man, he
bids him come and die. It may be a death like that of the first disciples who had to leave home and work to follow him, or it may be a
death like Luther's, who had to leave the monastery and go out
into the world. But it is the same death every time—death in Jesus
Christ, the death of the old man at his call. Jesus' summons to the
rich young man was calling him to die, because only the man who
is dead to his own will can follow Christ. In fact every command of
Jesus is a call to die, with all our affections and lusts. But we do not
want to die, and therefore Jesus Christ and his call are necessarily
our death as well as our life. The call to discipleship, the baptism in
the name of Jesus Christ, means both death and life. The call of
Christ, his baptism, sets the Christian in the middle of the daily
arena against sin and the devil. Every day he encounters new temptations, and every day he must suffer anew for Jesus Christ's sake.
The wounds and scars he receives in the fray are living tokens of
this participation in the cross of his Lord. But there is another kind
of suffering and shame which the Christian is not spared. While it
is true that only the sufferings of Christ are a means of atonement,
yet since he has suffered for and borne the sins of the whole world
and shares with his disciples the fruits of his passion, the Christian
also has to undergo temptations, he too has to bear the sins of others; he too must bear their shame and be driven like a scapegoat
from the gate of the city. But he would certainly break down under
this burden, but for the support of him who bore the sins of all. The
passion of Christ strengthens him to overcome the sins of others by
forgiving them. He becomes the bearer of other men's burdens—
"Bear ye one another's burdens, and so fulfill the law of Christ"
(Gal 6.2). As Christ bears our burdens, so ought we to bear the burdens of our fellowmen. The law of Christ, which it is our duty to
fulfill, is the bearing of the cross. My brother's burden which I must
bear is not only his outward life, his natural characteristics and
gifts, but quite literally his sin. And the only way to bear that sin is
by forgiving it in the power of the cross of Christ in which I now
share. Thus the call to follow Christ always means a call to share

the word of forgiving men their sins. Forgiveness is the Christlike
suffering which it is the Christian's duty to bear.

Dietrich Bonhoeffer

R TWENTY-THIRD SUNDAY IN ORDINARY TIME

E PROPER 18

L SIXTEENTH SUNDAY AFTER PENTECOST

What an extraordinary thing it is, the efficiency of prayer! Like a
queen, it has access at all times to the royal presence, and can get
whatever it asks for. And it's a mistake to imagine that your prayer
won't be answered unless you've something out of a book, some
splendid formula of words, specially devised to meet this emer-
gency. If that were true, I'm afraid I should be in a terribly bad position. You see, I recite the Divine Office, with a great sense of
unworthiness, but apart from that I can't face the strain of hunting
about in books for these splendid prayers—it makes my head spin.
There are such a lot of them, each more splendid than the last; how
am I to recite them all, or to choose between them? I just do what
children have to do before they've learnt to read: I tell God what I
want quite simply, without any splendid turns of phrase, and some-
how God always manages to understand me. For me, prayer means
launching out of the heart towards God; it means lifting up one's
eyes, quite simply, to heaven, a cry of grateful love, from the crest
of joy or the trough of despair; it's a vast, supernatural force which
opens out my heart, and binds me close to Jesus. I love prayers said
in common; hasn't our Lord told us that he'll be in our midst when
we gather in his name? On those occasions, I'm conscious that the
warmth of my sisters' piety is making up for the coldness of my
own.

I want our Lord to draw me into the furnace of his love, to unite me
ever more closely with himself, till it is he who lives and acts in me.
Still, as that flame kindles, I shall cry out to be drawn closer, closer;
and its effect on those around me will be the same, although I am
only a poor piece of iron filing, that outside the furnace would be
inert. They will be as active as I am—like those women of the Canti-
cles who ran, allured by his perfumes, where the royal lover went.

The soul that it enfolded by divine love can't remain inactive; though it may, like Mary, sit at the feet of Jesus and listen to those words of his, so full of fire, so full of comfort; not appearing to contribute anything, but really contributing so much!

All the saints have seen the importance of Mary's attitude, and perhaps particularly the ones who have done most to fill the world with the light of gospel teaching. Surely those great friends of God, people like St. Paul and St. Augustine and St. John of the Cross and St. Thomas and St. Francis and St. Dominic, all went to prayer to find the secret of their wisdom, a divine wisdom that has left the greatest minds lost in admiration.

"Give me a lever and a fulcrum," said the man of science, "and I'll shift the world." Archimedes wasn't talking to God, so his request wasn't granted; and in any case he was only thinking of the material world. But the saints really have enjoyed the privilege he asked for; the fulcrum God told them to use was nothing less than God's self, and the lever was prayer. Only it must be the kind of prayer that sets the heart all on fire with love; that's how the saints shift the world in our own day, and that's how they'll do it to the end of time.

Thérèse of Lisieux

R TWENTY-FOURTH SUNDAY IN ORDINARY TIME

E PROPER 19

L SEVENTEENTH SUNDAY AFTER PENTECOST

The evil of remembering past offenses is twofold: it is inexcusable before God, and it serves to recall past sins already forgiven and places them against us. And this is what happened here. For nothing, nothing whatsoever does God so hate, and turn away from, as cherishing remembrance of past offenses, and fostering our anger against another. Instructed therefore in all these things, and with this parable inscribed in our hearts, let us, when the thought comes of what our fellow servants have done to us, think also of what we have done against our Lord; and then through remembrance of our own sins, we shall be able at once to banish the anger we feel at others' sins against us.

And if we must remember offenses, let us remember only our own. And if we remember our own sins, we shall never store up the sins of others. And again, should we forget the sins of others, our thoughts will then readily turn to the remembrance of our own. For if this man had remembered the ten thousand talents, he would never have remembered the hundred pence. It was when he had forgotten his own great debt, that he throttled his fellow servant; and determined to get back a few pence, and failing, he brought back upon his own head the debt of the ten thousand talents.

Therefore, I shall make bold to say, that this sin is more grievous than any sin. Let us therefore be zealous in nothing so much as in keeping ourselves free from anger, and from not seeking to be reconciled with those who are opposed to us; since we know that neither prayer nor alms nor fasting nor partaking of the sacraments nor any of these will profit us, if on that last day we are found remembering past offenses. But should we triumph over this fault, though stained with a thousand other crimes, we shall be enabled to obtain forgiveness. And neither is this my word only, but the word of that God who shall come to judge us.

Therefore, that here on earth we may lead a mild and gentle life, and there obtain pardon and remission for our sins, let us be eager, let us strive earnestly so that those who are enemies, may be recon-

ciled to us: so that, even if we have sinned a thousand times, we
may be reconciled to our Lord and may come to the joys of heaven.

John Chrysostom

R TWENTY-FIFTH SUNDAY IN ORDINARY TIME

E PROPER 20

L EIGHTEENTH SUNDAY AFTER PENTECOST

Let all the pious and all lovers of God rejoice in the splendor of this
feast; let the wise servants blissfully enter into the joy of their Lord;
let those who have borne the burden of Lent now receive their pay,
and those who have toiled since the first hour, let them now receive
their due reward; let any who came after the third hour be grateful
to join the feast, and those who may have come after the sixth, let
them not be afraid of being too late, for the Lord is gracious and he
receives the last even as the first. He gives rest to those who come
on the eleventh hour as well as to those who have toiled since the
first: yes, he has pity on the last and he serves the first; he rewards
the one and is generous to the other; he repays the deed and praises
the effort.

Come you all: enter into the joy of your Lord. You the first and you
the last, receive alike your reward; you rich and you poor, dance together; you sober and you weaklings, celebrate the day; you who
have kept the fast and you who have not, rejoice today. The table is
richly loaded: enjoy its royal banquet. The calf is a fatted one: let no
one go away hungry. All of you enjoy the banquet of faith; all of
you receive the riches of his goodness.

Let none grieve over their poverty, for the universal kingdom has
been revealed; let none weep over their sins, for pardon has shone
from the grave; let none fear death, for the death of our Savior has
set us free: he has destroyed it by enduring it, he has despoiled
hades by going down into its kingdom, he has angered it by allow-
ing it to taste of his flesh.

When Isaiah foresaw all this, he cried out: "O hades, you have been
angered by encountering him in the nether world." Hades is angered because frustrated, it is angered because it has been mocked,
it is angered because it has been destroyed, it is angered because it

has been reduced to naught, it is angered because it is now captive. It seized a body, and, lo! it discovered God; it seized earth, and, behold! it encountered heaven; it seized the visible, and was overcome by the invisible.

O death, where is your sting? O hades, where is your victory? Christ is risen and you are abolished, Christ is risen and the demons are cast down, Christ is risen and the angels rejoice, Christ is risen and life is freed, Christ is risen and the tomb is emptied of the dead: for Christ, being risen from the dead, has become the Leader and Reviver of those who had fallen asleep. To him be glory and power for ever and ever.

John Chrysostom

R TWENTY-SIXTH SUNDAY IN ORDINARY TIME
E PROPER 21
L NINETEENTH SUNDAY AFTER PENTECOST

I have come to know, and with me so will any one who has reflected even a little, that there is no man who fears God who will not amend his life unless the man thinks he has a longer time to live. It is this brings death to so many, as they keep saying, "tomorrow, tomorrow" (cras, cras); and of a sudden the door is closed. He remains without, with his raven's croak, because his voice was not the grieving voice of the dove. Tomorrow, tomorrow (Cras, cras): the voice of the raven. Mourn like the dove, and beat your breast; but as you beat your breast, let what you beat amend itself, lest you seem not so much to be beating your conscience as ramming it hard with blows, making a bad conscience more unyielding instead of more obedient. Mourn, but not in fruitless grieving.

It may be that you say to yourself, God has promised me forgiveness, whenever I reform; so I am safe. Tomorrow, when I amend my life, God will pardon me my sins. And what am I to say? Am I to cry out against God? Am I to say to God: Do not extend pardon? Am I to say that this is not written in the scriptures, that God has not made this promise? If I were to say that, I would say what was false. You are right; what you say is true. That God has promised you pardon when you amend your life, I cannot deny. But tell me, pray: I agree and I grant you and I know that God has promised you forgiveness. But who has promised you tomorrow? Where you read that you will receive forgiveness, when you do penance, read for me also how much longer you have to live. It is not there, you say. Therefore you do not know how long more you have to live. Then reform your life, and be always prepared.

Augustine

R TWENTY-SEVENTH SUNDAY IN ORDINARY TIME

E PROPER 22

L TWENTIETH SUNDAY AFTER PENTECOST

Picture in your mind a tree whose roots are watered by an ever-flowing fountain that becomes a great and living river with four channels to water the garden of the entire church. From the trunk of this tree, imagine that there are growing twelve branches that are adorned with leaves, flowers and fruit. Imagine that the leaves are a most effective medicine to prevent and cure every kind of sickness, because the word of the cross is the power of God for salvation to everyone who believes. Let the flowers be beautiful with the radiance of every color and perfumed with the sweetness of every fragrance, awakening and attracting the anxious hearts of those who desire. Imagine that there are twelve fruits, having every delight and the sweetness of every taste. This fruit is offered to God's servants to be tasted so that when they eat it, they may always be satisfied, yet never grow weary of its taste. This is the fruit that took its origin from the virgin's womb and reached its savory maturity on the tree of the cross under the midday heat of the eternal sun, that is, the love of Christ. In the garden of the heavenly paradise—God's table—this fruit is served to those who desire it.

Although this fruit is one and undivided, it nourishes devout souls with varied consolations in view of its varied states, excellence, powers and works. These can be reduced to twelve. This fruit of the tree of life, therefore, is pictured and is offered to our taste under twelve flavors on twelve branches. On the first branch the soul devoted to Christ perceives the flavor of sweetness, by recalling the distinguished origin and sweet birth of its Savior; on the second branch, the humble mode of life which he condescended to adopt;

on the third, the loftiness of his perfect power; on the fourth, the plenitude of his most abundant piety; on the fifth, the confidence which he had in the trial of his passion; on the sixth, the patience which he exhibited in bearing great insults and injuries; on the seventh, the constancy which he maintained in the torture and suffering on his rough and bitter cross; on the eighth, the victory which he achieved in the conflict and passage of death; on the ninth, the novelty of his resurrection embellished with remarkable gifts; on the tenth, the sublimity of his ascension, pouring forth spiritual charisms; on the eleventh, the equity of the future judgment; on the twelfth, the eternity of the divine kingdom.

I call these fruits because they delight with their rich sweetness and strengthen with their nourishment the soul who meditates on them and diligently considers each one, abhoring the example of unfaithful Adam who preferred the tree of the knowledge of good and evil to the tree of life.

Bonaventure

R TWENTY-EIGHTH SUNDAY IN ORDINARY TIME
E PROPER 23
L TWENTY-FIRST SUNDAY AFTER PENTECOST

Let no one delay in coming to the supper. Let us put aside all idle wicked excuses, and come to the supper in which our souls are fed. Let no swelling of pride keep us back, or lift us above ourselves; and neither let unlawful superstition frighten us, or turn us away from God. Let not the delights of the senses keep us from the delights of the soul. Let us come, and let us be feasted. And who have come but the poor and the feeble and the lame and the blind? But the rich have not come there, nor the healthy, who as it were could walk well and see clearly, sure of themselves, and the more arrogant were they, the more endangered.

Let the poor come, for he who invites us, though rich, became poor for our sakes, that by his poverty we might be made rich.

Let the feeble come, for they who are in health need not the physician, but they that are ill. Let the lame come. Let the blind come.

Compel them to come in. I have prepared a great supper, a great house: I shall suffer no place there to remain empty.

The Gentiles came from the streets and the lanes. Let the heretics come from the hedges; here they will find peace. For they who make hedges are seeking to bring about divisions. Let them be drawn from the hedges; let them be plucked free of the thorns. They refuse to be compelled, and they cling to their hedges. Let us, they say, come in of our own will. But this is not what the Lord commanded. Compel them, he says, to come in.

Augustine

R TWENTY-NINTH SUNDAY IN ORDINARY TIME
E PROPER 24
L TWENTY-SECOND SUNDAY AFTER PENTECOST

We have no anxieties any longer because we are as young children. We are accepted and affirmed by God and so do not need to prove ourselves to him. We do not need to impress him, for his love has taken the initiative — his Son died for us whilst we were yet sinners. We have full confidence in God, as children have full confidence in their parents. We have been set free and our liberation is total and comprehensive — it includes being set free from political, social and economic structures that are oppressive and unjust since these would enslave us, and make us less than God intends us to be. There is little about "pie in the sky when you die" in the gospel of Jesus Christ, for, as Archbishop Temple said, "Christianity is the most materialistic of the major religions." You qualify yourself for heaven or hell according to whether you did or did not do certain thoroughly secular and "unreligious" (in the narrow sense) things such as feeding the hungry, clothing the naked, visiting the sick and the imprisoned because these are they whom Christ calls the least of his brethren. There is nowhere that the writ of God does not run, for everything belongs to him. Caesar must be accorded what is appropriate for him, and God must have all—including Caesar's domain; otherwise there would be a part of the universe, of life, that did not fall under God's control.

Desmond Mpilo Tutu

R THIRTIETH SUNDAY IN ORDINARY TIME

E PROPER 25

L TWENTY-THIRD SUNDAY AFTER PENTECOST

Because it is a great thing to know this mystery, how he is David's Lord and David's Son, how the one person is both man and God, how in the form of a man he is less than the Father, in the form of God equal to the Father; because this is a great mystery, and that we may grasp it, you must be trained in virtue. For this mystery is sealed to the unworthy, revealed to those who are worthy. Nor is it with stones, nor iron bars, nor fists, nor feet that we come to the Lord's door and knock. It is our life that knocks; it is to our life that the door is opened. The heart seeks, the heart asks, the heart knocks; God opens to the heart. But the heart that seeks worthily, that knocks and asks worthily, must be virtuous. It must first love God for his own sake; for this is the true love of God: nor seek from him for other reward than himself. For than God there is nothing more perfect. God gives us the earth, and you rejoice lover of the earth, and made from earth. If you rejoice, when God gives us the earth, how much more should you not rejoice when God gives you himself, who made heaven and earth?

Augustine

R THIRTY-FIRST SUNDAY IN ORDINARY TIME

E PROPER 26

L TWENTY-SIXTH SUNDAY AFTER PENTECOST

O Jesus, who humbled thy majesty that thou might raise up the unfortunate who had grown proud, may thy grace be increased in us, that step by step we may ascend to thy love. Grant us, holy Father, that through our good works we may take upon us thy likeness, so that the true image of thy humility may be impressed upon our person. Grant us to feel within us the sweet taste of thy love, so that the powers of our mind may at all times be transported to thee. Water our thirsting soul, that it may bring forth the fruit of glory, and become a holy temple wherein thy godhead dwells. Unite our members to thee, Lord the head of the whole body, so that no one of us may be shut out from partaking of thy sweetness.

O true Son of our Father, who receiving a kingdom forsook it, do not when you come in the clouds deny the children of thy Father. Grant us, good Jesus, the vision for which our souls thirst, the glory of thy revelation, in hope and pledge of our sharing it; so that though lowly, and dust from our birth, our souls may rise up through thy exaltation; for we have become the offspring of God.

O sea of infinite mercy, and of all forgiveness! O immeasurable goodness, love beyond telling, our vision is too narrow to embrace the riches of thy love. O our Creator! How deep thy goodness, how far surpassing all things created! Not for the gain of a few has the Son of the King become a son of our race. He came down to prepare a kingdom for all our nature. Though you were despised and scorned by insults without number, yet never because of this shall I deny the magnitude of the hope that is laid up in you.

Ephraem

R THIRTY-SECOND SUNDAY IN ORDINARY TIME
E PROPER 27
L TWENTY-FOURTH SUNDAY AFTER PENTECOST

The first coming, namely, when God became a human being, lived humbly, and died out of love for us, is one which we should imitate exteriorly through the perfect practice of the virtues and interiorly through charity and genuine humility. The second coming, which is in the present and which takes place when Christ comes with his graces into every loving heart, is one which we should desire and pray for every day, so that we might persevere and progress in new virtues. The third coming, at the judgment or at the hour of our death, is one which we should await with longing, confidence, and awe, so that we might be released from this present misery and enter the palace of glory.

Recall that at the beginning of his parable Christ says, "See," by which he means that we should see by means of charity and a purified conscience. Next he shows us what we are to see, namely, these three comings. Now he tells us what we are to do, when he says, "Go out." If you possess the first point and so are able to see by means of grace and charity, and if you have attentively observed your model, Christ, and his own going out, then from this charity and this loving observation of your Bridegroom there arises in you a righteousness which makes you desire to follow him in the practice of virtue. Then Christ will be saying within you, "Go out."

This going out is to be done in three ways: We must go out to God and to ourselves and to our neighbor, and this must be done with charity and righteousness. Charity constantly strives upward toward the kingdom of God, that is, to the very God who is the source from which charity has flowed forth without intermediary and in which it abides by means of union. Righteousness, which arises from charity, desires the perfection of all those virtues and forms of behavior that are honorable and proper to the kingdom of God, which is the soul. These two, charity and righteousness, lay a foundation in the kingdom of the soul in which God is to dwell; this foundation is humility.

These three virtues bear the entire weight of the edifice of all the virtues and of all nobility. Charity keeps a person constantly facing the fathomless goodness of God from which charity flows forth, in order that one might live honorably for God and persevere and grow in all the virtues and in genuine humility. Righteousness keeps a person facing the eternal truth of God, in order to be open to the truth and become enlightened and fulfill all the virtues without going astray. Humility keeps a person facing the great majesty of God, in order to remain small and lowly and surrender the self to God. This is the way a person should act before God so as constantly to grow in new virtues.

John Ruusbroec

R THIRTY-THIRD SUNDAY IN ORDINARY TIME

E PROPER 28

L TWENTY-FIFTH SUNDAY AFTER PENTECOST

And you may see that now the soul is like a housewife who has put all her household in good order and prudently arranged it and well disposed it: she has taken good care that nothing will damage it, her provision for the future is wise, she knows exactly what she is doing, she acquires and discards, she does what is proper, she avoids mistakes, and always she knows how everything should be. So it is with the soul: the soul is all love, and love rules in the soul, mighty and powerful, working and resting, doing and not doing, and all which is in the soul and comes to the soul is according to love's will.

And like the fish, swimming in the vast sea and resting in its deeps, and like the bird, boldly mounting high in the sky, so the soul feels its spirit freely moving through the vastness and the depth and the unutterable richness of love.

It is love's power that has seized the soul and led it, sheltered and protected it, given it prudence and wisdom and the sweetness and the strength which belong to love. Yet still at this time love hides from the soul its own power, that it has mounted to yet greater heights and that it is master of itself and that it is love which reigns triumphantly in it. And now the soul feels indeed that love is within it, as mighty and as active when the body is at rest as when it performs many deeds.

The soul knows well and feels that love is not found in the labors and sufferings of those in whom it rules, but that all who want to attain to love must seek it in fear and pursue it in faith, exercising themselves in longing, not sparing themselves in great labors, in many sufferings, underdoing many sorrows and enduring much contempt. The soul must not despise these things: small though they be, they must seem great, until it attains to the state where love rules in it and performs its own mighty works, making great things small, labor easy, suffering sweet, and all debts paid.

Beatrice of Nazareth

L TWENTY-SEVENTH SUNDAY AFTER PENTECOST

I find, therefore, that there is a temple. Learn, then, how it is to be built in the name of the Lord. Before we believed in God, the dwelling of our heart was perishable and weak, like a temple actually built with hands, for it was full of idolatry and was the home of demons, because we did what was opposed to God. "But it will be built in the name of the Lord." But take heed that the temple of the Lord may be built in glory. Learn how. When we received forgiveness of sins and set our hope on the name, we became new, created again from the beginning, and therefore God really lives in us, in the dwelling which we are. How? God's word of faith, the call of his promise, the wisdom of his decrees, the commands of his teaching, that very God prophesying within us and dwelling in us, opening the temple door, that is, the mouth, and giving us repentance, leads us, who were enslaved to death, into the indestructible temple. This is the spiritual temple that is being built for the Lord.

Letter of Barnabas

R LAST SUNDAY IN ORDINARY TIME,
CHRIST THE KING

E PROPER 29

L CHRIST THE KING, LAST SUNDAY AFTER
PENTECOST

There lived a certain monk of very venerable life named Martyrius, who on one occasion went to visit another monastery, ruled over by a holy abbot. And on his way he met a certain leper, whose members were all afflicted with elephantiasis, who was trying to return to his dwelling, but could not through weakness. His house, he said, was on the road along which Martyrius was going.

The man of God had compassion on the weakness of the poor leper, and so he spread his own cloak upon the ground, and, placing the leper upon it, wrapped him securely in the cloak, and lifting him upon his shoulders, brought him along with him. And when they drew near the monastery gates, the abbot of the monastery began to cry out with a great voice, "Hurry, hurry, run quickly and open the gates. Brother Martyrius is coming, and bringing the Lord with him."

As soon as Martyrius reached the entrance of the monastery, the man he thought was a leper leaped down from his shoulders, and Jesus Christ, true God and true man, appearing in that form in which the Redeemer of humankind was known on earth, returned again to heaven before the eyes of Martyrius. And as he was ascending he said to him, "Martyrius, you were not ashamed of me on earth; I shall not be ashamed of you in heaven."

And when the holy man went into the monastery the abbot said to him, "Brother Martyrius, where is he you were carrying?" Martyrius answered, "Had I known who it was, I would have held him by the feet." Then he told them that while he was carrying him he had felt no weight. And it is not to be wondered at that he could not feel his weight who upheld him who was carrying him.

For what in human flesh is more sublime than the body of Christ, which was exalted above the angels? And what in human flesh is more abject than the body of a leper, filled with running sores and giving off repulsive smells? But see how he appeared in a leper's flesh. Why is this, if not that he might teach us who are slower of understanding that whosoever is eager to come before him who is in heaven not refuse to be humble on earth, nor have compassion on those who are abject or despised?

Gregory the Great

SUNDAYS AND MAJOR HOLY DAYS

CYCLE B

It is Advent and we are a people, pregnant. Pregnant and waiting. We long for the God/Man to be born, and this waiting is hard. Our whole life is spent, one way or another, in waiting. Information puts us on hold and fills our waiting ear with thin, irritating music. Our order hasn't come in yet. The elevator must be stuck. Our spouse is late. Will the snow never melt, the rain never stop, the paint ever dry? Will anyone ever understand? Will I ever change? Life is a series of hopes, and waitings, and half-fulfillments. With grace and increasing patience and understanding of this human condition of constantly unsatisfied desire, we wait on our in-completed salvation.

Waiting, because it will always be with us, can be made a work of art, and the season of Advent invites us to underscore and under-stand with a new patience that very feminine state of being, wait-ing. Our masculine world wants to blast away waiting from our lives. Instant gratification has become our constitutional right and delay an aberration. We equate waiting with wasting. So we build Concorde airplanes, drink instant coffee, roll out green plastic and call it turf, and reach for the phone before we reach for the pen. The more life asks us to wait, the more we anxiously hurry. The tempo of haste in which we live has less to do with being on time or the ef-ficiency of a busy life—it has more to do with our being unable to wait. But waiting is unpractical time, good for nothing but mysteri-ously necessary to all that is coming. As in a pregnancy, nothing of value comes into being without a period of quiet incubation: not a healthy baby, not a loving relationship, not a reconciliation, a new understanding, a work of art, never a transformation. Rather, a shortened period of incubation brings forth what is not whole or strong or even alive. Brewing, baking, simmering, fermenting, rip-ening, germinating, gestating are the feminine processes of becom-ing and they are the symbolic states of being which belong in a life of value, necessary to transformation. Waiting could use a fresh new look. The discipline of delayed gratification—not celebrating Christmas until the twenty-fourth of December—and the hope-filled rituals of our Advent preparations will give new value to the waiting period in our lives.

Gertrud Mueller Nelson

The way to freedom runs through the wilderness. Hence the first message is that the people must prepare a way, more accurately a street, straight through the wilderness. In both Isaiah and Mark this is what the people have to do first of all.

To understand what is meant here by what we may find the bizarre idea of a "street through the wilderness," we must have a fair idea of what life was like for the anonymous prophet who has taken the name of Isaiah, living in Babylon. From Babylonian hymns and from archaeological evidence we know that "the boulevard," the high street or main street in Babylon, exercised an enormous fascination on the mass of people. It was rather like the Champs Elysees in Paris, leading to the Arc de Triomphe, or the Via Vittorio Emmanuele in Rome, leading to the colossal, pretentious monument to the king. The Lenin, Marx, and Eisenhower allées all lead up to great monumental buildings. So Isaiah too wants a highway for the Lord, running through the wilderness and leading to the temple in Jerusalem, which was to be rebuilt. In Babylon the streets bearing the names of gods or the resounding names of great kings, memorial to former victories, to jubilation and triumph, were also the place where every year colossal, majestic statues of gods were carried along in colorful state cavalcades and religious processions for all the world to see: the greatest show on earth! The Jewish exiles, including our prophet "Isaiah," had watched this pagan demonstration of power sadly every year, but nevertheless fell under its bewitching spell. In it they felt the living power of Babylon.

Nevertheless, Isaiah presented precisely this picture of the pagan triumphal route to the Jews, not as a street for Babylonian gods but as the Lord's street, a straight road for our God the Lord, called the highway of Yahweh. However — and this is the secret key to the whole account — Israel's God is no Babylonian god, and Jews were forbidden to make images. God's glory is not revealed in splendid cavalcades on great streets or in processions with imposing effigies, but only in everyday history, and above all in the event of the liberation of his people from slavery, through the difficult journey through the wilderness, back to the freedom of Zion. That, Isaiah says, is the way in which God's glory is made manifest and revealed to all. That is where God's jealous honor is to be found: in the exaltation of the insignificant, the poor and the lowly, those who are oppressed.

Edward Schillebeeckx

R E L THIRD SUNDAY OF ADVENT

It was a custom of the ancients, that if a man were not willing to retain the woman who was his wife, that he should untie the shoes of the one who came by right of kinship to claim her as bride. How has Christ appeared among humankind, except as the bridegroom of the church? This may be understood in yet another way. Who does not know that sandals are made from the skins of dead animals? The Lord, in becoming incarnate, appears among humankind as though shod; over his divinity, he has put on as it were the mortal covering of our corruptibility. The Lord declares that through the flesh he became known to the Gentiles, as if the divinity had come to us with feet shod.

But the human eye does not suffice to penetrate the mystery of this incarnation. For in no way may we search out how the Word became embodied, how the supreme life-giving Spirit was quickened within the womb of a mother, how that which has no beginning was both conceived and came into existence.

The latchets of his shoe are therefore the seals of a mystery. John was not worthy to loose his shoe, because he was unable to search into the mystery of his incarnation. It is as though he were to say: what wonder that he is preferred before me, whom I know to be born after me, but the mystery of whose birth I am unable to comprehend. Behold John, filled with the Spirit of prophecy, shining with knowledge, yet he plainly declares that as to this mystery he knows nothing.

Gregory the Great

R E L FOURTH SUNDAY OF ADVENT

We must both read and meditate upon the Nativity. If the meditation does not reach the heart, we shall sense no sweetness, nor shall we know what solace for humankind lies in this contemplation. The heart will not laugh nor be merry. As spray does not touch the deep, so mere meditation will not quiet the heart. There is such richness and goodness in this Nativity that if we should see and deeply understand, we should be dissolved in perpetual joy. Wherefore St. Bernard declared there are here three miracles: that God and humankind should be joined in this Child; that a mother should remain a virgin; that Mary should have such faith as to believe that this mystery would be accomplished in her. The last is not the least of the three. The virgin birth is a mere trifle for God; that God should become human is a greater miracle; but most amazing of all is it that his maiden should credit the announcement that she, rather than some other virgin, had been chosen to be the mother of God. She did indeed inquire of the angel, "How can these things be?" And he answered, "Mary, you have asked too high a question for me, but the Holy Spirit will come upon you and the power of the Most High will overshadow you and you will not know yourself how it happens." Had she not believed, she could not have conceived. She held fast to the word of the angel because she had become a new creature. Even so must we be transformed and renewed in heart from day to day. Otherwise Christ is born in vain. This is the word of the prophet: "Unto us a child is born, unto us a son is given." This is for us the hardest point, not so much to believe that he is the son of the virgin and of God as to believe that this Son of God is ours. Truly it is marvelous in our eyes that God should place a little child in the lap of a virgin and that all our blessedness should lie in him. And this Child belongs to all humankind. God feeds the whole world through a Babe nursing at Mary's breast. This must be our daily exercise: to be transformed into Christ, being nourished by this food. Then will the heart be suffused with all joy and will be strong and confident against every assault.

Martin Luther

R CHRISTMAS MASS AT MIDNIGHT
E CHRISTMAS DAY I
L THE NATIVITY OF OUR LORD, 1

It is no use saying that we are born two thousand years too late to give room to Christ. Nor will those who live at the end of the world have been born too late. Christ is always with us, always asking for room in our hearts.

But now it is with the voice of our contemporaries that he speaks, with the eyes of store clerks, factory workers, and children that he gazes; with the hand of office workers, slum dwellers, and suburban housewives that he gives. It is with the feet of soldiers and tramps that he walks, and with the heart of anyone in need that he longs for shelter. And giving shelter or food to anyone who asks for it, or needs it, is giving it to Christ.

It would be foolish to pretend that it is always easy to remember this. If everyone were holy and handsome, with "alter Christus" shining in neon lighting from them, it would be easy to see Christ in everyone. If Mary had appeared in Bethlehem clothed, as St. John says, with the sun, a crown of twelve stars on her head, and the moon under her feet, then people would have fought to make room for her. But that was not God's way for her, nor is it Christ's way for himself, now when he is disguised under every type of humanity that treads the earth.

To see how far one realizes this, it is a good thing to ask honestly what you would do, or have done, when a beggar asked at your house for food. Would you—or did you—give it on an old cracked plate, thinking that was good enough? Do you think that Martha and Mary thought that the old and chipped dish was good enough for their guest?

In Christ's human life, there were always a few who made up for the neglect of the crowd. The shepherds did it; their hurrying to the crib atoned for the people who would flee from Christ. The wise men did it; their journey across the world made up for those who refused to stir one hand's breadth from the routine of their lives to go to Christ. Even the gifts the wise men brought have in themselves an obscure recompense and atonement for what would follow later in this Child's life. For they brought gold, the king's emblem, to make up for the crown of thorns that he would wear; they offered incense, the symbol of praise, to make up for the mockery and the spitting; they gave him myrrh, to heal and soothe, and he was wounded from head to foot and no one bathed his wounds.

The women at the foot of the cross did it too, making up for the crowd who stood by and sneered.

We can do it too, exactly as they did. We are not born too late. We do it by seeing Christ and serving Christ in friends and strangers, in everyone we come in contact with.

Dorothy Day

R CHRISTMAS MASS DURING THE DAY
E CHRISTMAS DAY III
L THE NATIVITY OF OUR LORD, 2

The birth of Jesus Christ is no ordinary event in the recorded history of peoples. Ordinary historic events are marked down, remembered, and possibly commemorated year after year. In time a given occurrence may fade into insignificance as others capture the imagination. But the birth, life, and death of Jesus Christ do not belong to this kind of history. Once born, once having lived through the Pascal mysteries of death and resurrection, Jesus Christ is an ever present reality; in him we live and breathe and have our being even now. This is our faith. To say this and to believe this is to say something different about time and the manner of our participation in it. Human history is measured by dates on a time line that mark the deeds, events, and lives of great persons, nations, and peoples. This is historic time. We live in it. It is the time of human achievements, discoveries, explorations, settlements, scientific and technological advances, the production of artistic masterpieces, as well as the time of wars, pestilences, and famine.

Redemptive history is something else. It is not measured at all. It is a continuum of events in which God has acted for our salvation. Some call it mythic time. It encompasses and envelopes and moves through our human history, but it is not contained by it. By our faith and sacramental life we are caught up in it. It lives in us. Christians, you and I are called to live in the tension point where historic and redemptive time converge.

We are called to know the joy, the peace, the hope, the love that Christ infallibly confers upon those who join themselves to him. We are called not only to know his joy, his peace, his hope, and his love for ourselves, but to be bearers of these redemptive gifts into the lives of others. We are called to participate in the anguish, the pain, the deprivation, and the suffering of those around us. And we are called to minister to our world—to bring the certainty of our hope, known by us in redemptive time, into active work to better the circumstances of contemporary people so many of whom are doomed to suffering. In short, we are called to mediate the reality of the salvation which we experience in redemptive time into the unsaved, unredeemed, corrupted world of which we are a part.

Nadine Foley

R HOLY FAMILY
L FIRST SUNDAY AFTER CHRISTMAS

Sometimes it seemed to Marie d'Oignies that for three or more days she held Christ close to her so that he nestled between her breasts like a baby, and she hid him there lest he be seen by others. Sometimes she kissed him as though he were a little child and sometimes she held him on her lap as if he were a gentle lamb. At other times the holy Son of the virgin manifest himself in the form of a dove, or he would walk around the church as if he were a ram with a bright star in the middle of his forehead and, as it seemed to her, he would visit his faithful ones. And just as the Lord showed himself to his doubting disciples in the form of a pilgrim and took the shape of a merchant when he sent St. Thomas to the Indies, just so he deigned to manifest himself to his friends for their consolation under the form of a friend. Thus St. Jerome testified that when St. Paula came to Bethlehem, she saw him as a baby lying in a crib. He manifested himself to Marie in a form that was in keeping with the feast. Thus he showed himself at the nativity as though he were a baby sucking at the breasts of the virgin Mary or crying in his cradle. In this way the various feasts took on new interest according to how he manifested himself. At the Feast of the Purification she saw the blessed Virgin offering her Son in the temple and Simon receiving him in his arms. In this vision she exulted no less from joy than if she had been present herself when this happened in the temple. Sometimes during this same feast, after she had been walking in procession for a long time with her candle snuffed out, suddenly it burned with a most brilliant light which only God had kindled. Sometimes at the

Passion the Lord appeared to her on the cross, but this happened rarely because she could scarcely endure it. When any great solemnity approached she would sometimes feel joy for a full eight days before the feast. Thus was she transformed throughout the course of a whole year in different ways and was wondrously filled with love.

Jacques de Vitry

R L SECOND SUNDAY AFTER CHRISTMAS
E FIRST SUNDAY AFTER CHRISTMAS

Then I saw a most splendid light, and in that light, the whole of which burnt in a most beautiful, shining fire, was the figure of a man of a sapphire color, and that most splendid light poured over the whole of that shining fire, and the shining fire over all the splendid light, and that most splendid light and shining fire over the whole figure of the man, appearing one light in one virtue and power. And again I heard that living light saying to me: This is the meaning of the mysteries of God, that it may be discerned and understood discreetly what that fullness may be, which is without beginning and to which nothing is wanting, who by the most powerful strength planted all the rivers of the strong places.

On which account thou seest this most splendid light, which is without beginning and to whom nothing can be wanting: this means the Father, and in that figure of a man of a sapphire color, without any spot of the imperfection of envy and iniquity, is declared the Son, born of the Father, according to the divinity before all time, but afterwards incarnate according to the humanity, in the world, in time. The whole of which burns in a most beautiful, shining fire, which fire without a touch of any dark mortality shows the Holy Spirit, by whom the same only-begotten Son of God was conceived according to the flesh, and born in time of the virgin, and poured forth the light of true brightness upon the world.

But that splendid light pours forth all that shining fire, and that shining fire all that splendid light, and the splendid shining light of the fire, the whole of the figure of the man, making one light existing in one strength and power. Through that fountain of life came

the paternal love of the embrace of God, which educated us to life,
and in our dangers was our help, and in the most deep and beautiful light teaching us repentance.

Hildegard of Bingen

E SECOND SUNDAY AFTER CHRISTMAS

Herod was seeking an unripe grape by which he would make
an unseasonable harvest.
Winter was settling in when Mary produced the unfertilized grape,
And he did not find a ripened fruit but reaped a green harvest. For
the fruit of the only pure virgin

Is going to flee to Egypt along with the vine
To be planted there and bring forth fruit—
Flee to the land of the Jews,
Arid and barren of anything beautiful,
And arrive at the Nile, which is fertile—
Not as Moses on the river, thrown in the marsh, protected
by a wicker basket,
But rather as one to overthrow all their idols there.
As Herod is a friend of these idols, he sees
That his power will soon be destroyed.

Romanos

R E L THE EPIPHANY OF OUR LORD

Let us now see, after the star had come to rest, after the journey of
the magi, what wondrous dignity accompanies the newborn King.
For immediately the magi, falling down before the Lord, adore him
newlyborn, and lying in a manger, and offering gifts they venerate
the infancy of a weeping babe. With the eyes of their body they saw
one thing, another with the eyes of the mind. The lowliness of the
assumed body is before their eyes, yet the glory of the divinity is
not concealed. It is a child that is adored. And together with it the
unspeakable mystery of the divine condescension! That invisible
and eternal nature has not disdained, for our sakes, to take to itself
the infirmities of our flesh.

The Son of God, who is the God of all things, is born a man in body.
He permits himself to be placed in a crib, who holds the heavens in

his hand. He is confined in a manger whom the world cannot contain; he is heard in the voice of a wailing infant, at whose voice in the hour of his passion the whole earth trembled. The magi, beholding a child, profess that this is the Lord of glory, the Lord of majesty.

To him the magi offer gifts, that is: gold, frankincense and myrrh. As the Holy Spirit had in time past testified concerning them, the prophecy is manifestly fulfilled by the magi, who both announce the salvation of the Lord, born Christ the Son of God, and by their gifts proclaim him Christ and God, and king of humanity. For by gold the power of a king is signified, by frankincense the honor of God, by myrrh the burial of the body; and accordingly they offer him gold as king, frankincense as God, myrrh as man.

anonymous

R L BAPTISM OF OUR LORD
E FIRST SUNDAY AFTER EPIPHANY

Without delay therefore hear him whom in all things I am well pleased; in preaching whom I am made known; in whose lowliness I am glorified; for he is the truth and the life, he is my power, my wisdom. Hear him whom the mysteries of the Law foretold, whom the mouths of the prophets proclaimed. Hear him, whose blood has redeemed the world, who has chained the demon, taken from him what he held, and has blotted out the deed of sin, the covenant of evildoing. Hear him who opens the way to heaven, and through the humiliation of his cross prepared for you a way to ascend to his kingdom.

Why do you fear to be redeemed? Why tremble at being healed of your wounds? Let that be done which I willing Christ wills. Put away bodily fear, and arm yourselves with steadfast faith: for it is unfitting you should fear, in the passion of your Savior, what by his gift to you you shall not fear in your own end.

These words were spoken for the profit, not alone of those who heard them with their bodily ears, but in these three apostles the whole church learns what their eyes saw and their ears heard. Let the faith of all be strengthened by means of the preaching of the most holy gospel; and let no one fear to suffer for justice's sake, or doubt of the fulfillment of his promises: for it is through toil we come to rest, and through death we cross over to life. Since he has taken upon himself all the infirmity of our humanity, in him we shall overcome what he has overcome, and receive what he has promised, provided that we persevere in faith and love of him.

Leo

R SECOND SUNDAY IN ORDINARY TIME
E L SECOND SUNDAY AFTER EPIPHANY

Every one of us forms an idea of Christ that is limited and incomplete. It is cut according to our own measure. We tend to create for ourselves a Christ in our own image, a projection of our own aspirations, desires and ideals. We find in him what we want to find. We make him not only the incarnation of God but also the incarnation of the things we and our society and our part of society happen to live for.

Therefore, although it is true that perfection consists in imitating Christ and reproducing him in our own lives, it is not enough merely to imitate the Christ we have in our imagination. We read the gospels not merely to get a picture or an idea of Christ but to enter in and pass through the words of revelation to establish, by faith, a vital contact with the Christ who dwells in our souls as God.

The problem of forming Christ in us is not to be solved merely by our own efforts. It is not a matter of studying the gospels and then working to put our ideas into practice, although we should try to do that too, but always under the guidance of grace, in complete subjection to the Holy Spirit. For if we depend on our own ideas, own judgment and our own efforts to reproduce the life of Christ, we will only act out some kind of pious charade which will ultimately scare everybody we meet because it will be so stiff and artificial and so dead.

It is the Spirit of God that must teach us who Christ is and form Christ in us and transform us into other Christs. After all, transformation into Christ is not just an individual affair: there is only one Christ, not many. He is not divided. And for me to become Christ is to enter into the life of the whole Christ, the mystical body made up of the head and the members, Christ and all who are incorporated in him by his Spirit.

Therefore if you want to have in your heart the affections and dispositions that were those of Christ on earth, consult not your own imagination but faith. Enter into the darkness of interior renunciation, strip your soul of images and let Christ form himself in you by his cross.

Thomas Merton

R THIRD SUNDAY IN ORDINARY TIME
E L THIRD SUNDAY AFTER EPIPHANY

Beloved, you have today put on Christ and march under our direction, you are raised up by the word of God, like a fish on a hook, from the ocean of the world. With us normal life is transformed, for fish die as soon as they are taken from the seas of this life and we sinners although dead return to life.

As long as we were in the world we remained in the depths and our life was submerged in the mire. But since we have been rescued from the waters we have begun to see the sun, we have commenced to look on the true light. We cry, I say, to the Lord, and let us interpret the profound mysteries of the scripture by other witnesses of the scripture. Everything which we cannot discover in the abyss of the Old Testament we will find revealed in the New in the roar of God's cataracts, that is to say in God's prophets and apostles. All the lofty wastes of the Lord, the seas and the impetuous rivers which gladden the city of God, have been broken under us in Christ Jesus, to whom be glory and power forever and ever.

Jerome

R FOURTH SUNDAY IN ORDINARY TIME
E L FOURTH SUNDAY AFTER EPIPHANY

The Lord rebuke thee, O devil, the Lord who came into the world and tabernacled among men to destroy thy tyranny and deliver mankind: who upon the tree did triumph over the powers that were against him; when the sun was darkened and the earth did quake, when the graves were opened and the bodies of saints arose:

who by death destroyed death, and left him powerless who had the power of death, that is, the devil. I adjure thee by God, who set forth the tree of life, who appointed the cherubim and the living sword that turned to guard it: be rebuked and depart, O unclean spirit. I adjure thee by him who walked upon the surface of the sea as upon dry land, and rebuked the raging of the winds whose glance doth dry up the depths and his threat melt the mountains. For he himself now commands you through us. Be afraid, go hence and depart from these creatures, come not back to hide in them, approach them not, seek not to command or tear them, neither in night nor day, nor in the hour of mid-day: but depart to thine own dark abode, until the great day of judgment which is prepared for thee. Fear God that sitteth upon the throne of the cherubim, and looks down upon the abyss, whom the angels dread, with archangels, thrones, lordships, majesties, powers, the many-eyed cherubim and the six-winged seraphim, whom the heaven doth dread, and the earth, the sea, and all that is in them. Go hence and depart from the sealed, new-chosen servants of Christ our God. I adjure thee by him who walketh upon the wings of the wind, who maketh his angels spirits and his ministers a flaming fire: go hence and depart from these creatures with all thy power and thine angels, that the name of the Father, the Son, and the Holy Spirit be glorified now and ever unto all ages.

exorcism from Byzantine rite

R FIFTH SUNDAY IN ORDINARY TIME
E L FIFTH SUNDAY AFTER EPIPHANY

The church considers healing as a sacrament. But such was its misunderstanding during the long centuries of the total identification of the church with "religion" (a misunderstanding from which all sacraments suffered, and the whole doctrine of sacraments) that the sacrament of oil became in fact the sacrament of death, one of the "last rites" opening to man a more or less safe passage into eternity. There is a danger that today, with the growing interest in healing among Christians, it will be understood as a sacrament of health, a useful "complement" to secular medicine. And both views are wrong, because both miss precisely the sacramental nature of this act. A sacrament—as we already know—is always a passage, a transformation. Yet it is not a "passage" into "supernature," but into the kingdom of God, the world to come, into the very reality of this world and its life as redeemed and restored by Christ. It is the transformation not of "nature" into "supernature," but of the old into the new. A sacrament therefore is not a "miracle" by which God breaks, so to speak, the "laws of nature," but the manifestation of the ultimate truth about the world and life, man and nature, the truth which is Christ.

And healing is a sacrament because its purpose or end is not health as such, the restoration of physical health, but the entrance of man into the life of the kingdom, into the "joy and peace" of the Holy Spirit. In Christ everything in this world, and this means health and disease, joy and suffering, has become an ascension to, and entrance into this new life, its expectation and anticipation.

In this world suffering and disease are indeed "normal," but their "normalcy" is abnormal. They reveal the ultimate and permanent defeat of man and of life, a defeat which no partial victories of medicine, however wonderful and truly miraculous, can ultimately overcome. But in Christ suffering is not "removed"; it is transformed into victory. The defeat itself becomes victory, a way, an entrance into the kingdom, and this is the only true healing.

Alexander Schmemann

R SIXTH SUNDAY IN ORDINARY TIME
E SIXTH SUNDAY AFTER EPIPHANY, PROPER 1
L SIXTH SUNDAY AFTER EPIPHANY

People have bodies and feelings; they feel well, they hurt, they feel lonely, they sense delight. For Mark, the gospel can be felt and sensed, and he had an unparalleled way of expressing the corporeality of the experience of joy, well-being, and sorrow. For us in a western Christianity, where the body is forgotten or suppressed, or is a vehicle for achieving one's ends, many passages in his gospel sound remarkably archaic.

In Mark, Jesus himself is more of a human being, more physical than in the other gospels. He enjoys the gesture of anointing. He trembles with anguish in Gethsemane. He dies with an inarticulate cry, and the whole attitude of obedience which was added later has still not destroyed the image of the feeling, suffering man who looks for human proximity. He is also more sensitive towards examples of wretchedness. He is often grieved. He has a heart. He surrenders himself in his whole person.

This Jesus needs people. He is not the solitary hero. He is not so sovereign that he can do without his neighbor. The betrayal by the disciples grieves him, and in Gethsemane this grief makes him tremble physically. The luxurious anointing comes from the comforting proximity of women: delight, enjoyment, pleasure, in a solitude that is becoming increasingly painful. If we did not have the gospel of Mark, we would have a much cooler, more 'divine' picture of Jesus. Mark has brought us the gentle Jesus.

However, the physical nature of this Jesus, which he brings with him, this openness for himself, his sorrow, his joy, his nearness to others, also provokes conflicts with those around. Every culture has its phobias about touch. These appear above all in taboos about sexuality and their social effects. In ancient society the human body was taboo, i.e., untouchable, when it was unclean, leprous or dead. Anyone who touched such a body transgressed ritual laws and themselves became unclean, i.e., they could not participate in any religious cults.

In a sovereign way, Jesus puts himself above these taboos. For him they do not exist. He touches the lepers and heals them. He allows himself to be touched by them, and they become healthy. What we find miraculous plays a central role in the gospel: the breakthrough to a body of our own which is regarded as entirely God's good creation, which is not isolated by any illness and which no ritual laws can despise and present as untouchable.

Corporeality is no sphere reserved for women. In Mark, men too experience a healing change in their bodies. However, particular women experienced physical liberation more directly than men. Therefore, also in Mark, there emanates from them a wordless, healing, comforting power which embraces the whole person. On Easter morning they risk the same great transgression of a taboo as their master: they want to anoint a dead body and in an undisturbed way continue the physical proximity which they have experienced. However, the dead body is no longer there. The physical experience is not the only one, nor the last one. It is threatened by the death and destruction of the body, but despite this it is essential, because it bears within it the hope for the new heaven and the new earth.

Elisabeth Moltmann-Wendel

R SEVENTH SUNDAY IN ORDINARY TIME
E SEVENTH SUNDAY AFTER EPIPHANY, PROPER 2
L SEVENTH SUNDAY AFTER EPIPHANY

This bed the man is told to take up, what does it mean but that he is told to raise up the human body? This is the bed of pain upon which our soul lies sick in the grievous torment of a burthened conscience. But if anyone bear this bed according to the commandments of Christ, it is no longer a bed of pain, but of rest. Because what was death, begins now to be rest, by the mercy of the Lord who has changed our sleep of death into the grace of the delight of the Lord. He is bidden not only to take up his bed, but also to return to his house; that is, he is told to return to paradise; for that is his true home and the first to receive him: lost, not by law, but by fraud. Rightly therefore is his home restored to him, since he has come who destroyed the deed of fraud, and restored his right.

You alone I follow, Lord Jesus, who heals my wounds. For what shall separate me from the love of God, which is in you? Shall tribulation, or distress, or famine? I am held fast as though by nails, and fettered by the bonds of charity. Remove from me, O Lord Jesus, with your potent sword, the corruption of my sins. Secure me in the bonds of your love; cut away what is corrupt in me. Come quickly and make an end of my many, my hidden and secret afflictions. Open the wound lest the evil humor spread. With your new washing, cleanse in me all that is stained. Hear me, those of you who in your sins bring forth drunken thoughts. I have found a physician. He dwells in heaven and distributes his healing on earth. He alone can heal my pains who himself has none. He alone who knows what is hidden can take away the grief of my heart, the fear of my soul: Jesus Christ. Christ is grace, Christ is life, Christ is resurrection.

Ambrose

R EIGHTH SUNDAY IN ORDINARY TIME

E EIGHTH SUNDAY AFTER EPIPHANY, PROPER 2

L EIGHTH SUNDAY AFTER EPIPHANY

Our Redeemer is become our bridegroom! The bride is intoxicated by the sight of his glorious countenance. In her greatest strength she is overcome; in her blindness, she sees most clearly; in her greatest clearness, she is both dead and alive. The richer she becomes, the poorer she is. The more she storms, the more loving God is to her. The higher she soars, the more brightly she shines from the reflection of the Godhead the nearer she comes. The more she labors, the more sweetly she rests. The more she understands, the less she speaks. The louder she calls, the greater wonders she works with his power and her might. The more God loves her, the more glorious the course of love, the nearer the resting place, the closer the embrace. The closer the embrace, the sweeter the kiss. The more lovingly they gaze at each other, the more difficult it is to part. The more he gives her, the more she spends, the more she has. The more humbly she takes leave, the sooner she returns. The more the fire burns, the more her light increases. The more love consumes her, the brighter she shines. The vaster God's praise, the vaster her desire for him.

Ah! whither fares our bridegroom and Redeemer in the jubilation of the holy Trinity? As God willed no longer to remain in himself alone, therefore created he the soul and gave himself in great love to her alone.

Mechthild of Magdeburg

E LAST SUNDAY AFTER EPIPHANY

L TRANSFIGURATION OF OUR LORD

Christ brings before them the one who had died and one that had not yet died. Both had lost their life, and found it. For both the one and the other had courageously withstood a tyrant: one the Egyptian, the other Ahab; and this on behalf of a people who were both ungrateful and disobedient.

Both were simple, unlearned men. One was slow of speech and weak of voice, the other a rough countryman. And both were men who had despised the riches of this world. For Moses possessed nothing. And Elijah had nothing but his sheepskin. And this too when they were yet under the old law, and had the privilege of seeing signs and wonders. And though Moses had divided the sea in two, Peter had walked upon the waters, and could move mountains. And if Elijah had raised a dead man to life, these raised thousands, though they had not yet received the Holy Spirit.

Christ brought these men before the disciples, for he wished them to imitate their courage of soul, and their steadfastness in leading their people; and so that they might be gentle as Moses, and possessed of the zeal of Elijah, and as devoted as both were. He brought all this before their mind through this vision. He brought these before them in glory; and not alone that they might be as they were, but that they might surpass them. That Christ might uplift their courage against all such dangers, he here brings before them those two men who were such shining lights of the Old Testament.

John Chrysostom

R E L ASH WEDNESDAY

Hear our prayer; do not ignore our plea. We are neither so insolent nor so obstinate as to claim that we are righteous, without sin, for we have surely sinned.

We abuse, we betray, we are cruel.
We destroy, we embitter, we falsify.
We gossip, we hate, we insult.
We jeer, we kill, we lie.
We mock, we neglect, we oppress.
We pervert, we quarrel, we rebel.
We steal, we transgress, we are unkind.
We are violent, we are wicked, we are xenophobic.
We yield to evil, we are zealots for bad causes.

Compared to you, all the mighty are nothing, the famous are nonexistent, the wise lack wisdom, the clever lack reason. For most of their actions are meaninglessness, the days of their lives emptiness. All life is a fleeting breath.

What can we say to you, what can we tell you?
You know all things, secret and revealed.

You always forgive transgressions. Hear the cry of our prayer. Pass over the transgressions of a people who turn away from transgression. Blot out our sins from your sight.

confession from Yom Kippur evening service

R E L FIRST SUNDAY IN LENT

Mystical and salutary is this number, forty. For when in the beginning human iniquity covered the face of the earth, God, dissolving the clouds of heaven for the space of this number of days, covered the whole earth with a flood. For as it then rained for forty days, to cleanse the world, so now does it also. Yet the deluge of those days must be called a mercy; in that through it iniquity was crushed and justness upheld. For it took place out of mercy, to deliver the just, and that the wicked might no longer sin. We see clearly it was through mercy it came, as a sort of baptism, in which the face of the earth was renewed.

The flood of those days was, as I say, a figure of baptism. For that was then prefigured which is now fulfilled; that is, just as when the fountains of water overflowed, iniquity was imperilled, and justness alone reigned. Sin was swept into the abyss, and holiness upraised to heaven. For as Noah was saved in the ark, while human iniquity was drowned in the flood, so by the waters of baptism the church is borne close to heaven, all the superstitions of idols overthrown, and the faith reigns on earth which came forth from the ark of the Savior.

And so we, though we also are sinners, announce to you, as the blessed Noah in his time, the coming destruction of the world. And we tell you that they alone shall escape who find shelter in the bosom of the threefold ark of the faith. For threefold is the ark of the church, since it contains within it the mystery of the Trinity. For when the scripture relates that the ark had a middle and a third story, it is showing us that the church is adorned by the threefold presence of the Trinity. As Noah received his children into the ark, so do we also earnestly desire to receive our children into this ark.

Maximus

R   SECOND SUNDAY IN LENT
E   L   SECOND SUNDAY IN LENT

So why are you afraid to take up the cross, when it leads us to the kingdom?

In the cross is salvation, in the cross is life; in the cross is defense from enemies, in the cross heaven's sweetness is outpoured; in the cross is strength of mind, in the cross is joy of spirit; in the cross is highest virtue, in the cross is perfect holiness. There is no salvation for the soul nor hope of eternal life except in the cross. Take up your cross then, and follow Jesus, and you will enter eternal life. He went before you, carrying his cross, and on the cross he died for you, so that you too should carry your cross, and long for a death on the cross. For if you share his death, you will also share his life. If you are with him in his suffering, you will be with him in his glory.

All that matters is the cross and dying on that cross—there is no other way to life and real inward peace except the way of the holy cross, and of daily dying to self. Go where you like, look for what you like, you will not find a higher way above or a safer way below than the way of the holy cross.

The cross is always close by and waits for you everywhere. You cannot escape it, wherever you may run; for everywhere you go you take yourself, and always you will find yourself. Look up or down, out or in, there too you will find the cross; and all the time you must go on being patient if you wish to have inward peace and to win a crown that will last for ever.

If you carry your cross with gladness, it will carry you and lead you to that longed-for goal where there will be no more suffering, though there will always be suffering here. If you carry it grudgingly, you will make it a burden and weigh yourself down, but all the same you will have to bear it. If you throw one cross aside you will certainly find another, and possibly one that is heavier to bear.

Thomas à Kempis

R E L THIRD SUNDAY IN LENT

One would not inconsiderately receive a king—why say I a king? nay, were it but a royal robe, one would not inconsiderably touch it with unclean hands. Yet the robe is naught but certain threads spun by worms. And if you admire the dye, this too is the blood of a dead fish; nevertheless, one would not choose to venture on it with polluted hands. I say now, if even a garment be what one would not venture inconsiderately to touch, what shall we say of the body of the one who is God over all, spotless, pure, associate with the divine nature, the body whereby we are, and live; whereby the gates of hell were broken down and sanctuaries of heaven opened? Let us with all awe and purity draw nigh to it; and when you see it set before you, say to yourself, "Because of this body am I no longer earth and ashes, no longer a prisoner, but free: because of this I hope for heaven, and to receive the good things therein, immortal life, the portion of angels, converse with Christ; this body, nailed and scourged, was more than death could stand against; this body both the veil was rent in that moment, and rocks were burst asunder, and all the earth was shaken. This is even that body, the blood-stained, the pierced, and that out of which gushed the saving fountains, the one of blood, the other of water, for all the world."

Would you also learn its power from another source? Ask of her diseased with an issue of blood, who laid hold not of itself, but of the garment with which it was clad; nay, not of the whole of this, but of the hem: ask of the sea, which bore it on its back: ask even of the devil, and say, "Whence have you that incurable stroke? Whence have you no longer any power? Whence are you captive? By whom have you been seized in your flight?" And the devil will give no other answer than this, "The body that was crucified." By this were the goads of the devil broken in pieces; by this was the serpent's head crushed; by this were the powers and the principalities made a show of.

John Chrysostom

That is what the text means which begins: "God has sent his only-begotten Son into the world." You must not by this understand the external world in which the Son ate and drank with us, but understand it to apply to the inner world. As truly as the Father in his simple nature gives his Son birth naturally, so truly does he give him birth in the most inward part of the spirit, and that is the inner world. Here God's ground is my ground, and my ground is God's ground.

Where the creature stops, there God begins to be. Now God wants no more from you than that you should in creaturely fashion go out of yourself, and let God be God in you. The smallest creaturely image that ever forms in you is as great as God is great. Why? Because it comes between you and the whole of God. As soon as the image comes in, God and all his divinity have to give way. But as the image goes out, God goes in. God wants you to go out of yourself in creaturely fashion as much as if all his blessedness consisted in it. O my dear one, what harm does it do you to allow God to be God in you? Go completely out of yourself for God's love, and God comes completely out of himself for love of you. And when these two have gone out, what remains there is a simplified One. In this One the Father brings his Son to birth in the innermost source.

Meister Eckhart

E FOURTH SUNDAY IN LENT

O eternal Trinity!
Eternal Trinity!
O fire and deep well of charity!
O you who are madly in love
with your creature!
O eternal truth!
O eternal fire!
O eternal wisdom
given for our redemption!
But did your wisdom come into the world alone?
No.
For wisdom was not separate from power,
nor was power without mercy.
You, wisdom, did not come alone then,
but the whole Trinity was there.
O eternal Trinity,
mad with love,
of what use to you was our redemption?
None at all,
for you have no need of us,
you who are our God.
For whose good was it?
Only humanity's.

O boundless charity!
Just as you gave us yourself,
wholly God and wholly human,
so you left us all of yourself as food
so that while we are pilgrims in this life
we might not collapse in our weariness
but be strengthened by you, heavenly food.

Catherine of Siena

R E L FIFTH SUNDAY IN LENT

You must have already heard about God's marvels manifested in
the way silk originates. The silkworms come from seeds about the
size of little grains of pepper. (I have never seen this but have heard

of it, and so if something in the explanation gets distorted it won't be my fault.) When the warm weather comes and the leaves begin to appear on the mulberry tree, the seeds start to live, for they are dead until then. The worms nourish themselves on the mulberry leaves until, having grown to full size, they settle on some twigs. There with their little mouths they themselves go about spinning the silk and making some very thick little cocoons in which they enclose themselves. The silkworm, which is fat and ugly, then dies, and a little white butterfly, which is very pretty, comes forth from the cocoon. Now if this were not seen but recounted to us as having happened in other times, who would believe it? Or what reasonings could make us conclude that a thing as nonrational as a worm or bee could be so diligent in working for our benefit and with so much industriousness? And the poor little worm loses its life in the challenge.

Well, once this silkworm is grown, it begins to spin the silk and build the house wherein it will die. I would like to point out here that this house is Christ.

Therefore, courage! Let's be quick to do this work and weave this little cocoon by taking away our self-love and self-will, our attachment to any earthly thing, and by performing deeds of penance, prayer, mortification, obedience, and of all the other things you know. Would to heaven that we would do what we know we must; and we are instructed about what we must do. Let it die; let this silkworm die, as it does in completing what it was created to do! And you will see how we see God, as well as ourselves placed inside God's grandeur, as is this little silkworm within its cocoon.

Oh, now, to see the restlessness of this little butterfly, even though it has never been quieter and calmer in its life, is something to praise God for! And the difficulty is that it doesn't know where to alight and rest. Since it has experienced such wonderful rest, all that it sees on earth displaces it, especially if God gives it this wine often. Almost each time it gains new treasures. It no longer has any esteem for the works it did while a worm, which was to weave the cocoon little by little; it now has wings. How can it be happy walking step by step when it can fly?

Teresa of Avila

R E L SUNDAY OF THE PASSION

Even in Christ's very passion and crucifixion, before they had come to the shedding of his blood and the final cruelty of his death, what infamies of reproach did he not patiently endure, what revilings, what mockeries; so that he who a little before had healed with his spittle the eyes of a blind man was spat upon by those who insulted him. He was scourged in whose name and by whose servants the devil and his angels are scourged. He who crowns the martyrs with unfading garlands was himself crowned with thorns. They struck him on the face with the palms of their hands who gives the palm of victory to those who endure to the end. He who clothes others with the garment of everlasting life was stripped of his earthly garments. They gave him gall who gives us the food of heaven. He was given vinegar to drink who has given us the cup of salvation. He the just one, the innocent, nay, more, innocence itself, he who is justice, was reputed among thieves, and truth itself was surrounded by false witnesses. The judge of all was placed standing before an earthly judge. The Word of God was led wordless to be sacrificed.

And when the heavens were fearful at sight of the Lord upon the cross, and when the elements were thrown into confusion, and the earth trembled, and night shut out day, and the sun withdrew its beam and veiled its eyes, he did not speak, he did not move; not even in his very agony did he speak of his own divine majesty. He bore with everything, patiently and steadfastly to the end, so that in Christ patience might have its perfect fulfillment.

Cyprian

R HOLY THURSDAY

E L MAUNDY THURSDAY

The mystery of the lamb which God commanded should be sacrificed at the Passover was a figure of Christ, with whose blood, in accord with their faith in his word, they who believe in him anoint their houses, that is, themselves. But that this command was given only for a time I shall prove to you.

God did not permit that the lamb of the Passover should be sacrificed in any other place than where his name was named: knowing that the days would come, after the passion of Christ, in which the city of Jerusalem would be delivered up to your enemies, and all your sacrifices would come to an end. And this lamb which was commanded to be roasted whole was a symbol of the suffering on the cross which Christ was to undergo. For the lamb which is eaten is dressed and roasted in the form of a cross: one spit is transfixed right through from the lower part to the head, and one across the back, to which the forelegs of the lamb are attached.

The offering of fine flour, which was prescribed to be offered by those who were purified from leprosy was also a figure of the eucharistic bread which our Lord Jesus Christ prescribed should be eaten in memory of his passion by those whose souls are purified from all iniquity, that we may at the same time thank God for having created the world, with all that is in it, for our benefit, for delivering us from the evil in which we were held fast, and for casting down to nothing the principalities and powers, through him who of his own will became subject to suffering.

Justin

R E L GOOD FRIDAY

O sweet Christ, supreme love, have compassion for me and do not abandon me. I take refuge near you who are my assurance, for you have all my hope. To you alone do I find the possibility of addressing my petition. If you wish, you can indeed show me that in this life you have no obligation to me; but I know that by rights I should have nothing. Nevertheless, the wood of the cross sets me on fire. Those hands that were pierced to make visible their generosity give me hope of finding you, and those arms that remain open on the cross tell me that I can put my trust in becoming rich through that gesture. And the breast that was struck by the lance tells me how great is the divine love reserved for me. These stigmata, reminding me of your suffering, encourage me not to despair of my sins.

O Lord, you came for sinners, not for the saved. And you yourself, O Christ, said you would establish this pact. Forgive me my going astray, and hold me in your arms that are open for me on the cross.

O Holy Spirit, you who are the consoler, who grant as a gift the love of Christ, give me again those gifts that I have lost. Rekindle in my heart the torch of the love of Christ my Lord, by the love of the Virgin Mary, mother of Christ, my singing mistress, who taught me a melody for your love. Give me grace that my soul may contemplate your Son in every moment. So may it be.

Umilta of Faenza

R E L EASTER VIGIL

Now since you are celebrating the holy Pasch, you should know, what the Pasch is. Pasch means the crossing-over; and so the festival is called by this name. For it was on this day that the children of Israel crossed over out of Egypt, and the Son of God crossed over from this world to his Father. What gain is it to celebrate the Pasch unless you imitate him whom you worship; that is, unless you cross over from Egypt, that is, from the darkness of evildoing to the light of virtue, and from the love of this world to the love of your heavenly home?

For there are many who celebrate this holy festival, and honor this solemnity, and yet do so unworthily and because of their own wickedness; because they will not cross over from this world to their Father, that is, they will not cross over from the desires of this world, and from bodily delights, to the love of heaven. O unhappy Christians, who still remain in Egypt, that is, under the power of the devil, and taking delight in this evil!

Because of these things I warn you, that you must celebrate Pasch worthily, that is, that you cross over. Whosoever among you who are in sin, and celebrate this festival, let you cross over from evil doing to the life of virtue. Whosoever among you are just living, let you pass from virtue to virtue; so that there shall be none among you who has not crossed over.

Ambrose

If you would learn of the Father, listen to this word. If you would
be wise, ask him who is wisdom. When it is too dark for you to see,
seek Christ, for he is the light. Are you sick? Have recourse to him
who is both doctor and health. Would you know by whom the
world was made and all things are sustained? Believe in him, for he
is the arm and right hand. Are you afraid of this or that? Remember
that on all occasions he will stand by your side like an angel. If you
find it hard to meet face to face the high majesty of the only-begotten, do not lose hope. Remember, he was made human to make it
easy for everyone to approach God. If you are innocent, like a lamb
he will join your company. If you are saddened by pagan persecution, take courage. Remember that he himself went like a lamb to
the slaughter, and, priest that he is, he will offer you up as a victim
to the Father. If you do not know the way of salvation, look for
Christ, for he is the road for souls. If it is truth that you want, listen
to him, for he is the truth. Have no fear whatever of death, for
Christ is the life of those who believe. Do the pleasures of the world
seduce you? Turn all the more to the cross of Christ to find solace in
the sweetness of the vine that clustered there. Are you a lost sinner?
Then you must hunger for justice and thirst for the redeemer, for
that is what Christ is. Because he is bread, he takes away all hunger.
If you are stumbling, fix your foot firmly on him, for he is a rock;
and like a wall he will protect you. Are you weak and sick? Ask for
a medicine from him, because he is a doctor. Especially if you are
still unbaptized, you may suffer from the ardors of passion. Then
hurry to the well of life to put out the flame and to gain for your
soul eternal life. If anger is tormenting you and you are torn by dis-
sension, appeal to Christ, who is peace, and you will be reconciled
to the Father and will love everyone as you would like to be loved
yourself. If you are afraid that your body is failing and have a
dread of death, remember that he is the resurrection, and can raise
up what has fallen.

Nicetas

R E L SECOND SUNDAY OF EASTER

I think there is no suffering greater than what is caused by the doubts of those who want to believe. I know what torment this is, but I can only see it, in myself anyway, as the process by which faith is deepened. A faith that just accepts is a child's faith and all right for children, but eventually you have to grow religiously as every other way, though some never do.

What people don't realize is how much religion costs. They think faith is a big electric blanket, when of course it is the cross. It is much harder to believe than not to believe. If you feel you can't believe, you must at least do this: keep an open mind. Keep it open toward faith, keep wanting it, keep asking for it, and leave the rest to God.

When we get our spiritual house in order, we'll be dead. This goes on. You arrive at enough certainty to be able to make your way, but it is making it in darkness. Don't expect faith to clear things up for you. It is trust, not certainty.

Flannery O'Connor

R E L THIRD SUNDAY OF EASTER

Penetrate me, O Lord Jesus, to the bottom of my heart with the sweet and salutary wound of your love. Fill me with that ardent, sincere and tranquil love which caused your apostle St. Paul to desire that he might be separated from his body to be with you.

May my soul languish for you, filled incessantly with the desire for your eternal dwelling. May I hunger for you, the bread of angels, the food of holy souls, the living bread we should eat every day, the nourishing bread which sustains the hearts of men and women and contains in itself all sweetness.

May my heart always hunger for you, O most desirable bread, and feed on you without ceasing. May I thirst for you, O fountain of life, living source of wisdom and knowledge, torrent of delight which rejoices and refreshes the house of God. May I never cease to long for you whom the angels desire to see, whom they behold always with fresh ardor.

May my soul desire you, may it seek you, may it find you, may it tend to you, may it reach you. Be the object of my desires, the subject of my meditations and colloquies. May I do all things for your glory and humility, consideration, prudence and discretion, with love and joy and perseverance enduring to the end.

And be, yourself alone, my hope, my trust, my riches, my pleasure, my joy, my rest, my tranquility, the peace of my soul. Draw me to your sweetness, your perfume, your sweet savor; be to me a solid and pleasant nourishment.

May I love you, may I serve you without distaste and without relaxing in fervor. Be my refuge, my consolation, my help and my strength. And be my wisdom, my portion, my good, my treasure, wherein my heart may always be — and may my soul remain eternally, firmly and immovably rooted in you alone.

Bonaventure

R E L FOURTH SUNDAY OF EASTER

I saw a brazen ladder of wondrous length reaching up to heaven, but so narrow that only one could ascend at once; and on the sides of the ladder were fastened all kinds of iron weapons. There were swords, lances, hooks, daggers, so that if any man went up carelessly or without looking upwards he was mangled and his flesh caught on the weapons. And just beneath the ladder was a dragon couching of wondrous size who lay in wait for those going up and sought to frighten them from going up. Now Saturus went up first, who had given himself up for our sakes of his own accord, because our faith had been of his own building, and he had not been present when we were seized. And he reached the top of the ladder, and turned, and said to me, "Perpetua, I await you; but see that the dragon bite you not." And I said, "In the name of Jesus Christ he will not hurt me." And he put out his head gently, as if afraid of me, just at the foot of the ladder; and as though I were treading on the first step, I trod on his head. And I went up, and saw a vast expanse of garden, and in the midst a man sitting with white hair, in the dress of a shepherd, a tall man, milking sheep; and round about were many thousands clad in white. And he raised his head, and looked upon me, and said, "You have well come, my child." And

he called me, and gave me a morsel of the milk which he was milking and I received it in my joined hands, and ate; and all they that
stood around said, "Amen." And at the sound of the word I woke,
still eating something sweet.

R E L FIFTH SUNDAY OF EASTER

High eternal Trinity!
O Trinity, eternal Godhead!
Love!
We are trees of death
and you are the tree of life.
O eternal Godhead!
What a wonder,
in your light,
to see your creature as a pure tree,
a tree you drew out of yourself,
supreme purity,
in pure innocence!
You planted it and fused it
into the humanity you had formed
from the earth's clay.
You made this tree free.
You gave it branches:
the soul's powers
of memory,
understanding,
and will.
With what fruit did you endow the memory?
With the fruit of holding.
And understanding?
With the fruit of discerning.
And the will?
With the fruit of loving.
O tree
set in such purity
by the one who planted you!
Once we have been engrafted into you,

the branches you gave our tree
begin to produce their fruit.
Our memory is filled
with the continual recollection of your blessings.
Our understanding gazes into you
to know perfectly your truth
and your will.
And our will chooses to love and to follow
what our understanding has seen and known.
So each branch offers its fruit to the others.
You made us into trees of life again
when we were trees of death
by engrafting yourself, life,
into us.
Eternal Truth,
take those you have given me
to love with a special love:
join and engraft them into yourself
so that they may bring forth the fruit of life.

Catherine of Siena

R E L SIXTH SUNDAY OF EASTER

Good works do not receive their last perfection till they, as it were,
lose themselves in God. This is a kind of death to them, resembling
that of our bodies, which will not attain their highest life, their immortality, till they lose themselves in the glory of our souls, or
rather of God, wherewith they shall be filled. And it is only what
they had of earthly and mortal, which good works lose by this spiritual death.

Fire is the symbol of love; and the love of God is the principle and
the end of all our good works. But truth surpasses figure, and the
fire of divine love has this advantage over material fire, that it can
reascend to its source, and raise thither with it all the good works
which it produces. And by this means it prevents their being corrupted by pride, vanity, or any evil mixture. But this cannot be
done otherwise than by making these good works in a spiritual
manner die in God, by a deep gratitude, which plunges the soul in

him as in an abyss, with all that it is, and all the grace and works for which it is indebted to him: a gratitude whereby the soul seems to empty itself of them, that they may return to their source, as rivers seem willing to empty themselves when they pour themselves with all their waters into the sea.

John Wesley

R E L ASCENSION DAY

Be thou exalted: thou who wast enclosed in the womb of a mother. Thou who wast formed in her whom thou made. Thou who hast lain in a manger. Thou who as a true child in the flesh drank milk from the breast. Thou who while borne in thy mother's arms sustained the world. Thou whom the venerable Simeon beheld a child and extolled as mighty. Thou whom the widow Anna saw at the breast and knew omnipotent. Thou who hast hungered because of us, suffered thirst for us, grown weary on the way (but did the bread of life hunger, the fountain thirst, the way grow weary?). Thou who hast borne all these things for us. Thou who hast slept, yet unsleeping watches over Israel. And lastly, thou who wast seized, bound, scourged, crowned with thorns, hung upon the tree, pierced with a lance, died, and was buried. Be thou exalted, O God!

Be thou exalted, exalted above the heavens: for thou art God. Take thou thy seat in heaven who hung from the cross. As judge to come thou art awaited who awaited and received judgment. Who could believe this without his help, who raised the needy from the earth and uplifted the poor from the dunghill? He has raised up his own needy flesh and placed it with the princes of his people, with whom he shall judge the living and the dead.

Augustine

R E L SEVENTH SUNDAY OF EASTER

So thanks be to the Lord our God, who has delivered us from the power of darkness, and brought us into the kingdom of the beloved Son. Separated then from this darkness by the light of the gospel, and delivered from these powers of evil through his precious blood, let you watch and pray so that you may not enter into temptation. For whosoever among you has that faith which works by charity, the prince of this world is cast forth from your hearts. But outside, he goes about like a roaring lion, seeking whom he may devour.

Do not then yield place to the devil, whatever the quarter he seeks to enter by. But suffer Christ to dwell within you, and against him, for Christ through suffering for your sake cast him forth. For when he ruled you, you were then darkness, but now you are light in the Lord. Walk then as children of the light. Watch then in this Mother Light against the darkness, and the rulers of it, and from the bosom of this Mother Light pray to the Father of lights.

Augustine

R PENTECOST SUNDAY
E L DAY OF PENTECOST

The Holy Spirit is therefore a river, and the supreme river, which, according to the Hebrews, flowed from Jesus down to the earth. Mighty is this river, which flows for ever, and never grows less: and not alone the river, but also the rushing of the torrent, and its overflowing splendor.

Nor is that Jerusalem, which is above, watered by the course of any earthly river, but by that flowing from the fountain of life, the Holy Ghost, of which we are filled at a single draught; that delights to pour out ever more abundantly upon the heavenly thrones, dominations, and powers, upon the angels and archangels, rushing forth in the full stream of its sevenfold spiritual power. For if a river, overflowing the tops of its banks, spreads out, how much more will not the spirit, overtopping every created thing, make joyful with a more abundant richness of grace the creatures of heaven, when it pours out over the lowlier fields of our soul!

Do not be troubled that John has said "rivers" and in another place "the seven spirits of God." By these tokens of the sevenfold Spirit is meant the fullness of power: the spirit of wisdom, and of understanding, the spirit of counsel, and of fortitude, the spirit of knowledge, and of godliness, the spirit of the fear of the Lord. One therefore is the river, but many the channels of its spiritual gifts. This then is the river that flows forth from the fountain of life.

And do not turn your mind aside towards inferior things, because there is an obvious difference between a fountain and a river. For the divine scripture provides for all things, so that the limited human mind may not be led into error by the poverty of human speech. For whatever be the river you imagine to yourself, it comes from a fountain; they are of the one substance, the one clarity, and the one beauty. Let you then say, the Holy Spirit is one in substance with the Son of God, and with God the Father, one in brightness, and one in glory.

Ambrose

R E L TRINITY SUNDAY

O eternal Trinity,
my sweet love!
You, light,
give us light.
You, wisdom,
give us wisdom.
You, supreme strength,
strengthen us.
Today, eternal God,
let our cloud be dissipated
so that we may perfectly know and follow your Truth
in truth,
with a free and simple heart.

Catherine of Siena

R BODY AND BLOOD OF CHRIST

Consider with what honor you have been honored, at what table you feast, that which the angels trembled to behold, and dare not gaze upon because of its flashing brightness. It is with this we are nourished, to this we are joined, made one body and one flesh with Christ.

Reflect on this truth: he was born of our nature. But, you may say, this is not a matter that concerns all. And yet it does concern all. For if he came because of our nature, it is plain that he came for all. And if he came for all, he came for each one. And how is it all have not been enriched by his coming? This is not his fault, who of his own will did this for all, but rather the fault of those who have no will to profit by him. By this mystery he unites himself to each believing soul; and those to whom he has given life he nourished from himself—not giving to others to nourish—by this also proving to you that he has taken your flesh.

Let us then not hold his honor lightly, we who have been held worthy of such honor. You see how eager infants are for the maternal breast, how thirstily they drink from it? Let us with alike eagerness approach this table, and to the breast of the spiritual chalice. Let us with even more eagerness drink deep, like infants at the breast, of the love of the Spirit; and let it be our one grief that we should be deprived of this food. These gifts set before us do not come from human power. He who then made them at that supper, the same now makes what is here before us.

John Chrysostom

R NINTH SUNDAY IN ORDINARY TIME

E   PROPER 4

L SECOND SUNDAY AFTER PENTECOST

Any modern legalism which regards the law of love as a simple possibility and thinks it can be fulfilled if only it is stated persuasively and obeyed with real fervor, does not understand that part of the gospel which searches the human heart and discovers the sinful and self-loving man in need of grace both to fulfill the law and to be pardoned because he can not fulfill it. To make the law of love into a simple possibility means that it also becomes an instrument for evading the necessity of grace. It even becomes an instrument of competitive righteousness. All responsibility for the community, for the safety of loved ones, for the preservation of civilization, is disavowed for the sake of the individual's perfection, for the purpose of keeping him unspotted from the world.

This kind of legalism may be prompted by the honest illusion that it can shame the evil man into goodness, or by the false hope that history is in the process of gradually substituting "methods of force" with "method of love." But there is no doubt another motive, the same motive which prompted the monastic life in the Middle Ages. That motive is to purchase perfection at the price of responsibility. What is true in this approach is the conviction that a measure of guilt is involved in these loyalties and responsibilities. But love is also involved in these loyalties and responsibilities. Therefore the disavowal of responsibility for the sake of the law of love means a disavowal of the love involved in responsibility.

The law has its own uses in the ordering of the human community and in the discipline of the individual. But it is not an instrument of salvation, ultimately considered. Ultimately every fact of experience proves the simple gospel affirmations about the supremacy of grace to be true. We need both the power and the pardon of divine grace. We are not free to do good by our own resources and finally we are not good at all. The contradiction between man and God can not be healed by any human contrivance. If the attempt is made, religion produces not the fruits of the spirit—not love, joy and peace—but a frantic self-righteousness and a confusing self-deception.

Reinhold Niebuhr

R TENTH SUNDAY IN ORDINARY TIME
E PROPER 5
L THIRD SUNDAY AFTER PENTECOST

Then our Lord said in her mind, "I thank you, daughter, that you would be willing to suffer death for my love, for as often as you think so, you shall have the same reward in heaven as if you had suffered that same death. And yet no one shall slay you, nor fire burn you, nor water drown you, nor winds harm you, for I may not forget you and how you are written upon my hands and my feet. I am well pleased with the pains that I have suffered for you. I shall never be angry with you, but I shall love you without end. Though all the world be against you, don't be afraid, for they cannot understand you. I swear to your mind, that if it were possible for me to suffer pain again as I have done before, I would rather suffer as much pain as I ever did for your soul alone, rather than that you should be separated from me without end.

"And what more should I do for you, unless I were to take your soul out of your body and put it in heaven, and that I will not do yet. Nevertheless, wheresoever God is heaven is; and God is in your soul, and many an angel is round about your soul to guard it both night and day. For when you go to church, I go with you; when you sit at your meal, I sit with you; when you go to bed, I go with you; and when you go out of town, I go with you.

"Daughter, with my grace I sometimes behave towards you as I do with the sun. Sometimes, as you well know, the sun shines so that many people can see it, and sometimes it is hidden behind a cloud so that it cannot be seen, and yet it is the sun nevertheless, in its heat and its brightness. And just so I proceed with you and with my chosen souls.

"Although it may be that you do not always weep when you please, my grace is nevertheless in you. Therefore I prove that you are a daughter indeed to me, and a mother also, a sister, a wife and a spouse. When you strive to please me, then you are a true daughter; when you weep and mourn for my pain and my passion, then you are a true mother having compassion on her child; when you weep for other people's sins and adversities, then you are a true sister; and when you sorrow because you are kept so long from the bliss of heaven, then you are a true spouse and wife, for it is the wife's part to be with her husband and to have no true joy until she has his company."

Margery Kempe

R ELEVENTH SUNDAY IN ORDINARY TIME

E PROPER 6

L FOURTH SUNDAY AFTER PENTECOST

If the kingdom of heaven is like to a grain of mustard seed, and faith is like to a grain of mustard seed, faith is then truly the kingdom of heaven, and the kingdom of heaven is faith. Whoever therefore that has faith, possesses the kingdom of heaven. The kingdom of heaven is within us, and faith is within us.

Now let us, from the nature of the mustard seed, estimate the force of this comparison. Its seed is indeed very plain, and of little value:

but if bruised or crushed it shows forth its power. So faith first seems a simple thing: but if it is bruised by its enemies, it gives forth proof of its power, so as to fill others who hear or read of it with the odor of its sweetness.

At one time the faith is bruised, at another time oppressed, at other times it is sown. The Lord himself is the grain of mustard seed. He was without injury, but the people were unaware of him as a grain of mustard seed of which they took no notice. He chose to be bruised, he chose to be crushed; he chose to be planted in the earth as a seed. For it was in a garden that Christ was taken prisoner, and likewise buried: he sprung up in a garden, where he also rose from the dead, and became a tree.

You also then sow Christ in your garden—for a garden is a place that is full of flowers and various fruits—in which by virtue of your labor he may grow and breathe forth the multiple sweetness of his many virtues. There where fruit is, let Christ be found. Plant the Lord Jesus. He is a seed when a man takes hold of him: he is a tree when he rises again, a tree that give shade to the world; he is a seed when he is buried in the earth; he is a tree when raised to heaven.

Ambrose

R TWELFTH SUNDAY IN ORDINARY TIME

E PROPER 7

L FIFTH SUNDAY AFTER PENTECOST

Why therefore are you troubled, O you of little faith? If you have known me to have power on the land, why do you not believe that I have power also upon the sea? If you believe me to be God, the Creator of all things, why do you not also believe that the things which I have made are subject to my power? Why do you doubt, O you of little faith?

Now rising up he commands, and there comes a great calm. He commands the winds and the sea as their Lord, and, for the first time, in the presence of the disciples, so that hearing him command them they would be confirmed in their faith. Upon a sea tossed about and swollen by a great wind, and a great tempest, there comes a great calm. It was befitting that he that is mighty should do great things. And so, girt with mighty power, he shakes the sea to its depths: and again, showing the splendor of his might, he commands that there shall arise a great calm, so that the apostles, who had feared exceedingly, being now delivered might rejoice.

By means of all these happenings the Lord gave us a figure and image of his teaching, so that we might be patient in the face of every storm and persecution; that we may be steadfast; that we betray not our faith. And if all this world should boil up as the sea, and rise in fury against us, though on every side there should rage the winds and the whirlpools of the demons; though, as we have said, every menace of the sea, that is, every principality and power of this world, be roused against us, foaming with the swelling of their wrath, so as to torment the sanctified; and though like to the sea they whip up wickedness and treacheries to the very skies, stirring up against you the murmuring of the evilminded: yet, be not afraid; be not troubled; do not tremble; do not yield.

For as many as are in the little ship of faith are sailing with the Lord; as many as are in the bark of holy church will voyage with the Lord across this wave-tossed life; though the Lord himself may sleep in holy quiet, he is but watching your patience and endurance, looking forward to the repentance and to the conversion of those who have sinned.

Origen

R THIRTEENTH SUNDAY IN ORDINARY TIME

E PROPER 8

L SIXTH SUNDAY AFTER PENTECOST

How often have I felt my soul awakened by thy Light and warmed by the fire of thy Love—then I approach thee—I find Thee—but Alas instantly after I lose thee—often I think myself received—then fear I am rejected—and in this continual change of interior dispositions I walk in darkness and often go astray—I desire and know not how to desire, I love, and know not how to love, —nor how to find what I love.

Thus my soul loses itself without ceasing to hope in thee—It knows by its own experience that it desires much, and is unable to do any

thing—you seest its trouble O Lord—and in that happy moment
when fatigued with so many vicissitudes it falls at last into entire
diffidence of itself then you openest its eyes and it sees the true way
to Peace and Life—it knows you wast nearer than it imagined—you
instructest it all at once without Voice or Words, it thinks only of
what possesses it, abandoning all things else it then possesses
Thee—It sees without knowing what it sees, it hears, and is ignorant of what is hears, it knows only Who he is to whom it is atten-
tive it contents itself with loving HIM, it loves Him continually
more and more—Words cannot express, nor the mind comprehend
what it receives from THEE O MY GOD even in this place of BAN-
ISHMENT—

How happy is that moment O divine JESUS! how pure is that
Light, how ineffable is that communion of thy Blessings! You know
O Lord how precious that gift is, and thy Creature that receives it
knows also—Ah! if it were faithful, if it never departed from Thee—
if it knew how to preserve the Grace it had received, how happy
would it be! and yet this is but a drop of that infinite Ocean of Blessings which thou art one day to communicate to it—

O Soul of my Soul—what is my Soul and What Good can it have
without possessing you—Life of my Life! What is my Life when I
live not in you—Is it possible that my Heart is capable of possessing you—of enjoying you all alone—of extending and dilating itself
in you—can thy creature thus be elevated above itself to repose in
thy Breast, and after that depart from you? bury itself in the
Earth?—Ah Lord I know not what I ought to say to You: but hear
the voice of your love and of my misery; live always in me, and let
me live perpetually in You and for You as I live only by You.

Enlighten me, O Divine Light!
Conduct me, O Supreme Truth!
Raise me again, O increated Life!
Separate me from every thing that displeases Thee
Suffer me to remain at thy Feet

Elizabeth Seton

R FOURTEENTH SUNDAY IN ORDINARY TIME
E PROPER 9
L SEVENTH SUNDAY AFTER PENTECOST

There is a lot of unnecessary pain in the world that is the product of human brokenness or sin. But there are other kinds of suffering which are the outcome of our service to Christ. Last Christmas Eve an older priest was attacked as he was going to say mass. As a consequence of this act of violence, a few hours later he died in a hospital in the city of Cordoba, a holiday-resort place about 800 miles from the city of Buenos Aires. His only "sin" was that he had identified with the oppressed, the poor, and the underprivileged. He had no affiliations with any political parties, nor did he belong to a guerrilla group. It can be a very dangerous thing to take the message of deliverance seriously.

What does Peter call those Christians who are suffering for Christ's sake? He calls them "beloved," "dear friend of mine," "my dear friends." He addresses them affectionately. He shares their pain. If Christ's love abides in us, we cannot but share the pain of those who suffer along the road of faithfulness to a Lord of justice and love.

If we are going to take very seriously the message of the Bible: the releasing of captives, the giving of sight to the blind, liberty to the oppressed, and the proclamation and acts of the acceptable year of the Lord; if we are going to try to obey the word of the prophets and of Jesus Christ and the testimony of the early church, we are going to run into trouble. We are going to be involved in Christ's work, which is world-judging, world-condemning, world-transforming. This may bring to us not only unpopularity among our friends, family, and churches, but probably some things that are more costly. So, we should not enter into discipleship unless we are willing to pay the price, to pay the cost— avoiding all martyr complexes, all masochism, and all messianism—with the spirit of the joy which is grounded on the promises of God himself. Not only on the promises written in the Bible, but the promises of many Christians "written" in their experience of a living hope which is born from an encounter with a living God and with a whole host of witnesses in the Christian community through the centuries and around the world today.

Beatriz Melano Couch

R FIFTEENTH SUNDAY IN ORDINARY TIME
E PROPER 10
L EIGHTH SUNDAY AFTER PENTECOST

Yes, my friends, we who now are sent to preach the gospel in the name of our Lord Jesus Christ have less reason to whimper when we are labeled worse than blind guides, deliberate deceivers, false prophets, and ravenous wolves. It must be clear to us that the more freely we are contradicted, abused, and insulted, the more persuasive and credible our witness will be, because our situation comes to resemble that of the Lord and his apostles. The more vigorous spirit of truth will then witness through us to all who are of the truth that we speak only because we believe and that the road we point to is the narrow road which leads to the land of the living. We point to no other way than our Lord Jesus Christ who himself is the way, the truth, and the life.

The truth is that since our Lord Jesus Christ himself is the way, the only living way, to the heavenly Father's house, then all the heaven-bound roads we ourselves can discover or prepare are misleading and dead-end roads, whether they are broad or narrow. On the other hand, it is not sufficient to say that we see the right road in Jesus Christ; we must also follow it if it is to lead us to the goal. Although it is not sufficient for salvation to preach Jesus Christ and him alone as the way, the truth, and the life, it is sufficient for those who hear these words and act on them, so that deeds follow words and Jesus Christ really becomes their heavenly way, truth, and life. Then they will know that we were not false but true prophets, since our prediction was fulfilled: that Jesus Christ whom we proclaimed proved for them to be the sound tree which bore not evil but good and eternal fruit.

Therefore let this stand: the Lord Jesus Christ whom we confess in baptism with the word of faith from his own lips, who regenerates us in baptism with his heavenly Father's word and Spirit, and who nourishes us in the eucharist, he is the way, the truth, and the life. With him, but not without him, all believing hearts and truth-loving souls come to heaven. The louder and the more acridly the world labels us false prophets and ravenous wolves in sheep's clothing, the deeper will be the impression of our prediction upon the friends of truth, and the more clearly will they see that we are true prophets, not like the wolves but faithful shepherds who gather the flock and lead it to streams of living waters, sheltering and protecting it.

N. F. S. Grundtvig

R SIXTEENTH SUNDAY IN ORDINARY TIME

E PROPER 11

L NINTH SUNDAY AFTER PENTECOST

With regard to the eucharist, give thanks in this manner:

First, for the cup:
"We thank you, our Father,
for the holy vine of David your servant
which you have revealed to us through Jesus your Child.
Glory be yours through all ages!"

Then for the bread broken:
"We thank you, our Father,
for the life and knowledge which you have revealed to us
through Jesus your Child.
Glory be yours through all ages!"

Just as the bread broken
"was first scattered on the hills,
then was gathered and became one,
so let your church be gathered
from the ends of the earth into your kingdom,
for yours is glory and power through all ages."

When your hunger has been satisfied, give thanks thus:
"We thank you, holy Father,
for your holy name
which you have made to dwell in our hearts,

and for the knowledge and faith and immortality
which you have revealed to us through Jesus your Child.
Glory be yours through all ages!"

All-powerful Master, you created all things
for your name's sake,
and you have given food and drink
to the children of the human race
for their enjoyment
so that they may thank you.
On us, moreover, you have graciously bestowed
a spiritual food and drink
that lead to eternal life,
through Jesus your Child.

Above all, we thank you
because you are almighty.
Glory be yours through all ages!
Amen.

Lord, remember your church
and deliver it from all evil;
make it perfect in your love
and gather it from the four winds,
this sanctified church,
into your kingdom which you have prepared for it,
for power and glory are yours through all ages!"

Didache

R SEVENTEENTH SUNDAY IN ORDINARY TIME
L TENTH SUNDAY AFTER PENTECOST

And so, taking the loaves and fishes, the Lord looked up to heaven, then blessed and broke them, giving thanks to the Father that, after the law and the prophets, he is himself become the evangelical bread. The bread is given to the apostles, because it is through them the gifts of the divine grace are to be given. Then the people ate of the five loaves and the two fishes and were filled. And of the fragments of the bread and of the fishes, after all who had sat down were satisfied, there remained over enough to fill twelve baskets:

that is, the hunger of the multitude is satisfied by the word of God coming to them from the teaching of the law and the prophets; and the abundance of the divine goodness, kept in reserve for the people of the Gentiles, has overflowed from the source of eternal food unto the filling of the twelve apostles.

The wonder of this deed surpasses human understanding. And while often things are done which the mind can grasp but words cannot explain, in these things even the acuteness of the mind to perceive is at a loss, astonished at the very thought of the complexity of the unseen action. The five loaves are not multiplied into many loaves; but to the portions broken off succeed other portions, which pass unnoticed from the hands breaking them. The substance progressively increases, whether at the place that served for tables, or in the hands of those taking it, or in the mouth of those who ate it, I know not.

Wonder not that the fountains run, that there are grapes in the vines, and that wine comes forth from the grapes. For the power of him who makes surpasses all nature exceeds our understanding of what he does; and all that remains is the mystery of his power, who with the Father and the Holy Ghost live and reign world without end.

Hilary

E PROPER 12

Syncletica said, "When you have to fast, do not pretend illness. For those who do not fast often fall into real sicknesses. If you have begun to act well, do not turn back through constraint of the enemy, for through your endurance, the enemy is destroyed. Those who put out to sea at first sail with a favorable wind; then the sails spread, but later the winds become adverse. Then the ship is tossed by the waves and is no longer controlled by the rudder. But when in a little while there is a calm, and the tempest dies down, then the ship sails on again. So it is with us, when we are driven by the spirits who are against us; we hold to the cross as our sail and so we can set a safe course."

She also said, "We must arm ourselves in every way against the demons. For they attack us from outside, and they also stir us up from within; and the soul is then like a ship when great waves break over it, and at the same time it sinks because the hold is too full. We are just like that: we lose as much by the exterior faults we commit as by the thoughts inside us. So we must watch for the attacks of people that come from outside us, and also repel the interior on-slaughts of our thoughts."

She also said, "Here below we are not exempt from temptations. We sail on in darkness. The psalmist calls our life a sea and the sea is either full of rocks, or very rough, or else it is calm. We are like those who sail on a calm sea, and seculars are like those on a rough sea. We always set our course by the sun of justice, but it can often happen that the secular are saved in tempest and darkness, for they keep watch as they ought, while we go to the bottom through negligence, although we are on a calm sea, because we have let go of the guidance of justice."

Syncletica

R EIGHTEENTH SUNDAY IN ORDINARY TIME

E PROPER 13

L ELEVENTH SUNDAY AFTER PENTECOST

You, Oh Christ, are the kingdom of heaven; You, the land promised to the gentle; You the grazing lands of paradise; You, the hall of the celestial banquet; You, the ineffable marriage chamber; You, the table set for all,
You, the bread of life; You, the unheard of drink;
You, both the urn for the water and the life-giving water;
You, moreover, the inextinguishable lamp for each one of the saints;
You, the garment and the crown and the one who distributes crowns;
You, the joy and rest; You, the delight and glory;
You, the gaiety; You, the mirth;
and Your grace, grace of the Spirit of all sanctity, will shine like the sun in all the saints; and You, inaccessible sun, will shine in their midst and all will shine brightly, to the degree of their faith, their asceticism, their hope and their love, their purification and their illumination by your Spirit.

Symeon

You have tasted the fruit of disobedience. You have learned how bitter the food of that bitter counselor. Taste now the food of obedience, which keeps evil away. Then you will learn that it is sweet and profitable to obey God. You ate fruit out of due season, and you died; eat now in a seasonable time, and you shall live. By trial you have come to know the consequences of disobedience; by trial now learn how profitable obedience is. Through knowledge of evil you have gained an understanding of what disobedience means; through knowing goodness, learn how different is obedience. Taste and see that I the Lord am sweet!

Adam to his own hurt stretched forth his hand, having no reverence for my commandment of salvation. Since he would not acknowledge the commandment of the Lord, and the obedience of a servant, since he would not, trusting in God, turn away from the apostasy of his mistrust, he put forth his hand. There he made an evil bargain. He sold the life of happiness he held within his hands, and in exchange received a miserable death. Of his own will he put on corruption. Of his own will he was made subject to death.

Because of all these things once more I place the fruits of obedience before those who died through disobedience. Taste and see that I the Lord am most truthful in all things. Truth cannot bring forth falsehood; nor is the flower of death found growing from life: for things contrary to one another cannot join together as one. Eat of me who am life, and live. For this is what I desire. Eat of life which never comes to an end. Eat my bread: for I am the life-giving grain of the wheat, and I am the bread of life. Drink the wine I have mingled for you; for I am the draught of immortality. Put away the folly of sin, and live. Your first parent was driven from paradise through unbelief; let you enter in again through faith. Put away his impiety, and in its place receive love of me, your maker. Seek after wisdom, that you may live; and perfect your understanding in the knowledge of me.

Cyril of Alexandria

Come then, and follow after the riches of secret places, as partakers of a heavenly vocation, in faith unfeigned, and having on a wedding garment, and let us hasten to the mystical Supper. This day Christ receives us as his guests. This day Christ waits upon us; Christ the lover of all humankind give us refreshment. Awesome is what has been spoken; fearful what has here been wrought. The fattened calf is slaughtered. The Lamb of God who takes away the sins of the world is slain. The Father rejoices, of whose own will the Son is sacrificed; not by the enemies of God today, but by himself, that by this he may show that his sufferings were freely borne, and for our salvation.

These words are for you symbols of things now fulfilled. These words speak to you of the pleasures of this banquet now prepared. The Giver of gifts is at hand. The divine gifts are set before us. The mystical table is prepared. The life-giving chalice is mingled. The King of glory invites us. The Son of God receives us. God the word incarnate entertains us. She who has built herself a house, not made with hands, the substantial Wisdom of God the Father, distributes his body as her bread, and gives his blood as her wine to us to drink.

O ineffable work of the divine wisdom! O incomprehensible goodness! Come, eat my body, he exhorts us, and drink the wine I have mingled for you. I have prepared myself as food. I have mingled myself for those who desire me. Of my own will I became flesh, I who am life itself.

Cyril of Alexandria

R TWENTY-FIRST SUNDAY IN ORDINARY TIME
E PROPER 16
L FOURTEENTH SUNDAY AFTER PENTECOST

I ask you, brothers or sisters, tell me: which to you seems the
greater, the word of God, or the body of Christ? If you wish to say
what is true, you will have to answer that the word of God is not
less than the body of Christ. Therefore just as when the body of
Christ is administered to us, what care do we not use so that nothing of it falls from our hands to the ground, so should we with
equal care see that the word of God which is being imparted to us
shall not be lost to our soul, while we speak or think of something
else. For they who listen carelessly to the word of God are not less
guilty than they who through their own inattention suffer the body
of Christ to fall to the ground.

Caesarius

R TWENTY-SECOND SUNDAY IN ORDINARY TIME
E PROPER 17
L FIFTEENTH SUNDAY AFTER PENTECOST

As our souls prosper we shall be more and more sensible, not only
of the outside, but of the inside; we first battle with the outward
man, but as we advance in the divine life, we have nearer views of
the chambers of imagery that are in our hearts; and one day after
another we shall find more and more abomination there, and conse-
quently we shall see more of the glory of Jesus Christ, the wonders
of that Immanuel, who daily delivers us from this body of sin and
death; and I mention this, because there is nothing more common,
especially with young Christians. I used formerly to have at least a
hundred or two hundred in a day who would come and say, O
dear, I am so and so, I met with God; ah! that is quite well: a week
after they would come and say, O, sir, it is all delusion, there was
nothing in it; what is the matter? O never was such a wretch as I
am, I never thought I had such a wicked heart.

If your souls prosper, the more you will fall in love with the glorious Redeemer, and with his righteousness. I never knew a person

in my life that diligently used the word, and other means, but as they improved in grace, saw more and more of the necessity of depending upon a better righteousness than their own. Generally when we first set out, we have got better hearts than heads; but if we grow in the divine life, our heads will grow as well as our hearts, and the Spirit of God leads us out of abominable self, and causes us to flee more and more to that glorious and complete righteousness that Jesus Christ wrought out.

The more your souls prosper, the more you will see of the freeness and distinguishing nature of God's grace, that all is of grace. We are all naturally free-willers, and generally young ones say, O we have found the Messiah, of whom Moses and the prophets spoke; which is right, except that word "we"; for the believer a little after learns that the Messiah had found him. I mention this, because we ought not to make persons offenders for a word; we should bear with young Christians, and not knock a young child's brains out because he cannot speak in blank verse.

George Whitefield

R TWENTY-THIRD SUNDAY IN ORDINARY TIME
E PROPER 18
L SIXTEENTH SUNDAY AFTER PENTECOST

What then did we perform on Saturday last? The mystery of The Opening. And the mystery of The Opening was commemorated when the priest touched your ears and nostrils. And this our Lord Jesus Christ laid down for us in the gospel, when they brought him one who was deaf and dumb, and he touched his ears and his mouth: his ears because he was deaf; his mouth because he was dumb. And he said: Ephphath. This is a Hebrew word, and means "Be opened." The priest therefore touched your ears, that they might be opened to the words and to the exhortation of the priest.

But you will say to me: Why does he touch the nostrils? Christ touched the mouth, for it was there the man was dumb: so that he who could not speak of the heavenly mysteries might receive a voice from Christ. He touched him there because he was a man. Here, however, since women also are to be baptized, and since the purity of the servant is not the same as that of the master, the bishop does not touch the mouth, but the nostrils, that you may receive the good odor of eternal charity. Be filled with the fragrance of faith and devotion.

Ambrose

R TWENTY-FOURTH SUNDAY IN ORDINARY TIME

E PROPER 19

L SEVENTEENTH SUNDAY AFTER PENTECOST

One winter day, St. Francis was coming to St. Mary of the Angels from Perugia with Brother Leo, and the bitter cold made them suffer keenly. St. Francis called to Brother Leo, who was walking a bit ahead of him, and he said: "Brother Leo, even if the Friars Minor in every country give a great example of holiness and integrity and good edification, nevertheless write down and note carefully that perfect joy is not in that."

And when he had walked on a bit, St. Francis called him again, saying: "Brother Leo, even if a Friar Minor gives sight to the blind, heals the paralyzed, drives out devils, gives hearing back to the deaf, makes the lame walk, and restores speech to the dumb, and what is still more, brings back to life a man who has been dead for days, write that perfect joy is not in that."

And going on a bit, St. Francis cried out again in a strong voice: "Brother Leo, if a Friar Minor knew all languages and all sciences and scripture, if he also knew how to prophesy and to reveal not only the future but also the secrets of the consciences and minds of others, write down and note carefully that perfect joy is not in that."

And as they walked on, after a while St. Francis called again forcefully: "Brother Leo, little lamb of God, even if a Friar Minor could speak with the voice of an angel, and knew the courses of the stars and the powers of herbs, and knew all about the treasures in the earth, and if he knew the qualities of birds and fishes, animals, humans, roots, trees, rocks, and waters, write down and note carefully that true joy is not in that."

And going on a bit farther, St. Francis called again strongly:

"Brother Leo, even if a Friar Minor could preach so well that he should convert all infidels to the faith of Christ, write that perfect joy is not there."

Now when he had been talking this way for a distance of two miles, Brother Leo in great amazement asked him: "Father, I beg you in God's name to tell me where perfect joy is."

And St. Francis replied: "When we come to St. Mary of the Angels, soaked by the rain and frozen by the cold, and soiled with mud and suffering from hunger, and we ring at the gate of the place and the brother porter does not open for us, but makes us stand outside in the snow and rain, cold and hungry, until night falls—then if we endure all those insults and cruel rebuffs patiently, without being troubled and without complaining, O Brother Leo, write that perfect joy is there!

"And if we continue to knock, and the porter comes out in anger, and drives us away with curses and hard blows like bothersome scoundrels, and if we bear it patiently and take the insults with joy and love in our hearts, O Brother Leo, write that that is perfect joy!

"And if later, suffering intensely from hunger and the painful cold, with night falling, we still knock and call, and crying loudly beg them to open for us and let us come in for the love of God, and he grows still more angry and comes out with a knotty club, and grasping us by the cowl throws us onto the ground, rolling us in the mud and snow, and beats us with that club so much that he covers our bodies with wounds—if we endure all those evils and insults and blows with joy and patience, reflecting that we must accept and bear the sufferings of the blessed Christ patiently for love of him, oh, Brother Leo, write: that is perfect joy!"

The Little Flowers of St. Francis

R TWENTY-FIFTH SUNDAY IN ORDINARY TIME
E PROPER 20
L EIGHTEENTH SUNDAY AFTER PENTECOST

Does someone poor approach you? Remember how poor you once were, and how rich you were made. One in want of bread or of drink, perhaps another Lazarus, is cast at your gate; respect the sacramental table to which you have approached, the bread of which you have partaken, the cup in which you have communicated, being consecrated by the suffering of Christ.

If a stranger falls at your feet, homeless and a foreigner, welcome in him the one who for your sake was a stranger, even among his own, and who came to dwell in you by his grace, and who drew you towards the heavenly dwelling place. Be a Zaccheus, who yesterday was a publican, and is today of liberal soul; offer all to the coming in of Christ, that though small in bodily stature you may show yourself great, nobly contemplating Christ.

Someone sick or wounded lies before you; respect your own health, and the wounds from which Christ delivered you. If you see one naked, clothe him, in honor of your own garment in incorruption, which is Christ. If you find a debtor falling at your feet, tear up every document whether just or unjust. Remember the ten thousand talents which Christ forgave you, and be not a harsh exactor of a smaller debt — and that from whom? From your fellow servant, you who were forgiven so much more by the master.

Gregory of Nazianzus

R TWENTY-SIXTH SUNDAY IN ORDINARY TIME

E PROPER 21

L NINETEENTH SUNDAY AFTER PENTECOST

Do you want to honor Christ's body? Then do not scorn him in his nakedness, nor honor him here in the church with silken garments while neglecting him outside where he is cold and naked. Give him the honor prescribed in his law by giving your riches to the poor. For God does not want golden vessels but golden hearts.

Now, in saying this I am not forbidding you to make such gifts; I am only demanding that along with such gifts and before them you give alms. He accepts the former, but he is much more pleased with the latter. In the former, only the giver profits; in the latter, the recipient does too. A gift to the church may be taken as a form of ostentation, but an alms is pure kindness.

Of what use is it to weigh down Christ's table with golden cups, when he himself is dying of hunger? First, fill him when he is hungry; then use the means you have left to adorn his table. Will you have a golden cup made but not give a cup of water? What is the use of providing the table with cloths woven of gold thread, and not providing Christ himself with the clothes he needs? What profit is there in that? Tell me: If you were to see him lacking the necessary food but were to leave him in that state and merely surround his table with gold, would he be grateful to you or rather would he not be angry? What if you were to see him clad in worn-out rags and stiff from the cold, and were to forget about clothing him and instead were to set up golden columns for him, saying that you were doing it in his honor? Would he not think he was being mocked and greatly insulted?

Apply this also to Christ when he comes along the roads as a pilgrim, looking for shelter. You do not take him in as your guest, but you decorate floor and walls and the capitals of the pillars. You provide silver chains for the lamps, but you cannot bear even to look at him as he lies chained in prison. Once again, I am not forbidding you to supply these adornments; I am urging you to provide these other things as well, and indeed to provide them first. Do not, therefore, adorn the church and ignore your afflicted brother, for he is the most precious temple of all.

John Chrysostom

R TWENTY-SEVENTH SUNDAY IN ORDINARY TIME

E PROPER 22

L TWENTIETH SUNDAY AFTER PENTECOST

O God most pure, the Creator of every living thing, who didst transform the rib of our forefather Adam into a wife, because of thy love towards mankind, and didst bless them, and say unto them: Increase, and multiply, and have dominion over the earth; and didst make of the twain one flesh: for which cause a man shall leave his father and mother and cleave unto his wife, and the two shall be one flesh: and what God hath joined together, that let no man put asunder: Thou who didst bless thy servant Abraham, and opening the womb of Sarah didst make him to be the father of many nations; who didst give Isaac to Rebecca, and didst bless her in child-bearing; who didst join Jacob unto Rachel, and from that union didst generate the twelve Patriarchs; who didst unite Joseph and Asenath, giving unto them as the fruit of their procreation Ephraim and Manasses; who did accept Zacharias and Elizabeth, and didst make their offspring to be the Forerunner; who through thine unutterable gift and manifold goodness didst come to Cana of Galilee, and did bless the marriage there, that thou mightest make manifest that it is thy will that there should be lawful marriage and the begetting of children: Do thou, the same all-holy Master, accept the prayer of us thy servants. As thou wert present there, so likewise be thou present here, with thine invisible protection. Bless this marriage, and vouchsafe unto these thy servants, a peaceful life, length of days, chastity, mutual love in the bond of peace, long-lived seed, gratitude from their posterity, a crown of glory which fadeth not away. Graciously grant that they may behold their children's children. Preserve their bed unassailed, and give them of the dew of heaven from on high, and of the fatness of the earth. Fill their houses with wheat, and wine, and oil, and with every beneficence, that they may bestow in turn upon the needy; granting also unto those who are here present with them all those petitions which are for their salvation.

prayer at marriage rite

O thou who knowest the frailty of man's nature, in that thou art his Maker and Creator; who didst pardon Rahab the harlot, and accept the contrition of the publican: remember not the sins of our ignorance from our youth up. For if thou wilt consider iniquity, O Lord, Lord, who shall stand before thee? Or what flesh shall be justified in thy sight? For thou only art righteous, sinless, holy, plenteous in mercy, of great compassion, and repentest thee of the evils of men. Do thou, O Master, who hast brought together in wedlock thy servants, unite them to one another in love: vouchsafe unto them the contribution of the publican, the tears of the harlot, the confession of the thief; that, repenting with their whole heart, and doing thy commandments in peace and oneness of mind, they may be deemed worthy also of thy heavenly kingdom.

prayer at second marriage

R TWENTY-EIGHTH SUNDAY IN ORDINARY TIME

E PROPER 23

L TWENTY-FIRST SUNDAY AFTER PENTECOST

Follow me—I am the way; I am truth and life. Without the way, there is no travelling, without the truth, no knowing, without the life, no living. I am the way you must follow, the truth you must believe, the life you must hope for. I am the way that cannot go astray, the truth that cannot mislead, the life that cannot end. I am the straightest way, the highest truth; I am the true life, the blessed life, the uncreated life.

If you have a mind to enter into life, keep the commandments. If you have a mind to know the truth, believe in me. If you have a mind to be perfect, sell all you have. If you have a mind to become my follower, renounce yourself. If you have a mind exalted in heaven, make yourself humble on earth. If you have a mind to share my kingdom, carry the cross with me; for it is only the servants of the cross that find the way of blessedness and true light.

I ask nothing more of you except that you should want to surrender yourself entirely to me. I do not care what you give me besides yourself, because I do not want your gifts, but you. If you possessed everything except me, you would not find satisfaction. In the same way, nothing you give me can please me if you do not give yourself. Give yourself to me. I gave my whole body and my blood to feed you, so that I should be entirely yours, and you should be kept mine. If you want to achieve liberty and grace, the willing surrender of yourself into the hands of God is more important than all your works.

Thomas à Kempis

R TWENTY-NINTH SUNDAY IN ORDINARY TIME

E PROPER 24

L TWENTY-SECOND SUNDAY AFTER PENTECOST

This seemingly impossible role of service is possible for us all because it is not just a command. It is a gift of God.

Service is God's gift because it is God who serves us. Think of it.

This God of the Hebrew-Christian tradition is like no other gods! God is the one who chooses to serve, not just to be worshipped or adored. Other gods have been revealed so that women and men could serve them. This God, the God of the Suffering Servant—the God of Jesus Christ, begins from the other end. God comes to the people, to liberate them so that they may celebrate their freedom by sharing it with others. In God's service, we see what Karl Barth calls the humanity of God. God is, first of all, not a king sitting on a pyramid of the world creating pyramids of domination and subjugation in the hierarchies of church and society. Rather, the humanity of God is seen in that God chooses to be related to human beings through service.

Service is also God's gift because Jesus not only calls his disciples to serve, he also provides the power and possibility of carrying this out.

In Jesus Christ we have the representation of a new humanity—the beginning of a new type of human being whose life is lived for others. Jesus came as Immanuel, God with us: to be with all people— the women as well as the men; the ignorant as well as the learned; the outcasts as well as the religiously acceptable; the oppressed as well as the oppressors. Jesus helps us to see the humanity of God so that we too can become representatives of new humanity. Here we see what it means to be truly and newly human. This is the image of God—freedom to serve others. This is the image into which humanity is created and redeemed. The whole story of the New Testament revolves around this one theme—*diakonia*, service. At last someone has come, not to be served but to serve! The disciples of Jesus are called to be servants, to be liberated for others.

Letty Russell

R THIRTIETH SUNDAY IN ORDINARY TIME

E PROPER 25

L TWENTY-THIRD SUNDAY AFTER PENTECOST

There was a multitude of people round about the person of Jesus. The blind man could not see the light of truth, but in his soul he could feel his presence, and with the desire of his heart he laid hold of what his eye could not see. What is the meaning of all these people, he asks? They tell him that Jesus of Nazareth is passing by. O wondrous event! He is told one thing, and cries another. He hears them saying it is Jesus of Nazareth, but he cries out, not Jesus of Nazareth, but Jesus, Son of David. They who could see made answer from what was known by common report, but the blind man makes known what he had learned from truth itself, for he cries out, "Jesus, Son of David, have mercy on me."

Jesus, the sun of justice, has arisen. The rays of this spiritual sun spread out in all directions. One indeed receives less grace, and another more; not that grace so gives itself, but that it is our own disposition that supplies the measure. For as the sun is one which gives light to the whole universe, and its ray is one, and its splendor, yet it does not shine with equal light upon all the world. Here is wondrous and abundant sunshine, here there is less. This house has little sunlight, this has it more abundantly; not because the sun gives more to this house, and less to that, but according to the windows which were opened to it by those who built the houses, and less to that, it has more room to enter, and pours in accordingly. And since our thoughts and purposes are the windows of our soul, when you open wide your heart you receive a larger, more generous, divine favor, when you narrow your soul, you can but receive a less abundant grace. Open wide and lay bare your heart and soul to God, that God's splendor may enter into you.

anonymous

R THIRTY-FIRST SUNDAY IN ORDINARY TIME
E PROPER 26
L TWENTY-FOURTH SUNDAY AFTER PENTECOST

Finally, let us not put our own works into the balance, and say they are good, and that we think well of them; but let us understand that the good works are those which God has commanded in the law and that all we can do beside these are nothing. Therefore, let us learn to shape our lives according to what God has commanded: to put our trust in him, to call upon him, to give him thanks, to bear patiently whatsoever it pleases him to send us, to deal uprightly with our neighbors, and to live honestly before all people. These are the works which God requires at our hands.

If we were not so perverse in our nature, there would be none of us but what might discern these things: even children would have skill enough to discern them. The works that God has not commanded are but foolishness and an abomination, whereby God's pure service is marred. If we wish to know what constitutes the good works spoken of by St. Paul, we must lay aside all human inventions, and simply follow the instructions contained in the word of God; for we have no other rule than that which is given by God.

Now let us fall down before the face of our good God, acknowledging our faults, praying God to make us perceive them more clearly and to give us such trust in the name of our Lord Jesus Christ that we may come to God and be assured of the forgiveness of our sins. May God make us partakers of sound faith, whereby all our filthiness may be washed away.

John Calvin

R THIRTY-SECOND SUNDAY IN ORDINARY TIME
E PROPER 27
L TWENTY-FIFTH SUNDAY AFTER PENTECOST

Yesterday I was crucified with Christ; today I will be glorified with him. Yesterday I died with Christ; today I will return to life with him. Yesterday I was buried with Christ; today I will rise with him from the tomb.

Let us then carry our first fruits to him who has suffered and risen for us. Do you think perhaps that I am talking of gold, silver, garments, or precious stones? Insubstantial earthly goods, transitory, tied to earth, owned for the most part by the wicked, the slaves of materialism and the prince of this world? No, let us offer ourselves: it is the most precious and dearest gift in the eyes of God. Give to God's image what resembles it most. Recognizing our greatness, honor our model, understanding the force of this mystery and the reasons for Christ's death.

Become like Christ, since Christ has become like us. Become gods for him since he became human for us. He has become inferior to make us superior; he has become poor to enrich us by his poverty; he has taken the condition of a slave to procure freedom for us; he has come on earth to bring us to heaven; he has been tempted to see us triumph; he has been dishonored to cover us with glory; he has died to save us; he has ascended to heaven to draw us to himself, we who lie prostrate because of falling into sin. Give all, offer all, to him who has given himself for us as a prize and ransom. We will give nothing as great as ourselves if we have grown by the nature of this mystery and have become for him all which he has become for us.

Gregory of Nazianzus

R THIRTY-THIRD SUNDAY IN ORDINARY TIME
E PROPER 28
L TWENTY-SEVENTH SUNDAY AFTER PENTECOST

How blessed and wonderful the gifts of God are, dear friends! Life in immortality, splendor in uprightness, truth with boldness, faith with confidence, self-control with sanctification, all these things are within our understanding. Then what are the things that are being provided for those that wait for God? The Creator and Father of the ages, the Most Holy One knows their number and beauty. Let us therefore strive to be found in the number of those that wait, so that we may share in the gifts God has promised. But how shall this be, dear friends? If our mind is fixed believingly on God, if we seek what is pleasing and acceptable to God, if we perform acts that are in harmony with God's blameless will and follow the way of truth, casting from us all iniquity and wickedness, covetousness, quarreling, ill-nature and deceit, gossip, slander, hatred of God, overbearingness and boastfulness, vain glory and inhospitality.

This is the way, dear friends, by which we find our salvation: Jesus Christ, the high priest of our offerings, the protector and helper of our weakness. Through him we fix our eyes on the heights of heaven. In him we see mirrored God's faultless and sublime face; through him the eyes of our mind have been opened, through him our foolish, darkened understanding springs up to the light;

through him the Master has willed that we should taste immortal
knowledge.

First Clement

L TWENTY-SIXTH SUNDAY AFTER PENTECOST

Wood ceases to be wood when in the fire; it becomes ashes and gas,
light and warmth. Jesus meant to say: such transmutation, such radical change is what I bring and give. Just so he purposely used that
other strong word: I am not come to bring peace, but a sword, the
sword that brings death, that is, not just a change and an improve-
ment in this existence with which we are acquainted, but a transi-
tion from this existence to an entirely unfamiliar one. Let us think
for a moment that that which Jesus is and that which he wants, this
Immanuel! God with us! is true. Something new, something different begins, something as different from all that now is, as ashes,
gas, light and warmth are different from wood, death from life.

God with us! That is too strong a contradiction, not only against
our sins and sufferings but also against the nature of our existence
even down to the very deepest depths of its roots. God with us!
That conflicts too much, not only with our unrighteousness, but
more yet, with our righteousness; not only with the atrocities of history, but more yet with history's supposed progress and achievements; not only with the misery on earth, but more yet, with the
supposed happiness and satisfaction on earth. God with us! That is
redemption, but real, all-embracing, serious, and therefore, radical
redemption. That is the fire of which Jesus spoke, the fire that
wants to come forth out of the glow that he started. Hence the im-
possibility for us to look right into the glow; hence our helplessness
in the presence of Jesus, now as then. Hence the earthquake, the dis-
quietude, the confusion which inevitably arises, when the word of
reconciliation is really preached and heard. Hence the alternative
with which we are inevitably confronted when we understand
what is at stake, when we come too close to the glow in Jesus.

Karl Barth

R LAST SUNDAY IN ORDINARY TIME, CHRIST THE KING

E PROPER 29

L CHRIST THE KING, LAST SUNDAY AFTER PENTECOST

Blessed are you, my Lord Jesus Christ. You foretold your death and at the last supper you marvelously consecrated bread which became your precious body. And then you gave it to your apostles out of love as a memorial of your most holy passion. By washing their feet with your holy hands, you gave them a supreme example of your deep humility.

Blessed may you be, my Lord Jesus Christ. After you had been led to Caiaphas, you, the judge of all, humbly allowed yourself to be handed over to the judgment of Pilate.

Glory to be you, my Lord Jesus Christ, for the mockery you endured when you stood clothed in purple and wearing a crown of sharp thorns. With utmost endurance you allowed vicious men to spit upon your glorious face, blindfold you, and beat your cheek and neck with cruelest blows.

Praise be to you, my Lord Jesus Christ. For with the greatest patience you allowed yourself like an innocent lamb to be bound to a pillar and mercilessly scourged, and then to be brought, covered with blood, before the judgment seat of Pilate to be gazed upon by all.

Honor be to you, my Lord Jesus Christ. For after your glorious body was covered with blood, you were condemned to death on the cross, you endured the pain of carrying the cross on your sacred shoulders, and you were led with curses to the place where you were to suffer. Then stripped of your garments, you allowed yourself to be nailed to the wood of the cross.

Blessed are you and praiseworthy and glorious for ever, my Lord Jesus. You sit upon your throne in your kingdom of heaven, in the glory of your divinity, living in the most holy body you took from a virgin's flesh. So will you appear on that last day to judge the souls of all the living and the dead, you who live and reign with the Father and the Holy Spirit for ever and ever.

Bridget of Sweden

SUNDAYS AND MAJOR HOLY DAYS

CYCLE C

The coming of the Son-of-man is longed for, so that by his presence there may be accomplished in the whole world of angels and of human beings that which is wrought in single souls, who with all fitting dispositions receive Christ. So the powers of heaven, at the coming of the Lord of salvation, will also attain to an increase of grace; for he is the Lord of the powers as well, and they will tremble at this appearance among them of the fullness of the glory of the divinity. Then too the powers that proclaim the glory of God shall also tremble before this fuller revealing of his glory, as they gaze on Christ.

You will behold him in the clouds. Not that I believe that Christ will come in lowering mist, or in the chill rain torrent, for when they appear, they cloak the sky in gloomy darkness. How then shall he set his tabernacle in the sun if his coming be in rain clouds?

But there are clouds which serve to veil the splendor of the divine mystery. There are clouds which moisten with the dew of spiritual refreshment. Consider the cloud in the Old Testament: God spoke to them, it says, in the pillar of cloud. God spoke indeed through Moses, and by the mouth of Josuah, who bade the sun stand still that he might have the light of the lengthened day. So Moses and Josuah were clouds. And observe also that the Holy Ones are clouds, who fly as clouds and as doves to their windows. Above me, like clouds, are Isaiah and Ezekiel, of whom the former has shown me through the cherubim and seraphim the holiness of the divine Trinity. The prophets all are clouds; in these clouds Christ came. He came in a cloud in the Canticle, serene and lovely, refulgent with the joy of the bridegroom. He came in a swift cloud, becoming incarnate through the virgin, for the prophet saw him come as a cloud from the east. And rightly did the prophet call him a swift cloud whom no stain of earth weighed down. Consider the cloud in which the Holy Spirit descended, and from wherein the power of the Most High shadowed forth. When therefore Christ shall appear in the clouds, the tribes of the earth shall mourn; for there is a certain number of offenses, a certain series of sins against God, which will suddenly be interrupted by the advent of Christ.

Ambrose

It was a wonderful and astonishing thing to see the endurance of John the Baptist in a human body. It was this in great measure that drew the attention of the Jews, who beheld in this man the great Elijah, and from what they saw in him the memory of that great and holy man was recalled to their minds. Indeed they were filled with an even greater admiration of John. The prophet had been reared in cities, and in the midst of peoples; the Baptist had dwelt from his childhood alone in the desert.

And it was necessary that the precursor of him who was to undo the age-long human burdens of toil, malediction, pain, and sweat, should in his own person give some token of the gifts to come, and stand himself above all these tribulations. And so it was that he neither tilled the earth, nor ploughed the furrow, nor did he eat bread of his own sweat, for his table was easily prepared, and his clothing more easily than his table, and his dwelling more easily than his clothing. For he had need neither of roof, nor bed, nor table, nor any such like; but even while still within this flesh of ours lived an almost angelic life. His clothing was put together from the hair of camels, so that even from his garments he might teach us that we free ourselves of human needs, and be not bound to this earth, but that we must return to the pristine dignity in which Adam first lived, before he had need of garments or of clothing. So his manner of dress was in itself a symbol, as well of our dignity as of our need of repentance.

Do not say to me, where did this desert dweller procure his garment of hair and his girdle of leather? For if you ask me that question, you raise many more: how did he fare in the winter, and how in the summer, and alone, especially while still tender of body and young in years? How could the constitution of a young boy endure such extremes of nature, upon such food, and in face of all the other hardships of that vast solitude?

What have the philosophers to say to this, especially those who follow the impudent school of the Cynics, who indulge themselves with rings, and goblets, with male and female servants and all the other signs of luxury, and despite their philosophy give themselves over to every excess? Truly great was this man, who dwelt in the desert as though in heaven, showing himself a model of true wisdom. From there he came to the city, as an angel from heaven; an athlete of every virtue, crowned before the world, a philosopher of the philosophy that is worthy of heaven.

John Chrysostom

R E L THIRD SUNDAY OF ADVENT

Look how shamefully the dear martyrs were murdered, and yet now they shine forth so brightly that by comparison the whole world is nothing but a stench. Thus before our own time John Hus was condemned in an abominable fashion that was unheard of before, and they supposed that his name was obliterated forever. Yet now he is shining forth with such glory that his cause and his teaching have to be praised before the whole world.

That is what happened to Christ himself. They had put him under the ground, and they thought he was buried so deep that no one would ever sing or speak his name again. But just then he flashed forth, and by his word he began to shine so brilliantly that it destroyed them. This ought to make us feel safe, too; for we have his word that though our teaching and our works may be hidden now, they must come to the light and be praised in the presence of all the world — that is, unless even God stays in the dark.

You see, this is the promise given to us for our comfort and our admonition. We should exercise ourselves in genuine good works, without worrying because the world takes no notice of them. For the world is too blind to notice them. It does not recognize the word and the works of God any more than it recognizes God. It will never attain to the vision of how marvelous a baptized child is, or a Christian who receives the sacrament and who gladly hears the word of God. It must always look at these things as merely a waterbath or a piece of bread, or useless palaver. In the same way it fails to see what people are doing when they properly fast or pray. Therefore we commend it to the one who can see it.

Martin Luther

And to teach us this, our Lord God showed me our Lady, Saint Mary, at that same time, that is to say, the lofty wisdom and strength she had when she beheld her maker, so great, so noble, so mighty, so good. The greatness and nobility she saw in God filled her full of reverent dread, and with it she saw herself so little, so low, so simple, so poor in comparison to her Lord God that her reverent dread filled her full of meekness. And thus, on these grounds she was filled full of grace and of all manner of virtues, and passed beyond all other creatures.

And thus it is between our Lord Jesus and us, for truly, it is the greatest joy possible, as I see it, that he who is highest and mightiest, noblest and worthiest, becomes lowest and meekest, friendliest and most courteous. And really and truly, this marvelous joy shall be shown us all when we see him. And our Lord wills that we believe, choose and trust him, enjoy and delight in him, comforting and solacing ourselves as best we can with his grace and his help until the time we see it in reality. For the greatest fulfillment of joy we shall have, as I see it, is the marvelous courtesy and unassuming friendliness of our Father who is our maker, in our Lord Jesus Christ, who is our brother and our savior. But this marvelous familiarity no one may experience in this present life unless doing so through a special showing of our Lord, or through great fullness of grace given inwardly by the Holy Spirit. But faith and belief, with charity, deserve their reward, and thus it is attained by grace. For in faith, with hope and charity, our life is grounded.

And when the showing, which is given at a single time, has passed away and is hidden, then the faith, by the grace of the Holy Spirit, preserves it to the end of our lives. Thus the showing is not other than the faith, neither less nor more, as can be seen in our Lord's teaching on the same matter, about when each shall come to its end.

Julian of Norwich

R CHRISTMAS MASS AT MIDNIGHT

E CHRISTMAS DAY I

L THE NATIVITY OF OUR LORD, 1

I behold a new and wondrous mystery. My ears resound to the shepherd's song, piping no soft melody, but chanting full forth a heavenly hymn. The angels sing. The archangels blend their voices in harmony. The cherubim hymn their joyful praise. The seraphim exalt God's glory. All join to praise this holy feast, beholding the godhead here on earth, and a man in heaven. The one who is above, now for our redemption dwells here below; and he that was lowly is by divine mercy raised.

Yet he has not forsaken his angels, nor left them deprived of his care, nor because of his incarnation has he departed from the god-head. And behold kings have come, that they might adore the heavenly King of glory; soldiers, that they might serve the leader of the hosts of heaven; women, that they might adore him who was born of a woman so that he might change the pains of childbirth into joy; virgins, to the son of the virgin, beholding with joy, that he who is the giver of milk, who has decreed that the fountains of the breast pour forth in ready streams, receives from a virgin mother the food of infancy; infants, that they may adore him who became a little child, so that out of the mouth of infants and of sucklings, he might perfect praise; children, to the child who raised up martyrs through the rage of Herod; men, to him who became a man, that he might heal the miseries of his servants; shepherds, to the Good Shepherd who has laid down his life for his sheep; priests, to him who has become a high priest according to the order of Melchisedech; servants, to him who took upon Himself the form of a servant that he might bless our servitude with the reward of freedom; fishermen, to him who from amongst fishermen chose catchers of human beings; publicans, to him who from amongst them named a chosen evangelist; sinful women, to him who exposed his feet to the tears of the repentant; and that I may embrace them all together, all sinners have come, that they may look upon the Lamb of God who takes away the sins of the world.

Since therefore all rejoice, I too desire to rejoice. I too wish to share the choral dance, to celebrate the festival. But I take my part, not plucking the harp, not shaking the thyrsian staff, not with the music of the pipes, nor holding a torch, but holding in my arms the cradle of Christ. For this is all my hope, this my life, this my salvation, this my life, this my salvation, this my pipe, my harp. And bearing it I come, and having from its power received the gift of speech, I too, with the angels, sing: Glory to God in the highest.

John Chrysostom

R CHRISTMAS MASS DURING THE DAY
E CHRISTMAS DAY III
L THE NATIVITY OF OUR LORD, 2

The omnipotent, all-creating, invisible God from heaven introduced among mortals the truth and the holy and incomprehensible word and has established it in their hearts, not as one might imagine, sending some servant or angel or ruler, or one of those who manage things on earth, or one of those who have been entrusted with the administration of affairs in heaven, but sent the very designer and creator of the universe by whom God created the heavens, by whom God enclosed the sea in its own limits, whose secrets all the elements faithfully keep, from whom the sun has received the measures of the courses of the day to keep, whom the moon obeys when commanded to shine at night, whom the stars obey, as they follow the course of the moon; by whom all things have been constituted and had their limits set and made subject, the heavens and the things in the heavens, the earth and the things on the earth, the sea and the things in the sea, fire, air, abyss, the things in the heights, the things in the deeps, the things between. Did God though do it as a man might suppose, like a tyrant with fear and terror? Not at all. But with gentleness and meekness, like a king sending his son, God sent the word as king, as God, as a human to humans, God sent as seeking to save, as persuading, not compelling, for compulsion is not the way of God. God sent as one calling, not pursuing, as one loving, not judging.

For what human being knew at all what God was, before the word came? Or do you accept the empty, silly accounts of the recognized philosophers, some of whom said that God was fire (they call that

God to which they will go!), and others, water, and others some other one of the elements created by God? And yet if any of these statements is worth accepting, every other created thing could be pronounced God. But this is marvel-talk and imposture of tricksters. No one has ever seen or discovered God, but God has revealed himself through faith, through which alone it is granted to see God. For God, the master and creator of the universe, who made all things and put them in order, was not only kind, but long-suffering as well. God always was, and is and will be so—kindly, good, free from anger, true, and alone is good. Having in the former time proved the inability of our nature to obtain life, and now having revealed the Savior able to save even what was incapable of being saved, for both these reasons God wished us to believe in divine goodness, to regard God as nourisher, father, teacher, counselor, physician, mind, light, honor, glory, strength, life, and not to be anxious about food and clothing.

Address to Diognetus

R HOLY FAMILY

L FIRST SUNDAY AFTER CHRISTMAS

Some think that the soul of Christ had equal wisdom with God. Others, fearful of making a creature seem equal with God, say that since he grew in age, so he also grew in wisdom. But of these opinions let each of you judge as you will. For me it suffices to know and believe that the Lord Jesus was perfect God, and whatsoever can be said of God, as to the divine nature, I doubt not that the same can be said of Christ, even within the womb of his mother.

Nor do we by this deny him, prior to his resurrection, either mortality or the power to suffer, since we confess that he was not a seeming man, but truly a man; and that he possessed the true nature of a man, in which he could increase in age.

The great God abiding in the divine nature is born a child according to the flesh, and grows for a certain space of time, and after the manner of the flesh, so that we who are children in mind, and almost without mind, may be spiritually reborn, and that we may grow up according to the grades of the spiritual ages and advance in wisdom and grace. So his bodily growth is our spiritual growth, and the things that are recorded as done by him in the successive ages are seen as done in us, as we advance through the diverse stages of spiritual growth.

So let his corporal birth be our spiritual birth, that is, the beginning of our conversion. Let his persecution, that which he suffered from Herod, be to us a sign of the temptation we suffer from the devil in the beginning of our conversion. Let his growing up in Nazareth express our advancement in perfection. The prodigal son, perishing with hunger, was invited to the house of bread where there is bread baked in ashes, not fine wheaten bread; so that he may eat bread like ashes, and mingle drink with weeping. But Christ is the pure wheaten bread, clean, without ashes, without ferment, without chaff, which we must seek.

Aelred

R L SECOND SUNDAY AFTER CHRISTMAS
E FIRST SUNDAY AFTER CHRISTMAS

The maidenhood of Mary was hidden from the ruler of this world, as were her giving birth and likewise the death of the Lord—three secrets to be cried aloud, which yet were accomplished in the silence of God. How, then, was he shown to the ages? A star blazed forth in heaven brighter than all the stars and its light was inexpressible, and its strangeness caused astonishment, and all the rest of the stars, along with the sun and moon, formed a chorus round the star, but it outshone them all; and there was perplexity as to where this strange thing, so unlike the rest, came from. In consequence of it all magic was dissolved, and every wicked spell vanished, ignorance was abolished, the old kingdom was destroyed, when God appeared in human form, to bring us new, eternal life; and what God had prepared had its beginning. Hence all things were in confusion, because the abolishing of death was being designed.

Ignatius

E SECOND SUNDAY AFTER CHRISTMAS

Far to the East there is the sacred grove of paradise. It is always flooded with spring's soft sunshine. The weather continually remains most agreeable. Neither sorrow nor sickness nor death are known there. The grove is watered by a crystal-clear spring; its high trees are laden with luscious fruit, which never falls to the ground. A phoenix, the bird of paradise, is the grove's sole inhabitant.

At the first gleam of dawn this bird bathes in the limpid stream and drinks from the spring. Then it flies to the tree of life and there awaits the sunrise. It greets the first beam of sunlight with a song more beautiful than any earthly music. After the sun is fully risen, it beats its wings with a ringing sound as its wings glitter in the sunlight like a rainbow.

When a thousand years have passed, the phoenix senses that its course is run. It leaves its home and paradise, and flies into the world where death holds sway. Soon its wings have carried it to Phoenicia, where it stops to rest in some remote place. It selects the highest palm tree and builds there a nest to serve as a grave. Now the phoenix dies only in order that it might live, and be created anew. Therefore it gathers the finest spices of every land, beds itself therein, and dies. The carcass, being set on fire by the sun's heat, generates life as it burns to ashes. For in these ashes is the germ of new life. Soon there comes forth a milk-white egg which, transforming itself like the caterpillar into a butterfly, becomes a phoenix and nourishes itself on heavenly dew.

Whoever sees it is amazed by its beauty. Its plumage shimmers with beautiful colors, its eyes sparkle like a hyacinth, and a crown of light encircles its head. No bird, and certainly no animal, rivals it in glory. It is royal in appearance and though gigantic in size flies gracefully and without effort. Thus the phoenix appears to admiring eyes. The birds of the sky gather as an escort. But the phoenix flies back alone to its haven, the sacred grove of paradise.

legend

R E L THE EPIPHANY OF OUR LORD

The magi come bearing gold, incense and myrrh. Gold is offered in tribute to a king, incense is offered in sacrifice to God, with myrrh the bodies of the dead are embalmed. The magi therefore proclaim also by their mystic gifts who it is they adore; with gold they proclaim him king, with incense that he is God, by myrrh that he is mortal.

There are heretics who believe that he is God, but they do not believe that he reigns everywhere. These indeed offer incense, but refuse to offer him gold. There are others who believe he is a king, but deny he is God. These offer gold, but deny him incense. And there are others who confess he is both God and king, but deny that he assumed a mortal body. Such as these offer him gold and incense, but refuse the myrrh of his assumed mortality.

Let us then offer gold to the newborn Lord, that we may confess he reigns everywhere; let us offer incense, inasmuch as we believe that he who appeared in time was God before all time; let us offer myrrh, that we believe that in our flesh he was mortal.

The gold, incense and myrrh we may interpret in yet another way. For by gold wisdom is also symbolized. By incense, which is burnt in honor of God, we signify the power of prayer. By myrrh is symbolized the mortification of our flesh, whence it is that holy church says of its workers who have labored for God until death.

To the newborn king we offer gold, if we shine before him in the brightness of heavenly wisdom. We offer him incense, if we consume the thoughts of the flesh upon the altar of our heart, so that in our heavenly desires we send up to God an odor of sweetness. We offer him myrrh, when we safeguard this mortal body of ours from the corruption of wantonness by the preservatives of chastity.

In that they return to their own land by another way, the magi intimate to us something of great importance. It is paradise that is our true country, to which, having come to know Jesus, we are forbidden to return by the way we came. For we left our land by the way of pride and disobedience, by following after the things of this world, by tasting forbidden food; and so we must return to it by the way of tears, by obedience, by contempt of the world, and by restraining the desires of the flesh. Let us return then to our own country by another way.

Gregory the Great

Then, when you were stripped, you were anointed with exorcized oil from the very hairs of your head to your feet, and were made partakers of the good olive tree, Jesus Christ. For you were cut off from the wild olive tree, and grafted into the good one, and were made to share the fatness of the true olive tree. The exorcized oil therefore was a symbol of the participation of the fatness of Christ, the charm to drive away every trace of hostile influence. For as the breathing of the saints and the invocation of the name of God like fiercest flame scorch and drive out evil spirits, so also this exorcized oil receives such virtue by the invocation of God and by prayer, as not only to burn and cleanse away the traces of sins, but also to chase away all the invisible powers of the evil one.

After these things, you were led to the holy pool of divine baptism, as Christ was carried from the cross to the sepulcher which is before our eyes. And each of you was asked, whether you believed in the name of the Father, and of the Son, and of the Holy Ghost, and you made that saving confession, and descended three times into the water, and ascended again; here also covertly pointing by a figure at the three-day burial of Christ. For as our Savior passed three days and three nights in the heart of the earth, so you also in your first ascent out of the water, represented the first day of Christ in the earth, and by your descent, the night; for as they who one in the night, see no more, but they who are in the day, remain in the light, so in descending, you saw nothing as in the night, but in ascending again, you were as in the day. And at the self-same moment, you died and were born, and that water of salvation was at once your grave and your mother. To you the time to die is also the time to be born; and one and the same season brings about both of these, and your birth went hand in hand with your death.

Cyril of Jerusalem

R SECOND SUNDAY IN ORDINARY TIME
E L SECOND SUNDAY AFTER EPIPHANY

Such are the wonders of Christ, more beautiful and more advantageous than those done by nature; and so also the other happenings, as when he healed an afflicted limb, he made it better than the sound one. That it was wine, and the best wine, not alone the waiters, but the chief steward and the bridegroom bear witness; and that it was made from water, they testify who drew the water. And, so though the miracle was not yet revealed, it could not in the end remain in silence, so many and so close linked were the testimonies provided for future times.

That he had made water into wine, he had the waiters as witnesses; that the wine was good, he had a witnesses the chief steward and the bridegroom. It is likely that the bridegroom made some answer, but the evangelist, having recorded this wonder, goes on, pressing on to what was more necessary. For what was strictly necessary was that it be truly known that he changed water into wine; what the bridegroom said to the chief steward he did not think needed to be recorded.

And many of the miracles at first obscure have become clearer in the course of time. Then those who saw the event from the very beginning narrated what had taken place. Jesus then made wine from water: and now as well as then he ceases not to change our weak and unstable wills into that which is better. For there are, I affirm, people who differ in nothing from water; they are cold, weak, and never stand firm. Let us bring those who are so afflicted to the Lord, that he may change their will to the quality of wine: that they no longer flow away, but be steadfast; and become to themselves and to others a source of comfort.

John Chrysostom

R THIRD SUNDAY IN ORDINARY TIME
E L THIRD SUNDAY AFTER EPIPHANY

Awe-inspiring, in truth, are the mysteries of the church: awesome, in truth, its altar. A fountain sprang up out of paradise, sending forth sensible streams; a fountain arises from this table, sending forth spiritual streams. Beside this fountain there have grown, not willows without fruit, but trees reaching to heaven itself, with fruit ever in season and incorrupt. Let whoever is intensely hot come to this fountain and cool down the feverish heat. It dispels parching heat and gently cools all things that are very hot, not those inflamed by the sun's heat, but those set on fire by burning arrows. It does so because it takes its beginning from above, and has its source from there, and from there it is fed. Many are the streams of this fountain, streams which the Paraclete sends forth; and the Son becomes its custodian, not keeping its channel open with a mattock, but making our hearts receptive.

This fountain is a fountain of light, shedding abundant rays of truth. And beside it the powers from on high have taken their stand, gazing on the beauty of its streams, since they perceive more clearly than we the power of what lies before us and its unapproachable flashing rays. Just as if one were to put one's hand or tongue into molten gold—if that were possible—one would at once make the object golden, the mystery lying before us here affects the soul, but much more so. The stream gushes up more vigorously than fire; it does not burn, however, but only cleanses what it touches.

This blood was formerly foreshadowed continually in altars, in sacrifices of the law. This is the price of the world; by it Christ purchased the church; by it he adorned it entirely. Just as a man in buying slaves gives gold and, if he desires to beautify them, does this with gold, so also Christ has both purchased us with his blood and adorned us with his blood. Those who share in this blood have taken their stand with angels, and archangels, and the powers from on high, clad in the royal livery of Christ and grasping spiritual weapons. But I have not yet mentioned anything great, for they are wearing the King himself.

However, since it is a great and wonderful thing, if you approach with purity you come unto salvation. Let us who enjoy such blessings take heed to ourselves, and when we are tempted to utter a sinful word, or when we find ourselves being carried away by anger or some other such passion, let us reflect on what privileges we have been granted, what Spirit it is whose presence we enjoy, and this thought will check in us the unruly passions. How long, in truth, shall we be attached to present things? How long shall we remain asleep? How long shall we not take thought for our own salvation? Let us remember what privileges God has bestowed on us, let us give thanks, and let us glorify God, not only by faith, but also by our very works.

John Chrysostom

R FOURTH SUNDAY IN ORDINARY TIME

E L FOURTH SUNDAY AFTER EPIPHANY

In this very year, in my monastery, a certain brother, turned to repentance, entered the monastery, was devoutly accepted, and became himself yet more devoutly changed in life. His brother followed him into the monastery: in the flesh, not in the spirit. For though detesting the monastic dress and the monastic life, he remained in the monastery as a guest; and he was unable to discontinue living there, though he shunned the life of the monks, because he had neither occupation nor the means to live.

His evil conduct was a burden to all; yet all endured him with patience out of love for his brother. And though he knew not what followed after this present life, yet, arrogant and uncertain, he scoffed if anyone wished to instruct him in this. And so, flippant in speech, restless in movement, empty in mind, disorderly in dress, dissipated in behavior, he lived on in the monastery, but in the dispositions of the world.

During the month of July last, he was stricken down in that epidemic of the pestilence that you remember; and as he was approaching his end he was urged to put his soul in order. The power of life now remained only in his heart and in his tongue, his extremities were already dead. The brethren stood by him, helping him in his end by their prayers, as far as God permitted. Suddenly, beholding the demon coming to take possession of him, he began to cry out in a loud voice, "Look, I am delivered over to the dragon to be devoured; but it cannot devour me because of your presence. Why do you delay me? Go away that the dragon may finish me!"

And when the brethren exhorted him to sign himself with the sign of the cross, he answered as well as he was able: "I want to bless myself but I cannot, because I am held fast by the dragon: my throat is held in its jaws, and the foam of its mouth has smeared my face. Look! My arms are imprisoned by the one who has my head in its jaws!"

While he was saying this, trembling, pale, and dying, the brethren began ever more earnestly to pray for him, to help by their intercession this man here tormented by the presence of an evil spirit. Then of a sudden he was delivered, and began to cry out aloud, "Thanks be to God." There and then he vowed to serve God, and to become a monk.

Who would have believed that this man would have been preserved and converted? Who can fathom the so great depths of the mercy of God? What tongue can speak of the bowels of the divine mercy? What soul is not awed at the richness of the divine kindness? Remembering that God sees our evildoing, and suffers it in patience, that God is unmindful of our offenses, and with all this brings us through repentance to final reward, he wished not to say that God was merciful, but called God mercy itself, saying: My God, my mercy.

Gregory the Great

R FIFTH SUNDAY IN ORDINARY TIME
E L FIFTH SUNDAY AFTER EPIPHANY

Springing up on Pentecost and Calvary, the church flows through the ages like a river, and that same river and no other will flow unchanging on through the ages until that great day when it will empty completely into the famed sea of eternal blessedness. Just as a river of water is made up of the same sort of drops, so all the children of that great river called the church have been and will be of the same sort through all generations. All human races have sprung from the same blood and thus have the same bloodline. In the same way all children of the church from the very beginning share the same spirit and are one spiritual race. As I in my age am a drop of the great river, a member of the church, so am I a brother of the fathers who came before me and the children who come after me. There is no distinction between the firstborn and the lastborn child of the church except the distinction of time, and in the course of things that too will disappear and finally leave no distinction at all. From beginning to end we are all one holy and blessed fellowship in God almighty. When God lives in us and we in God, we lack nothing we need in order to grasp the complete truth and joy in this thought.

I do not know how long the church will stand in history and overcome the ages. Nor can I say with absolute certainty whether the final period of the church's flourishing has come or how many more such periods may yet come. But there are two things I do know for certain. I know that the old church is presently flourishing in what we call our church. I know that the river of the centuries, the river which has existed since the beginning, flows through our land and that this river is not a new stream just because it flowed through Wittenberg three centuries ago or because we who are children of yesterday have been given the grace to live on its banks. I also know that the river will not cease to flow as long as the world stands, that the church will not die out as long as the sun and the moon continue to shine. That stream may be hemmed in or hidden from the gaze of a casual observer—for a time. But it cannot be overcome, for there must always be one holy church on earth. Just as the moon waxes and wanes and yet remains in the sky, so the church does not always appear in the same splendor but nevertheless goes its quiet way, undisturbed and full of promise. Just as the clouds sometimes cover the sun and moon, the church also has its cloudy days. But just as the clouds can never fully take away the splendor of sunshiny days and moonlit nights, just as cloudy days and cloudy moonlit nights still have some light, so the church is never so darkened that it cannot be found by the eye which seeks it.

Wilhelm Loehe

R SIXTH SUNDAY IN ORDINARY TIME

E SIXTH SUNDAY AFTER EPIPHANY, PROPER 1

L SIXTH SUNDAY AFTER EPIPHANY

This gospel from Luke teaches us today that human love is a religious, Christian event. Luke does not leave this vague. Within the church he is clearly concerned that possessions should be shared, so that there will not be poor Christians alongside rich Christians. For Luke the beatitudes of Jesus are praised of the rich who give half their possessions to the poor in the community. From a social perspective, that, and only that, is life according to the gospel. It is not the whole of Christian life, but it is also Christian life. Furthermore, it is striking that Luke deliberately but consistently changes the familiar liturgical words at the celebration of the eucharist in his community, 'Drink you all of this,' into, 'Share this cup with one another.' Everything is to be shared with one another. Luke translates Jesus' gospel for the poor into a gospel for the rich, since in his day the original church of the poor and the underdogs had become a community of both poor and rich. And Luke wants to exploit this new situation. In almost every chapter of his gospel his demand for the social solidarity of rich Christians with poor Christians has a prominent place.

Translated for today's world, above all in its beatitudes, the gospel of Luke is a direct indictment of our bourgeois existence, our bourgeois behavior and our bourgeois society. This bourgeois character has also attacked the hearts of Christians and of the church itself. Of course we cannot derive any suitable social program for our time from the gospel. But the plan that Luke sketches of a truly Christian community in accordance with the gospel — half of what you possess for the unimportant among us — remains a challenge which can make us lie awake at nights worrying whether we are taking Christ's gospel seriously. At all events this message of Luke does not let present-day Christians get off scot-free.

In terms of the modern world, what Luke says to us describes precisely the scandal in which the present church is involved: How is it possible for defenders of oppressive systems and those they oppress, all of us and the third world, to celebrate the one eucharist together as Christians? We drink from our full cups but do not share the one cup among one another. The great scandal among us is not intercommunion among Christians of different communions: that is a sign of hope. The scandal is the intercommunion of rich Christians who remain rich and poor Christians who remain poor while celebrating the same eucharist, taking no notice of the Christian model of sharing possessions: the sharing of the one cup of salvation among one another. For this salvation also has social and economic consequences. Everyone, not just an elite group, has to be full enough to be able to laugh because salvation has happened to him or her. Jesus said, "Today salvation has come to the house of Zacchaeus," because Zacchaeus gave away to the poor half of what he possessed.

Is not all this more urgent than our petty problems within the church, however real they may be at the time? God does not want human suffering; God wants life, and life in abundance, for all not simply for one-third of the world's population. What about our abundance? That is Luke's critical question, a concrete challenge to all of us, here and now.

Edward Schillebeeckx

R SEVENTH SUNDAY IN ORDINARY TIME
E SEVENTH SUNDAY AFTER EPIPHANY, PROPER 2
L SEVENTH SUNDAY AFTER EPIPHANY

Probably no admonition of Jesus has been more difficult to follow than the command to "love your enemies." Some men have sincerely felt that its actual practice is not possible. It is easy, they say, to love those who love you, but how can one love those who openly and insidiously seek to defeat you? Others, like the philosopher Nietzsche, contend that Jesus' exhortation to love one's enemies is testimony to the fact that the Christian ethic is designed for the weak and cowardly, and not for the strong and courageous. Jesus, they say, was an impractical idealist.

In spite of these insistent questions and persistent objections, this command of Jesus challenges us with new urgency. Upheaval after upheaval has reminded us that modern man is travelling along a road called hate, in a journey that will bring us to destruction and damnation. Far from being the pious injunction of a utopian dreamer, the command to love one's enemy is an absolute necessity for our survival. Love even for enemies is the key to the solution of the problems of our world. Jesus is not an impractical idealist: he is the practical realist.

I am certain that Jesus understood the difficulty inherent in the act of loving one's enemy. He never joined the ranks of those who talk glibly about the easiness of the moral life. He realized that every genuine expression of love grows out of a consistent and total surrender to God. So when Jesus said, "Love your enemy," he was not unmindful of its stringent qualities. Yet he meant every word of it. Our responsibility as Christians is to discover the meaning of this command and seek passionately to live it out in our daily lives.

Let us be practical and ask the question, How do we love our enemies?

First, we must develop and maintain the capacity to forgive. He who is devoid of the power to forgive is devoid of the power to love. It is impossible even to begin the act of loving one's enemies without the prior acceptance of the necessity, over and over again, of forgiving those who inflict evil and injury upon us. It is also necessary to realize that the forgiving act must always be initiated by the person who has been wronged, the victim of some great hurt, the recipient of some tortuous injustice, the absorber of some terrible act of oppression. The wrongdoer may request forgiveness. He may come to himself, and, like the prodigal son, move up some dusty road, his heart palpitating with the desire for forgiveness. But only the injured neighbor, the loving father back home, can really pour out the warm water of forgiveness.

Martin Luther King, Jr.

R EIGHTH SUNDAY IN ORDINARY TIME
E EIGHTH SUNDAY AFTER EPIPHANY, PROPER 3
L EIGHTH SUNDAY AFTER EPIPHANY

Nothing equals the merit of almsgiving. Great is the power of this action when it flows forth from untarnished sources. But when it comes from sources that are defiled, it is as if a fountain were to send forth mud. But when alms are given from our just gains, it is as if they flowed forth from a pure and limpid stream, one flowing from paradise, pleasant to the eye, pleasant to the touch, something cool and light given in the noonday heat. Such are alms. Beside this fountain grow not poplars nor pines nor cypresses, but trees more rare and precious: the love of God, the praise of others, glory before

God, the good will of all, the wiping away of sins, great confidence in God, small esteem for riches.

By this fountain the tree of love is nourished; for nothing so nourishes love as to be compassionate toward others. It lifts its branches on high. Let death light on this, and like a spark the fountain extinguishes it; for wherever it flows, such as these are its blessings. It extinguishes as though it were a spark in a river of flame. For should a drop of this water fall upon chains it dissolves them; should it be poured upon furnaces, it extinguishes all of them. As the fountain of paradise does not now give forth streams, now run dry—otherwise it would not be a fountain—but is ever springing up, so let our fountain give forth ever more generously of the stream of its alms, especially to those who stand in need, that it may remain a fountain. This makes cheerful the one who receives. This is almsgiving: to give forth, and not alone in a vigorous stream, but in an ever-flowing stream. If you desire that God should rain upon you from as it were the fountains of divine mercy, let you also have a fountain. Yet there is no comparison between the one and the other. If you open the gates of this fountain, such will be the gates of God's fountain that it overwhelms the deep. God but seeks from us an occasion, to pour forth blessings from heaven's stores.

Let no unfruitful tree stand by this fountain, to waste its moisture. Have you wealth? Then do not plant there the black poplar; for that is but luxury, conceit as it were. It consumes much and shows no return in itself, and spoils fruit. Neither plant the fir tree, nor the pine, nor any of these kinds, which consume moisture but bear no fruit: for such is the delight of rich clothing, beautiful to see, but profitable in nothing. Plant it around with young shoots of trees that bear fruit. Plant what you will, in the hands of the poor. There is no earth more fruitful than this. And though narrow the breadth of a hand, yet the tree planted there will rise to heaven itself and stand firm. This is truly to plant. For what is planted on the earth will fade away, if not now then a hundred years from now. Why plant trees you will not enjoy? For before you can enjoy them, death comes between and snatches you away. But this tree, when you have gone from here, then will you eat its fruits.

John Chrysostom

E LAST SUNDAY AFTER EPIPHANY
L TRANSFIGURATION OF OUR LORD

One day during Lent, the angel carried me to a towering mountain and placed me on the mountainside. When I looked up, I saw an immense precipice, with what looked like dark water underneath. And the angel said to me, "Here you see the abyss." And when we had made our way up the mountain, we came to a very handsome gate; passing through it, we came upon another, more magnificent, and a third even more beautiful than the first two. And when we passed through that third gate we found a large multitude of most beautiful people, rejoicing and praising God fervently, with a clear and joyous voice. And they all bowed their heads to my guide. But of the song they were singing, only these words have remained in my memory: Praise and glory to the God of fame. And I said to my guide, "Lord, who are these men we see?" The angel said, "These are the holy desert fathers, who lived in ancient times." And when I asked where blessed Paul, the first eremite, was, he was pointed out to me, preeminent among all the others in his glory. And blessed Antony too the angel pointed out to me, bearing witness that they had all gazed on God face to face.

Elizabeth of Schoenau

R E L ASH WEDNESDAY

As we are therefore beginning this sacred season, dedicated to the purification of the soul, let us be careful to fulfill the apostolic command that we cleanse ourselves from all defilement of the flesh and of the spirit, so that restraining the conflict that exists between the one and the other substance, the soul, which in the providence of God is meant to be the ruler of the body, may regain the dignity of its rightful authority, so that, giving offense to no one, we may not incur the contumely of evil mongers. With just contempt shall we be tormented by those who have no faith, and from our wickedness evil tongues will draw weapons to wound religion, if the way of life of those who fast be not in accord with what is needed in true self-denial. For the sum total of our fasting does not consist in merely abstaining from food. In vain do we deny our body food if we do not withhold our heart from iniquity, and restrain our lips that they speak no evil.

We must then so moderate our rightful use of food that our other desires may be subject to the same rule. For this is also a time for gentleness and patience, a time of peace and serenity, in which having put away all stains of evildoing we strive after steadfastness in what is good. Now is the time when generous Christian souls forgive offenses, pay no heed to insults, and wipe out the memory of past injuries. Now let the Christian soul exercise itself in the armor of justice, on the right hand and on the left, so that amid honor and dishonor, evil report and good, the praise of others will not make proud the virtue that is well-rooted and the conscience that has peace. The moderation of those who worship God is not melancholy, but blameless.

Neither should we now hear sound of discord coming from those to whom the consolations of holy joy are never wanting. And when you are engaged in works of mercy, do not fear a lessening of your own earthly possessions. Christian poverty is ever rich; for that which it possesses is greater than that which it does not possess. Neither should you fear to work on in poverty to whom it has been given to possess all things in the Lord of all things.

They therefore who desire to do good works, let them not fear that they shall be without the means; since even for giving two farthings, the generosity of the poor widow of the gospel was glorified, and even the free gift of a cup of cold water shall not be without its reward. By their desires we shall know the measure of the good will of the just; and whoever has a heart ever open to pity will never lack means to help those in need. We learn this from that holy widow who, in a time of famine, placed before the blessed Elijah all that she had, and that was but food sufficient for a day; and putting the prophet's hunger before her own, she gave without hesitation her handful of meal and her drop of oil. But she was not left to want for that which she had so piously bestowed: and in the vessels which charity had emptied there arose a fresh source of abundance, so that the amount of what she had had was not made less by the charity that had not feared to go wanting.

Leo

And after that, without voice or the opening of lips, the Lord formed these words in my soul: "Herewith is the fiend overcome." When he said these words, our Lord was referring to his blessed passion, as he had shown previously.

In this our Lord showed part of the devil's malice and all of his powerlessness, for he showed that his passion in the overcoming of the fiend. God showed that the devil has the same malice now that he had before the incarnation, and the harder he works, the more continually he sees that all salvation's souls escape from him gloriously, by virtue of Christ's precious passion. And that is his sorrow.

His end is attained very badly, for all that God allows him to do turns to joy for us and to shame, pain and woe for him. He has as much sorrow when God gives him permission to work as when he does not work. The reason for this is that he can never do as much evil as he would like to, because all his power is locked in God's hands.

But, as I see it, there can be no wrath in God. For our good Lord endlessly has regard for his own honor and for the profit of all who shall be saved. With might and right, our Lord withstands the discredited, who, with malice and shrewdness, busy themselves to contrive and work against God's will.

Also, I saw our Lord scorn his malice and reduce his powerlessness to nothing, and he wills that we do the same thing. On account of this sight, I laughed loud and long, which made those who were around me laugh too, and their laughter was a pleasure to me. Then I thought I would like all my fellow Christians to have seen what I saw, for then they should all laugh with me. I didn't see Christ laugh, but I knew well that it was the sight he had shown me that had made me laugh. For I understood that we may laugh, comforting ourselves and rejoicing in God that the devil has been overcome.

And after this, I fell into a more sober mood and said, "I see three things: a jest, scorn and earnest. I see a jest in that the fiend is overcome. I see scorn in that God scorns him, and he shall be scorned. And I see earnest in that he is overcome by the blessed passion and death of our Lord Jesus Christ, which was done in absolute earnest and with sorrowful, difficult labor."

Julian of Norwich

R SECOND SUNDAY IN LENT, *see 163*
E L SECOND SUNDAY IN LENT

But now it is necessary for me to say a little more about this "spreading forth," as I understood it in our Lord's meaning—how we are brought again, by the motherhood of mercy and grace, into our natural place, for which we were created by the motherhood of natural love. This natural love never leaves us.

A mother's service is nearest, readiest and surest. It is nearest because it is most natural. It is readiest because it is most loving. And it is surest because it is most true. This office no one but him alone might or could ever have performed to the full.

We realize that all our mothers bear us for pain and for dying, and what is that? But our true mother, Jesus—All love—alone bears us for joy and for endless living, blessed may he be! Thus he sustains us within himself in love and hard labor, until the fulness of time. Then he willed to suffer the sharpest thorns and the most grievous pains there ever were or ever will be, and to die at the last.

When he had done this and so borne us to bliss, all this still could not satisfy his marvelous love. Therefore it was necessary for him to feed us, for the most precious love of motherhood had made him a debtor to us. A mother can give her child her milk to suck, but our precious mother, Jesus, can feed us with himself. He does so most courteously and most tenderly, with the blessed sacrament, which is the precious food of true life. With all the sweet sacraments he sustains us most mercifully and graciously. That is what he meant in these blessed words, where he said, "I am that which holy church preaches and teaches you," that is to say, "All the health and the life of the sacraments, all the virtue and the grace of my word, all the goodness that is ordained for you in holy church, that I am."

Julian of Norwich

And after this our Lord showed himself more glorious in my sight than I had ever seen him before. In this I was taught that our soul shall never have rest until it comes to him, knowing that he is the fulness of joy, familiarly and courteously blissful, and life itself.

Our Lord Jesus frequently said, "I am it! I am the one! I am that which is the highest! I am what you love! I am what delights you! I am the one you serve! I am what you long for! I am what you desire! I am what you intend! I am all! I am what holy church preaches and teaches you! I am the one who has shown myself to you here."

The number of the words exceeded my wit, all my understanding and all my powers, and as I see it, this is the highest point, for in these words is comprehended—I cannot tell; but the joy I saw in the showing of them goes beyond anything heart may will and soul may desire. That is why the words are not repeated here.

After this, the Lord brought to my mind the longing I had had for him before, and I saw that nothing stood in my way but sin. I saw that this is generally true of all of us. It seemed to me if sin had not existed, we would all have been pure and like our Lord, as our Lord made us. Thus, in my folly, before this time, I often wondered why, by the great foreseeing wisdom of God, the beginning of sin had not been prevented, for then, I thought, all would have been well.

This stirring definitely ought to have been given up; nevertheless, I mourned and sorrowed on its account without reason or discretion. But Jesus, who in this vision informed me of all I needed to know, answered in these words, saying, "Sin is necessary, but all shall be well, and all shall be well, and all manner of things shall be well."

Julian of Norwich

Where does Jesus Christ appear in this story, or, if there are not direct traces in the story, where are we going to place him? Is not the
Father ready to forgive? Why, then, do we need the cross, why do
we need any mediatorship and reconciliation and the whole of
Christology? Does not this story, just as it stands, have about it a divine simplicity; and is it not a fact that there is no Christ in it?

Jesus, who tells this parable, is pointing to himself, between the
lines and back of every word. If this were just anyone telling us this
story of the good and kindly father, we could only laugh. We could
only say, "How do you know there is a God who seeks me, who
takes any interest in my lostness, who, indeed, suffers because of
me?"

But this is not just "anybody." This is Jesus Christ himself who is
speaking. And he is not merely telling us about this father; the Father is in him. He is not merely imagining a picture of an alleged
heaven that is open to sinners; in him the kingdom is actually in the
midst of us. Does he not eat with sinners? Does he not seek out the
lost? Is he not with us when we die and leave all others behind? Is
he not the light that shines in the darkness? Is he not the very voice
of the Father's heart that overtakes us in the far country and tells us
that incredibly joyful news, "You can come home. Come home!"?

The ultimate theme of this story, therefore, is not the prodigal son,
but the Father who finds us. The ultimate theme is not faithlessness
of human beings, but the faithfulness of God. The ultimate secret of
this story is this: There is a homecoming for us all because there is a
home.

Helmut Thielicke

R FIFTH SUNDAY IN LENT

The suffering of the soul was so great that it obliterated all other
thoughts. Incapable of feeling any joy, the soul seemed to be stifled
in melancholy, completely at a loss as to what to do. Neither
heaven nor earth offered it a place of rest, and it avoided human
company and the remembrance of past joys or sadness.

I find myself responsible,

the soul said,
for all the evil I have done
and I want to atone for it by myself.
Hell alone, I know, is the proper place for me,
but I can only go there after death.
Alas, my God, what shall I do with myself?
Where can I hide?
How can I appear in your presence sullied as I am?
Still, I find you everywhere, and find myself unbearable.
What am I to do with this filthy robe I wear?
Weeping does no good, nor sighing;
contrition is not acceptable and penance wins no pardon,
for it cannot make satisfaction
for the punishment my sins deserve.

Unable to call out to the mercy of God, with no confidence in itself, the soul nevertheless fought to ward off despair. Still, it suffered greatly, for it knew the weight it was carrying, the evil it had done; and in this distress the soul was sick with heartache, unshed tears and sighs, sick unto death. She could not eat, sleep, or talk, nor had she any taste for things, either spiritual or earthly. She had no sense of where she was, in heaven or on earth, and would gladly have hidden from everyone. So alienated was she by the offense given to God that she looked more like a frightened animal than a human being. The pain of enduring that vision of sin was as keen-edged and hard as a diamond.

God, however, then provided for her in the following way. One day there appeared to her inner vision Jesus Christ incarnate crucified, all bloody from head to foot. It seemed that the body rained blood. From within she heard a voice say, "Do you see this blood? It has been shed for your love, to atone for your sins." With that she received a wound of love that drew her to Jesus with such trust that it washed away all that previous fright, and she took joy in the Lord. She was also granted another vision, more striking yet, beyond telling or imagination. God showed her the love with which he had suffered out of love of her. That vision made her turn away from every other love and joy that did not come directly from God.

Catherine of Genoa

E L FIFTH SUNDAY IN LENT

Plantation of God,
holy vineyard of the catholic church,
you the chosen who have put your confidence
in the simplicity of the fear of the Lord,
you who have become, through faith,
heirs of his everlasting kingdom,
you who have received the power and gift of his Spirit,
who have been armed by him,
who have been strengthened in fear,
you who share in the pure and precious blood
poured out by the great God, Jesus Christ,
you who have received the freedom
to call the almighty God "Father,"
who are coheirs and friends of God's beloved Son:
listen to the teaching of God,
all you who hope in God's promises
and wait for their fulfillment!

Didascalia of the Apostles

R L SUNDAY OF THE PASSION

E PALM SUNDAY

This was the Pasch which Jesus desired to suffer for us. His suffering has freed us from sufferings, his death has vanquished death, the visible nourishment has procured his eternal life for us. Such is the salutary desire of Jesus, such his love which is the Spirit; to show the figures as figures and no more; to offer in their place his holy body to his disciples. He desires not so much to eat as to suffer so that he might deliver us from suffering in eating.

And so he plants a new tree in place of the old one; it is no longer the old hand of wickedness which yesterday was extended in an impious gesture; it is his pure hand in a gesture of piety he shows, his whole life truly stretched on the cross.

This cross is the tree of my eternal salvation nourishing and delighting me. I take root in its roots, I am extended in its branches, I am delighted by its dew, I am fertilized by its spirit as by a delightful breeze. In my tent I am shaded by its shade and fleeing the excessive heat I find this refuge moist with dew. Its flowers are my flowers; I am wholly delighted by its fruits and I feast unrestrainedly on its fruits which are reserved for me always. This is my nourishment when I am hungry, my fountain when I am thirsty, my covering when I am stripped, for my leaves are no longer fig leaves but the breath of life. This is my safeguard when I fear God, my support when I falter, my prize when I enter combat, and my trophy when I triumph. This is my narrow path, my steep way. This is the ladder of Jacob, the way of angels, at the summit of which the Lord is truly established. This is my tree, wide as the firmament, which extends from earth to the heavens, with its immortal trunk established between heaven and earth; it is the pillar of the universe, the support of the whole world, the joint of the world, holding together the variety of human nature, and riveted by the invisible bolts of the Spirit, so that it may remain fastened to the divinity and impossible to detach. Its top touches the highest heavens, its roots are planted in the earth, and in the midst its giant arms embrace the ever-present breaths of air. It is wholly in all things and in all places.

And although he had permeated all things with himself, Christ stripped himself naked to war against the powers of the air. For an instant he calls for a drink so as to show that he was truly also a man. Since he ran to victory in the spiritual contest he received on his sacred brow the crown of thorns, effacing the entire ancient curse of the race, and eradicating the thorny undergrowth of sin from the world with his divine head. And when he drank the bitter gall of the serpent he opened up for us instead the sweet fountains which issued from himself.

anonymous

R HOLY THURSDAY

E L MAUNDY THURSDAY

Eternal goodness,
I shall contemplate myself in you.
And I shall clothe myself in your eternal will,
and by this light I shall come to know
that you, eternal Trinity,

are table
and food
and waiter for us.
You, eternal Father,
are the table
that offers us as food
the Lamb, your only-begotten Son.
He is the most exquisite of foods for us,
both in his teaching,
which nourishes us in your will,
and in the sacrament
that we receive in holy communion,
which feeds and strengthens us
while we are pilgrim travelers in this life.
And the Holy Spirit
is indeed a waiter for us,
who serves us this teaching
by enlightening our mind's eye with it
and inspiring us to follow it,
and who serves us charity for our neighbors
and hunger to have as our food
souls
and the salvation of the whole world
for the Father's honor.

Catherine of Siena

R E L GOOD FRIDAY

The day of their victory dawned, and they proceeded from the
prison to the amphitheater, as if they were on their way to heaven,
with gay and gracious looks, trembling, if at all, not with fear but
joy. Perpetua followed with shining steps, as the true wife of Christ,
as the darling of God, abashing with the high spirit in her eyes the
gaze of all; Felicitas also, rejoicing that she had brought forth in
safety that so she might fight the beasts, from blood to blood, from
midwife to gladiator, to find in her second baptism her childbirth
washing. And when they were led within the gate, and were on the
point of being forced to put on the dress, the men of the priests of
Saturn, the women of those dedicated to Ceres, the noble Perpetua

resisted steadfastly to the last. For she said: "Therefore we came to this issue of our own free will, that our liberty might not be violated; therefore we pledged our lives, that we might do no such thing: this was our pact with you." Injustice acknowledged justice; the commanding officer gave permission that they should enter the arena in their ordinary dress as they were. Perpetua was singing a psalm of triumph, as already treading on the head of the Egyptian.

For the young women the devil made ready a mad heifer, an unusual animal selected for this reason, that he wished to match their sex with that of the beast. And so after being stripped and enclosed in nets they were brought into the arena. The people were horrified, beholding in the one a tender girl, in the other a woman fresh from childbirth, with milk dripping from her breasts. So they were recalled and dressed in tunics without girdles. Perpetua was tossed first, and fell on her loins. Sitting down she drew back her torn tunic from her side to cover her thighs, more mindful of her modesty than of her suffering. Then having asked for a pin she further fastened her disordered hair. For it was not seemly that a martyr should suffer with her hair disheveled, lest she should seem to mourn in the hour of her glory.

The Passion of St. Perpetua and St. Felicitas

R E L EASTER VIGIL

Since then this night is aglow with lights which mingle the brightness of its lights with the first rays of the dawn making one day with no interval of darkness, let us reflect on the prophecy that says, "This is the day which the Lord has made."

It is a saying in Wisdom that evils are forgotten on the day of joy. This day makes us forget the first sentence brought against us; or rather it eliminates its very existence and not just its memory. For it has completely erased the memory of our condemnation. At that time birth took place in travail; now our new birth is painless. At that time we were flesh born of flesh; now it is a spirit that is born of spirit. At that time we were children of humankind; now we are born children of God. At that time we were relegated from heaven to earth; now the one in heaven has made us sharers of heaven with God. At that time death reigned because of sin; now thanks to life it is justice which has taken over the power. At that time one man opened the gate of death; now through one man the gate of life is opened in its place. At that time we fell from life through death; now death is abolished by life. At that time we were hidden under the fig tree by shame; now by glory we approach the tree of life. At that time through disobedience we were expelled from paradise; now through faith we are admitted into paradise. Once again the fruit of life is offered to us to be enjoyed by us freely. Once again the fount of paradise with its four rivers of the gospels irrigates the whole face of the church, so that the furrows of our souls are inebriated which the sower of the word has ploughed with doctrine, and the seeds of virtue increase and multiply.

What else then should we do because of this except to imitate the mountains and the hills of prophecy? The mountains, we are told, skipped like rams, and the hills like lambs. Come, then, let us exult before the Lord who has broken the enemy's strength and power, and raised up the great trophy of the cross for us to destroy our adversary. Let us exult. For exultation or jubilation is the cry of victory raised by the victors over the vanquished. Since then the battle line of the enemy has collapsed, and the one who once held sway over the force of devils has been vanquished and disappeared, annihilated, let us say that God is a great Lord and a great King over the entire earth, who has crowned the year with kindness and has assembled us in the spiritual choir, in Jesus Christ our Lord, to whom is glory rendered for ever and ever.

Gregory of Nyssa

R E EASTER DAY

L THE RESURRECTION OF OUR LORD

Glorious is our paschal festival, and truly splendid this great assembly of the Christian people. And within this holy mystery are contained things both old and new. The celebration of this week, or rather its joyfulness, is shared by such a multitude, that not alone do we rejoice on earth, but even the powers of heaven are united with us in joyful celebration of Christ's resurrection. For now the angels and the hosts of the archangels also keep holiday this day, and stand waiting for the triumphant return from this earth of

Christ our Lord, who is king of heaven. And the multitude of the blessed likewise rejoice, proclaiming the Christ who was begotten before the day star rose. The earth rejoices, now washed by divine blood. The sea rejoices, honored as it was by his feet upon its waters. And ever more let each soul rejoice, who is born again of water and the Holy Spirit and at last set free from the ancient curse!

With such great joy does Christ fill our hearts this day by his resurrection, not alone because he gives us the gladness of this day, but because he has also given us salvation through his passion, immortality through his death, healing for our wounds, and resurrection from our fall! And long ago, beloved, this paschal mystery, begun in Egypt, was symbolically pointed out to us in the old law, in the sacrifice of the lamb. And now, in the gospel, let us celebrate the resurrection of the lamb, our Pasch.

Then a lamb of the flock was slain, as the law laid down; now Christ, the Lamb of God, is offered up. There a sheep from the sheepfold; here, in place of the sheep, the good shepherd lays down his life for his sheep. There the sprinkled blood upon the doorposts was a sign of deliverance for the people of God; here the precious blood of Christ was poured out for the deliverance of the whole world, that we might be forgiven our sins. There the firstborn of Egypt were slain; here the manifold children of sinners are made clean confessing the Lamb. There Pharaoh and his fearful host were drowned in the sea; here the spiritual Pharaoh with all his people are immersed in the deep of baptism. There the children of the Hebrews, crossing over the Red Sea, sang their song of victory to their Deliverer; here those found worthy of baptism sing their song of victory. The Hebrews, after the crossing of the Red Sea, ate manna in the desert; now, those who have come forth from the waters of baptism eat bread that came down from heaven. For his is the voice that says: I am the living bread.

Proclus

R E L SECOND SUNDAY OF EASTER

The mother can hold her child tenderly to her breast, but our tender mother, Jesus, can lead us in friendly fashion into his blessed breast by means of his sweet open side and there show us something of the godhead and the joys of heaven with a spiritual assurance of endless bliss. This he showed in where he said, "See how I loved you!" Look into his blessed side, rejoicing.

This fair, lovely word "mother" is so sweet and so natural in itself that it cannot truly be said of anyone but him, or to anyone but him, who is the true mother of life and of everything.

To motherhood as properties belong natural love, wisdom and knowledge—and this is God. For though it is true that our bodily bringing forth is very little, low and simple compared to our spiritual bringing forth, yet it is he who does the mothering in the creatures by whom it is done.

The natural loving mother, who recognizes and knows the need of her child, takes care of it most tenderly, as the nature and condition of motherhood will do. And continually, as the child grows in age and size, she changes what she does but not her love. When the child has grown older, she allows it to be punished, breaking down vices to enable the child to receive virtues and grace.

This work, with all that is fair and good, our Lord does in those by whom it is done. Thus he is our mother in nature, by the working of grace in the lower part for love of the higher. And he wills that we know it, for he wills to have all our love fastened to him.

In this I saw that all the debts that we owe, by God's command, to fatherhood and motherhood by reason of God's fatherhood and motherhood, are repaid in the true loving of God. This blessed love Christ works in us. And this was showed in everything, especially in the noble, plenteous words, where he says, "I am what you love."

Julian of Norwich

R E L THIRD SUNDAY OF EASTER

And this will be the seventh day: the first day as it were being all time from Adam until Noah; the second from Noah to Abraham; the third, as Matthew's gospel divides it, from Abraham to David; the fourth from David to the Babylonian transmigration; the fifth from the transmigration to the coming of our Lord Jesus Christ. The sixth therefore is counted from the coming of our Lord: we are in the sixth day. And so as in Genesis the human being on the sixth day was formed in the image and likeness of God, so we also in this time, upon as it were the sixth day of the whole of time, are reborn in baptism, that we may receive again the image and likeness of our Maker.

But when the sixth day has passed, the sanctified and the holy unto God will celebrate the sabbath, and there shall be rest after the winnowing. But after the seventh day, when the splendid heap, the glory and the merit of the sanctified, has appeared upon the threshing floor, we shall enter into life.

Then we as it were return to the beginning. For as these seven days end, the eighth then becomes as it were the first: so when the seven ages of this passing world are ended and complete, we shall return to that blessed happiness and immortality from which humankind has fallen. And concerning this question, the number seven multiplied seven times makes forty-nine; and one being added, as though to return again to the beginning, we have fifty: which number is celebrated by us in mystery till Pentecost. This is seen again by another reckoning, in the distribution of the number forty, to which is added a denarius as wages. Both reckonings come to the quinquagenary number; which multiplied three times, because of the Trinity, makes one hundred and fifty. Adding three, as token and witness both of the multiplication and of the Trinity, by this number of one hundred and fifty-three fishes we understand the church.

Augustine

R E L FOURTH SUNDAY OF EASTER

Here the innocent sheep, cleansed by the heavenly water,
are marked by the hand of the supreme Shepherd.

You who have been begotten in this water, come to the unity
to which the Holy Spirit calls you, to receive God's gifts.

You have received the cross:
learn to escape the storm of the world:
that is the great lesson of which this place reminds you.

inscription in consignatorium

R E L FIFTH SUNDAY OF EASTER

O eternal Father! O fiery abyss of charity! O eternal beauty, O eternal wisdom! O eternal goodness! O eternal mercy! O hope and refuge of sinners! O immeasurable generosity! O eternal, infinite God! O mad lover! And you have need of your creature? It seems so to me, for you act as if you could not live without her, in spite of the fact that you are life itself, and everything has life from you and nothing can have life without you. Why then are you so mad? Because you have fallen in love with what you have made! You are pleased and delighted over her within yourself, as if you were drunk with desire for her salvation. She runs away from you and you go looking for her. She strays and you draw closer to her: you clothed yourself in our humanity, and nearer than that you could not have come.

And what shall I say? I will stutter, "A—a," because there is nothing else I know how to say. Finite language cannot express the emotion of the soul who longs for you infinitely. I think I could echo Paul's words: The tongue cannot speak nor the ear hear nor the eye see nor the heart imagine what I have seen! What have you seen? "I have seen the hidden things of God!" And I—what do I say? I have nothing to add from these clumsy emotions of mine. I say only, my soul, that you have tasted and seen the abyss of supreme eternal providence.

But because I see that you are a fulfiller of holy desires, and that your truth cannot lie, I wish now that you would speak to me a little about the power and excellence of obedience just as you, eternal Father, promised me you would, so that I might fall in love with this virtue and never cut myself off from obedience to you. Please, in your infinite kindness, tell me how perfect it is, where I can find it, what would take it away from me, who gives it to me, and what is the sign that I do or do not have it.

Catherine of Siena

R E L SIXTH SUNDAY OF EASTER

For all who are under heaven who shall come to heaven, their way is by longing and desiring. This desiring and longing were showed in the servant standing before the lord, or else by the Son standing before the Father in Adam's tunic. The longing and desire of all of mankind that shall be saved appeared in Jesus. For Jesus is all that shall be saved. And all that are saved are Jesus, as is all of the charity of God, with the obedience, meekness, patience and the virtues that belong to us.

Christ lay in the grave until Easter morning. And from that time he never again lay down dead, for then the wallowing and writhing, the groaning and moaning were rightfully ended. Our foul, mortal flesh, which God's Son took upon himself—Adam's old tunic, tight, bare and short—was then, by our Savior, made fair, new, white and bright, of endless cleanness, ample and full, more fair and richer than was the clothing I saw on the Father. For the Father's clothing is bliss, and Christ's clothing is now a fair and becoming mixture that is so marvelous that I cannot describe it, for it is all of glory itself.

Now the Son does not stand before the Father as the servant stands before the lord, dreadfully clothed and partly naked, but he stands before the Father directly in front of him, richly clothed in blissful amplitude, with a crown of precious richness on his head. For it was showed that we are his crown, and this crown is the Father's joy, the Son's glory, the Holy Spirit's delight, and endless marvelous bliss to all who are in heaven.

Now the Son does not stand before the Father on the left side like a laborer, but he sits at the Father's right hand in endless rest and peace. But this does not mean that the Son sits at the Father's right hand beside him, as one man sits next to another in this life, for there is no such sitting in the Trinity, as I saw it. He sits at his Father's right hand with "right hand" meaning in the highest nobility of the Father's joy.

Now is the spouse, God's Son, in peace with his beloved wife, who is the fair maiden of endless joy. Now the Son, true God and true man, sits in his city in the rest and peace his Father has prepared for him in his endless purpose. And so sits the Father in the Son, and the Holy Spirit in the Father and the Son.

Julian of Norwich

If the Lord spent forty days with his disciples, he did not without reason spend forty days with them. Perhaps twenty might have been enough; thirty would have sufficed; but forty days is the divine arrangement for this whole world. The number ten signifies the fullness of wisdom. This wisdom is distributed throughout the four parts of the world, over the whole earth; and the fourfold times are disposed in due order. For the year has four seasons, and the world four cardinal points. Ten then multiplied by four gives us the number forty.

Because of this the Lord fasted for forty days, to show us that as long as we are in the world the faithful must abstain from all corruption. Elijah representing in his person the dignity of prophecy, fasted for forty days. Moses, in his own person standing for the law, fasted for forty days. For forty years the people of Israel were led in the desert. For forty days the ark was tossed upon the flood. The ark is a figure of the church: made from imperishable wood, for imperishable wood are the souls of the saints and the just, the ark also has within it both clean and unclean animals; for as long as we live in this world, and the church is made clean by baptism as by a flood, it cannot be without both good and bad; and so the former ark had within it both clean and unclean animals.

But after Noah emerged from the ark he offered no sacrifices to God save from the animals that were clean. From which we are to understand that though in this ark also there are clean and unclean, after this flood God accepts those only who have made themselves clean. Therefore consider all this time you now see passing as but forty days. All this time, as long as people are in this world, the ark is in the flood; as long as Christians are baptized and made clean through water, the ark, which for forty days was tossed upon the waters, is seen upon the waves.

The Lord remaining with his disciples for forty days deigned by this to show us that belief in the incarnation is necessary for all throughout this time, and this is needed because we are weak. If there had been an eye that had seen that "In the beginning was the Word," which had seen, which had grasped, which had embraced, which had rejoiced, there would have been no need that the Word should take flesh and dwell among us. But because the inner eye that could grasp and take delight in God had been blinded by the dust of sin, there was no way whereby humankind could come to know the Word; and that he might be sent whom human beings before could not see, then afterwards could see, the Word deigned to become flesh.

Augustine

R E L SEVENTH SUNDAY OF EASTER

How do I adore you within myself and yet I perceive you at a distance? How do I embrace you within me and I see you in the heavens? You alone know it, you, the author of these things who shine like the sun in my heart, my material heart, immaterially, you who made the light of your glory shine on me, O my God.

Because I see You, that is sufficient for me; that will be my glory, my joy, my royal crown and, above all the charms and all the attractions of the world, that will make of me the equal of angels, will even elevate me, O my Master, above them. For, if by your essence you are invisible to them and inaccessible by your nature, yet you show yourself to me.

Thus, uniting with your body, I participate in your nature and I really take as mine a part of your essence, uniting with your divinity, much more becoming heir in my body, I see myself superior to incorporeals, I become a child of God. Glory be to your mercy and to your divine plan, because you became human, you who by nature are God, without change or confusion, for ever divine and human, and that you have made me, a mortal by my nature, a god, god by adoption, god by your grace, by the power of your Spirit, uniting miraculously, God that you are, the two extremes.

Symeon

R PENTECOST SUNDAY
E L DAY OF PENTECOST

Isaiah makes known that the Holy Spirit is not alone light, but fire. Because of this the prophets call the Spirit a burning fire; because we observe the power of the divinity very frequently under these three aspects: it is of the nature of the Divinity to sanctify; to give light is a property of light and fire equally; and it is the divine way to be seen, or to be described, under the appearance of fire.

For Moses had seen fire in the bush, and had heard the Lord when a voice spoke to him, from the midst of the flames, saying, "I am the God of Abraham, the God of Isaac, and the God of Jacob." The voice then came from the flames, and the flames did not hurt it. The bush was on fire, yet it was not burnt; that the Lord might show us by this mystery, that Christ would come to cast light on the thorns of our body, that he would not consume the afflicted but would lighten our afflictions, that he would baptize in the Holy Spirit and in fire, that he would give us grace, and destroy our sins. And so the plan of God is laid bare to us under the figure of fire.

Also, in the Acts of the Apostles, the Holy Spirit descended upon the faithful under the image of fire. So was it when Gideon was about to defeat the Midianites, and commanded his three hundred men to take pitchers, and to carry burning torches in the pitchers, and a trumpet in their right hands. Our bodies are pitchers, formed from the clay of the earth, which shall burn with the fire of spiritual grace, and shall bear witness with the voice of confession to the passion of the Lord Jesus.

What therefore is this fire? Of a certainty it is not built up from a lowly bush; nor does it flame up from the burning brambles of the forest. This is a fire which, as with gold, makes what is good better, and devours sin as stubble. Here beyond doubt is the Holy Spirit, who is called the countenance of the Lord, and fire, and light. And as the Spirit is the light of the divine countenance, so also is the Spirit the fire that burns before the face of God.

Ambrose

R E L TRINITY SUNDAY

I earnestly ask for your very close attention, and for recollection of the presence of God. Only material bodies fill or occupy material space. The Godhead is beyond all space; let no one seek it as though it were in space. Everywhere it is invisible and indivisibly present: not greater in one direction, lesser in another, but whole and entire in all places, and nowhere divided.

Who can see this? Who can comprehend it? Let us humble ourselves, keeping in mind who we are, of whom we speak. Let this truth or that truth, or whatever it is that God is, be devoutly believed, piously meditated on, and, as far as it is given us, as well as we can, understood in silence. Let words cease, let the tongue be at rest, but let the heart be enkindled, let the heart be uplifted. For it is not such as enters into the human heart, but whither the human heart may ascend.

What then are we to say of God? For if you have grasped what you wish to say, it is not God. If you had been able to comprehend it, you would have comprehended something else in the place of God. If you had been almost able to comprehend it, your mind has deceived you. That then is not God, if you have understood it. But if it is God, you have not understood it. What therefore would you say of that which you could not understand?

Augustine

R BODY AND BLOOD OF CHRIST

Through your faith you are aware that our Lord Jesus Christ, who has just suffered for us and risen again, is the head of the church, and that the church is his body, and that in his body the unity of the members, and the bond of their mutual love, is as it were the token of its health. And whosoever has grown cold in charity, has grown weak in the body of Christ. But the one who has raised up our head is able also to heal our infirm members, provided they are not cut off by too grievous wickedness, but remain with the body till they are healed. For all who adhere to the body still have hope of healing; but they who have been cut off can neither be treated nor healed.

Since then he is the head of the church, and the church is his body, the whole Christ is then both head and body. He is now risen. Our head, without stain and immortal, now makes intercession with God for our sins, so that at the end of the world, we also being risen, and partaking of his heavenly glory, may follow our head. For where the head is, there also are the other members. And while here, we are his members; let us then be filled with hope that we shall follow our head.

For consider the love of this our head. He is now in heaven, yet while the church suffers here on earth, he too suffers here. Here Christ hungers, here he thirsts, here he is naked, here he is a stranger, he is sick, he is in prison. All that his body here suffers, he has said that he suffers.

For so also in our own body is the head above, and the feet on earth. Yet in any crowd when people press close together should someone tread on your foot, does not your head say, "You are treading on my foot." No one has trodden on your head, or on your tongue; it is above in safety, no harm has come to it, and yet, because of the bond of love, there is a oneness from your head down to your feet. Therefore just as the tongue, which no one has touched, says, "You are standing on my foot," so Christ, whom no one has touched, says, "I was hungry, and you gave me food."

Augustine

R NINTH SUNDAY IN ORDINARY TIME

E PROPER 4

L SECOND SUNDAY AFTER PENTECOST

Seven years after, a little before Advent, by your ordinance, who are the Source of all good, you did infuse a desire in me when I approached your body and blood, which broke forth in these words: "Lord, I am not worthy to receive the least of your gifts; but I beseech you, by the merits and prayers of all here present, to pierce my heart with the arrow of your love." I soon perceived that my words had reached your divine heart, both by an interior effusion of grace, and by a remarkable prodigy which you did show me in the image of your crucifixion.

After I had received the sacrament of life, and had retired to the place where I pray, it seemed to me that I saw a ray of light like an arrow coming forth from the wound of the right side of the crucifix, which was in an elevated place, and it continued, as it were, to advance and retire for some time, sweetly attracting my cold affections. And behold, you came suddenly before me, and did imprint a wound in my heart, saying these words: "May the full tide of your affections flow hither, so that all your pleasure, your hope, your joy, your grief, your fear, and every other feeling may be sustained by my love!"

May all the deprivation of those things which my malice and wickedness have caused be supplied through that love whose plentitude abides in him who, being seated on your right hand, has become bone of my bones, and flesh of my flesh! As it is by him, through the operation of the Holy Spirit, that you have placed in me this noble virtue of compassion, humility, and reverence, to enable me to speak to you my complaint of the miseries I endure, which are so great in number, and which have caused me to offend your divine goodness in so many ways by my thoughts, words, and actions, but principally by the bad use which I have made of aforesaid graces, by my unfaithfulness, my negligence, and my irreverence. For if you have given to one so unworthy even a thread of flax as a remembrance of you, I should have been bound to respect it more than I have done all these favors.

You know, O my God, from whom nothing is hidden, that the reason why I have written these things, so much against my inclination, is that I have profited so little by your liberality that I cannot believe they were made known to me for myself alone, since your eternal wisdom cannot be deceived. Grant, then, O Giver of gifts, who has so freely and unreservedly bestowed them on me, that whoever reads these things may be touched with tenderness and compassion for you; and, knowing that the seal which you have for the salvation of souls has induced you to leave such royal gems so long in my defiled heart, they may praise, adore, and extol your mercy, saying with their lips, and with their hearts, "Praise, honor, glory, and benediction be to you, O God the Father, from whom all things proceed," thus to supply for my deficiencies.

Gertrude the Great

R TENTH SUNDAY IN ORDINARY TIME

E PROPER 5

L THIRD SUNDAY AFTER PENTECOST

The widowed mother rejoiced over the young man restored to life.
Mother Church rejoices daily over those restored to life in the spirit.
He was dead in his body, they in the soul, his visible death was
mourned before all, their invisible death is neither seen nor thought
of. For unless the Lord had come to raise the dead, the apostle
would not have said, "Awake, O sleeper, and arise from the dead."
The word "Awake" you understand as addressed to one who
sleeps. But when you hear "and arise from the dead," understand
them of one dead. The visibly dead are often spoken of as sleeping.
And certainly to him who has power to waken them, they are sleeping. A dead man is to you a dead man; shake him, prod him as you
will, he will not waken. But to Christ he lay sleeping; to him Christ
said, "Arise," and immediately he arose. No one can so easily
waken one who sleeps in bed, as Christ wakens the dead from the
grave.

We read that the Lord visibly restored three persons to life, thousands invisibly. How many dead he visibly restored, who knows?
For all that he did is not written down. There were no doubt many
others raised to life; but it is not without purpose that three have
been commemorated. For our Lord Jesus Christ wished that what
he wrought corporally should also be understood spiritually. For he
did not work miracles simply as miracles, but so that what he did
might appear wondrous to those who saw them, and convey truth
to those who would understand them.

Augustine

R ELEVENTH SUNDAY IN ORDINARY TIME

E PROPER 6

L FOURTH SUNDAY AFTER PENTECOST

Grant me, Christ, to kiss your feet.
Grant me to embrace your hands,
these hands which created me by your word,
these hands which brought forth everything without effort.

Grant me to fill myself with these graces without being satisfied.
Grant me to see your face, O Word,
and to enjoy your inexpressible beauty,
to contemplate and to savor your vision,
ineffable vision, invisible vision,
awesome vision; however, grant me to tell
not its essence but its operations.
For you are beyond nature, beyond all essence,
completely, you, my God, my Creator.
But the reflection of your divine glory
lets itself be seen by us as a simple light, a gentle light;
light it reveals itself, light it unites itself
completely, I think, with us completely, your servants,
light that we contemplate in spirit and from afar,
light that suddenly becomes visible within ourselves,
light that springs like water, and burns like fire
in the heart which it really possesses.
Yes, how shall I bear it,
how shall I fully suffer, how endure
or how express this great marvel
which has happened to me, the prodigal?
We urgently ask you to save us gratuitously
and to justify us by your grace and your mercy.
It is that mercy which you have now poured out on me
with abundance,
and I will not hesitate to say it or to write it.

Symeon

R TWELFTH SUNDAY IN ORDINARY TIME

E PROPER 7

L FIFTH SUNDAY AFTER PENTECOST

This is how we destroy ourselves in our whole way of life, and we do not live with Christ and we do not carry the cross with the Son of God. We only carry it with Simon, who was hired to carry the cross of our Lord.

It is the same when we suffer and endure. We demand God as the reward for our good deed, we want to know God in this present life, because it seems to us that we are very deserving and that it is only right that God should give us some of what we ask in return for what we do. We think that what we do or suffer for God is a great matter, and there is no rest for us until we have our reward and feel that we are pleasing to God, and what we would choose would be to have our reward here and now, a reward of consolation and rest in God. And there is yet another reward which we choose, the reward of our own self-satisfaction and complacency. And our third reward is when we know that we are pleasing to others, and receive their respect and praise and honor.

All this is carrying the cross with Simon, who labored under the cross for a short while, but did not die upon it. People who live in this way, even though to others their lives may seem exalted and their works fine and splendid, so that sometimes they seem to live in wisdom and sanctity, well ordered and virtuous, have little about them which is pleasing to God, for they are neither upright nor enduring. The virtues which they seem to possess are in truth their failings; the most trifling opposition, if they encounter it, can expose them for what they are. One moment they are all exaltation and consolation, the next moment they are plunged into bitterness; because their lives are not built upon truth, their foundations are false and infirm. However much others may esteem them, in their works and in their lives they remain unstable and untrue. They are not upright, they are not persevering, and they do not die with Christ. They may perform the works of virtue, but their intention is neither pure nor true. There is so much falsehood mingled with their virtues that they can have no power to guide or illumine others, nor to persevere in a settled and firm truth, in which their everlastingness should be established.

For we are obliged to perform virtuous works not to gain admiration or happiness, not for wealth or power, nor for any pleasure in heaven or on earth, but only so that we may be pleasing to God's greatest honor, who created human nature for this, making it to God's honor and praise, and for our joy in eternal glory. And in all this there must be no other intention than that love should be enthroned, as it should be, in human beings and in all creatures, according to love's pleasure. This is to hang upon the cross with

Christ, this is to die with him and with him to rise again. May he help us always to do this; and for this help I entreat him in whom is every perfect virtue.

Hadewijch of Brabant

R THIRTEENTH SUNDAY IN ORDINARY TIME

E PROPER 8

L SIXTH SUNDAY AFTER PENTECOST

Never a pause, O Christ, in your persistent questioning, "Who do you say that I am?"

You are the one who loves me into endless life.

You open up the way of risk. You go ahead of me along the way of holiness, where happy are they who die of love, where the ultimate response is martyrdom.

Day by day you transfigure the "No" in me into "Yes." You ask me, not for a few scraps, but for the whole of my existence. You are the one who prays in me day and night. My stammerings are prayer: simply calling you by your name, Jesus, fills our communion to the full.

You are the one who, every morning, slips on my finger the ring of the prodigal son, the ring of festival.

So why have I wavered so long? You have been seeking me un-wearyingly. Why did I hesitate once again, asking for time to deal with my own affairs? Once I had set my hand to the plough, why did I look back? Without realizing it, I was making myself unfit to follow you.

Yet, though I had never seen you, I loved you.

You kept on saying: live the little bit of the gospel you have grasped. Proclaim my life. Light fire on the earth . . .
You, follow me . . .

Until one day I understood: you were asking me to commit myself to the point of no return.

Roger Schutz

R FOURTEENTH SUNDAY IN ORDINARY TIME

E PROPER 9

L SEVENTH SUNDAY AFTER PENTECOST

O Lord, you have led me from my father's loins and formed me in my mother's womb. You brought me, a naked baby, into the light of day, for nature's laws always obey your commands.

By the blessings of the Holy Spirit you prepared my creation and my existence; not because human beings willed it or flesh desired it, but by your ineffable grace. You sent me forth into the light by adopting me as your son, and you enrolled me among the children of your holy and spotless church through baptism.

You nursed me with the spiritual milk of your divine words. You kept me alive with the solid food of the body of Jesus Christ and you let me drink from the chalice of his life-giving blood, poured out to save the whole world.

Now you have called me by the hand of your bishop to minister to your people. Purify my mind and heart to lead your people in truth.

You, O church, are a most noble assembly whose assistance comes from God. You in whom God lives, receive from us an exposition of the faith that is free from error, to strengthen the church, just as our forebears handed it down to us.

John of Damascus

R FIFTEENTH SUNDAY IN ORDINARY TIME

E PROPER 10

L EIGHTH SUNDAY AFTER PENTECOST

And so when he came nigh to the half-dead man, and saw him lying in his blood, moved by compassion he came near to him, to be a neighbor to him. He bound up his wounds; he poured oil into them, mixed with wine. This is the Samaritan, whose help and healing all need who are sick. And he above all needed this Samaritan's help, who going down from Jerusalem to Jericho had fallen among robbers, and, wounded by them, had been abandoned half dead. But that you may know that this Samaritan descended in accordance with God's providence, to heal the one who had fallen among robbers, you shall be taught this clearly from the fact that he had brought with him bandages, that he had brought oil, that he had brought wine. And I believe that the Samaritan carried these things with him, not solely for this one half-dead man, but for others also who, for various reasons, had been wounded, and would need to have their wounds bound up, and would need both oil and wine.

He cleans the wounds with wine, and places the man who had been wounded upon his own beast, that is, upon his own body, which as a man he had deigned to assume. This Samaritan bears our sins, and suffers for us, and lifts up the half-dead man, and brings him to an inn, that is into the church, which receives everyone and denies its help to no one. And after he brought him there, he did not at once disappear, but remains at the inn for a day with the half-dead man, and takes care of his wounds not only by day, but also by night, giving him every care and attention.

And when in the morning he was setting out, he takes from his own honest silver, from his own honest money, two denarii, and pays the innkeeper, no doubt the angel of the church, to whom he gives the command to care for him diligently, and bring back to health this man whom he also, because of the urgency of his need, had cared for. The two denarii seem to me to be the knowledge of the Father and the Son, and the knowledge of the mystery of how the Father is in the Son, and the Son is in the Father, which are given as a reward to the angel. From the words of Christ that now follow it is possible therefore for us to imitate Christ, to have compassion on those who have fallen among robbers, to draw near them, to bind their wounds, pouring in oil and wine, to place them upon our own beast, and bear their burdens.

Origen

R SIXTEENTH SUNDAY IN ORDINARY TIME

E PROPER 11

L NINTH SUNDAY AFTER PENTECOST

Service or servanthood as the model of leadership has nothing to do with sanctifying dominance. But neither does it have anything to do with sanctifying the servitude of the oppressed. Jesus does not use the language of servanthood to idealize the role of women or slaves. Indeed the one time when he uses the term serving in a negative manner is when he is speaking to a woman, Martha. Martha's complaint against her sister Mary represents the woman conditioned to the traditional female role. Mary is the one who is out of place. Judaism did not believe that women were "called to the Torah." They were not supposed to study the scriptures as disciples of the teacher—and to be a disciple was also, eventually, to become, oneself, a rabbi. Women were to stay in the kitchen and send their husbands and sons to the synagogue. Mary, in effect, was claiming her right to be an equal member in the circle of disciples. Martha wants Jesus to endorse the traditional role of women by putting Mary back "in her place." But instead Jesus rebukes Martha, not only for finding her only identity in this "woman's place," but also for using this "woman's place" to keep other women from growing.

We need to rediscover the revolutionary potential of the concept of ministry suggested in the gospel sayings. Service is not a code word for a new power trip, nor a sanctimonious way of justifying the servitude of the enslaved. It is a revolution that overthrows all these models of relationship. It means the self-emptying of alienated male power, even alienated divine power. Those who have set themselves up to use power to dominate others relinquish it to become servants. Who has ever seen those in power do this voluntarily? Never. Perhaps that is why God "himself" has to inaugurate this revolution by giving up the alienation of divine power that buttresses this worldly power. It is God who begins the *kenosis*, or emptying, of alienated power projected on the throne of heaven as the apotheosis of alienated male kingly power. It is God who becomes a servant, pulling out the foundations of all other kings and lords who use the divine as the model of hierarchy.

This emptying of God into service in the world, in turn, liberates those who have been oppressed. Women, slaves, are called out of their servitude to become equals—sisters and brothers in the community of the liberated humanity. It is the poor and the oppressed who must lead the way into the kingdom of God. Those who have

been despised are seen as first in the community of the new humanity. Only by becoming one with their liberation do all of us, female
and male, black and white, poor and rich, discover our own whole-
ness, in ourselves and with each other. This is the liberated and reconciled humanity which the gospel proclaims, but which we, the
church, have yet to learn to believe and to fulfill.

Rosemary Radford Ruether

R SEVENTEENTH SUNDAY IN ORDINARY TIME
E PROPER 12
L TENTH SUNDAY AFTER PENTECOST

Have mercy on me! The phrase is short; but it holds within it a sea
of loving trust; for where there is mercy, there all good things are.
Though you move not your lips, cry out in your soul: for even the
prayer of the silent is heard by the Lord.

It is not a place that is to be looked for, but the Master of the place.
Jeremiah lay in squalor, and the Lord hearkened to his prayer. Job
prayed from his dunghill, and the Lord was gracious to him. Jonah
was in the belly of a whale, and the Lord listened to his prayer. And
you, even if you are in the baths, pray; wherever you are, pray; do
not seek for a place to pray in: you yourself are a temple.

The sea lay in the path of the Jews. Behind them were the Egyp-
tians. Between stood Moses, silent. For in great anguish of mind he
was praying. And you, when temptation shall come against you,
fly to God, call upon the Lord. Your prayer is scarce ended, and
God is offering you a remedy for your need. For if you have a mind
free from all impure affections, though you stand in the market
place or the street, or are present at a trial, or by the sea, or at an
inn, or in your workshop, in a word wherever you may be, by calling on the Lord you can obtain what you ask for.

What is the meaning of stretching out hands in prayer? They have
been the instrument of many iniquities, and because of this we are
bidden to lift them up, that the ministry of prayer may serve them
as a fetter against evildoing, as a withdrawal from iniquity, so that
should you be on the point of committing a theft, of oppressing or
striking another, you may remember that you must raise those

hands in pleading before God, and by means of them offer up a spiritual sacrifice. Do not dishonor them; do not deprive them of their office of pleading by using them in the service of evil. Purify them by almsdeeds, by works of mercy, by protecting those in distress, and thus you will uplift them in prayer. For if you would not raise them in prayer unwashed, much less will you, being just, stain them with sin. For if you fear to pray with unwashed hands, which is a small offense, much more fear what is graver. For to pray with unwashed hands is not such a grievous thing; but to uplift them in prayer, stained with innumerable crimes, brings down wrath and destruction.

John Chrysostom

R EIGHTEENTH SUNDAY IN ORDINARY TIME

E PROPER 13

L ELEVENTH SUNDAY AFTER PENTECOST

When I have these new barns filled, you say, then I will distribute something to the poor. You have given yourself a long time to live. Take care that the appointed day does not, coming swift, forestall you. And promises of that sort are not very helpful, and are an indication of a perverse heart rather than of kindness. For you promise, not that you will afterwards fulfill, but to relieve yourself of a present embarrassment. What keeps you from giving now? There are no hungry perhaps? The hungry are dying before your face. The naked are stiff with cold. The person in debt is held by the throat. And you, you put off your alms till another day?

What good counsel you are despising by shutting up your ears beforehand with avarice. And what thanks you should have offered to the most merciful God, how cheerful you should be, how joyful, because of the honor God has given you, namely, that you need not go knocking at the doors of other people, but that they must come knocking at yours! Instead you are sullen and repellent. You turn away from those you meet lest you be forced to let even a morsel escape your clutches. You have only one phrase, "I have nothing to give; I am poor." You are indeed poor, and in need of every good. You are poor in love for your neighbor, poor in humanity, poor in faith in God, poor in the hope of eternity! Make others sharers of your grain; and what may wither tomorrow, give to the needy today. For it is greed of the most horrible kind to deny to the starving even what you must soon throw away!

Who am I injuring, you will say, when I keep what is mine for myself? And what, tell me, is yours? And from where have you brought it with you into this life? You act like a man who has secured a place at the theater, and then excludes others from entering, claiming that the place was his which exists for the common use of all. And such are the rich. For taking possession of the things which are for the common use of all, they count them as theirs because they hold them in possession. Did you not come forth naked from your mother's womb, and will you not return naked to the earth? How then are these things yours? If you say that this is so by chance, then you are a godless creature, ignorant of your Creator, and giving no thanks to your benefactor. If you confess that they are from God, tell us then why it was you that received them. That bread you hold in your clutches, that belongs to the starving. That cloak you keep locked away in your wardrobe, that belongs to the naked. Those shoes that are going to waste with you, they belong to the barefooted. The silver you buried away, that belongs to the needy. Whomsoever you could have helped and did not, to so many have you been unjust.

Basil

R NINETEENTH SUNDAY IN ORDINARY TIME

E PROPER 14

L TWELFTH SUNDAY AFTER PENTECOST

Will you, then, shut your eyes against light, and stop your ears against admonition? It is but for a moment, compared with eternity, that you can thus deceive yourself, and cry Peace. The overwhelming consciousness must soon press upon your amazed heart, that you are without holiness and cannot see the Lord, and that the harvest is past, the summer ended, and you not saved. There is no hope in your case while you think your heart is good, and feel no need of a divine renovation. They that are whole need not the physician, but they that are sick; and Jesus Christ came to call, not the righteous, but sinners, to repentance. While the delusion prevails that you are rich and stand in need of nothing, you will reject the counsel of Christ, to apply to him for eye-salve that you may see, and for white raiment to cover the shame of your nakedness. You will do nothing to save your own soul, and God will do nothing to save it, while, under the concentrated light of evidence, you remain willfully ignorant of your malady, and wildly negligent of your only remedy. Admit, then, the painful, alarming fact, that you have no religion, and without delay commence the inquiry what you must do to be saved, and thus escape the coming wrath, and lay hold on eternal life. All who are now in heaven were once, like you, without God, and without Christ, and without hope; and all who are now on earth, strangers and pilgrims seeking a better country, were once, like you, without religion. But he who commanded the light to shine out of darkness has shined in their hearts, and the same blessed Spirit is able and willing to enlighten you; but you must confess, and not cover your sin; you must come to the light, and not shun it; you must be convinced of sin, of righteousness, and of a judgment to come; you must be born again, or you cannot see the kingdom of God.

Lyman Beecher

R TWENTIETH SUNDAY IN ORDINARY TIME

E PROPER 15

L THIRTEENTH SUNDAY AFTER PENTECOST

The following of Christ is inseparable from the cross of Calvary. Do you think that I have come to bring peace on earth? No, I tell you but rather division! To those who follow Christ fully is given the world's hatred, for they are a challenge to his spirit just as Christ himself was hated first. Humiliation, lack of appreciation, criticism — we must remember that the people whom he healed or forgave turned round and crucified him.

Failure is nothing but the kiss of Jesus.

Have compassion even in the face of adversity. See the compassion of Christ toward Judas, the man who received so much love, yet betrayed his own master — the master who kept silent and would not betray him to his companions. Jesus could have easily spoken in public and told the others of the hidden intentions and deeds of Judas but he did not do so. He rather showed mercy and charity and, instead of condemning him, he called him a friend; and if Judas would have only looked into the eyes of Jesus as Peter did, today Judas would have been the friend of God's mercy. Jesus always had compassion.

Today the world is an open Calvary. Mental and physical suffering is everywhere. Pain and suffering have to come into your life but remember pain, sorrow, suffering are but the kiss of Jesus — signs that you have come so close to him that he can kiss you. Accept them as his gift — all for Jesus. You are really reliving the passion of Christ, so accept Jesus as he comes into your life — bruised, divided, full of pains and wounds.

The spirit pours love, peace, joy into our hearts proportionately to our emptying ourselves of self-indulgence, vanity, anger and ambition, and to our willingness to shoulder the cross of Christ.

Without our suffering, our work would just be social work, very good and helpful, but it would not be the work of Jesus Christ, not part of the redemption. Jesus wanted to help us by sharing our life, our loneliness, our agony and death, all which he has taken upon himself and has carried into the darkest night. Only by being one with us has he redeemed us. We are allowed to do the same; all the desolation of the poor people, not only their material poverty, but their spiritual destitution must be redeemed; and we must share it, for only by being with them can we redeem them, that is by bringing God into their lives and bringing them to God.

Suffering, if it is accepted together, borne together, is joy. Remember that the passion of Christ ends always in the joy of the resurrection of Christ, so when you feel in your own heart the suffering of Christ, remember the resurrection has to come — the joy of Easter has to dawn. Never let anything so fill you with sorrow as to make you forget the joy of the risen Christ.

Teresa of Calcutta

R TWENTY-FIRST SUNDAY IN ORDINARY TIME
E PROPER 16
L FOURTEENTH SUNDAY AFTER PENTECOST

Be aroused, therefore, for these joys, you who are both mixed together and separated: mixed with the good and separated from the
evil; you who are the elect, the beloved, the foreknown, the called,
those who are to be justified, those who are to be glorified, so that,
growing, maturing, and becoming old in your faith and in the maturity of your powers, not in the corruption of your members, in a
fruitful old age you may serenely tell of works of the Lord who has
done great things for you, who is mighty because his name is great,
and of whose wisdom there is no reckoning.

You seek life; run to him who is the fountain of life, and when the
darkness of your smoldering passions has been dissipated, you will
see light in the light of the only-begotten, your most gracious Redeemer and your most brilliant Enlightener. If you seek safety, hope
in him who saves them who trust in him. If you seek satiety in
drinking and other delights, he will not refuse them. Only come
and adore; fall down and weep before him who made you. He will
inebriate you with the plenty of his house, and he will give you to
drink of the torrent of his delights.

However, beware lest the foot of pride come to you; and guard lest
the hands of sinners move you. Lest the former should happen,
pray that God may cleanse you from your secret sins; but, lest the
second should rush in and destroy you, beg God to spare you from
the sins of others. If you are lying down, rise up; if you are rising,
stand; if you are standing, sit down; if you are sitting, resist. Do not
willingly bear the yoke; rather, break their bonds asunder, and cast
away their yoke from you, that you may not be held fast again by
the bonds of servitude.

Now eat the bread of sorrow; the time will come when, after this
bread of sadness, God will give you the bread of gladness. However, the worth of the latter depends on the endurance of the former. Your apostasy and flight merited this bread of sorrow; turn
back, be sorry, and return to your Lord. He is ready to bestow his
bread of joy upon him who returns in penitence, if you are sincere.

Eat as poor people, and then you will be filled. When thus wholesomely nourished, give forth the glory of his bread. Run to him and be converted, for he it is who brings back those who have turned away; who searches after the fugitives; who finds those who have been lost; who humbles the proud; who feeds the hungry; who releases those who are in chains; who gives light to the blind; who cleanses the unclean; who refreshes the weary; who raises the dead; and who rescues those who are possessed and held by the spirits of iniquity.

Augustine

R TWENTY-SECOND SUNDAY IN ORDINARY TIME
E PROPER 17
L FIFTEENTH SUNDAY AFTER PENTECOST

God treats Jesus — and us — in the same way as the host in the parable: he cares for those who are humiliated and turns away the proud. We see that fully only in the death and resurrection of Jesus. In stories which anyone can understand, today's readings provide the essence of what we might call distinctive Christianity, specifically the way in which God deals with people. Here we have as it were the thought-form and at the same time the life-style which is characteristic of Christianity: any hopeful affirmation also contains a painful, humiliating radical negation: those who exalt themselves will be humiliated and those who are humiliated will be exalted. That is often the case in human life. Jesus and the Christians take up precisely this trivial fact to make clear to us something of God's own attitude toward people. We should not be misled by the way in which this is expressed in terms of reward and prestige. Luke himself breaks through that pattern: we must not invite the rich to our tables but the poor, because the rich simply repay the compliment by inviting us back: the poor can't do that. Only then is it evident what being good is.

God seems to have a predilection for those who do not belong to the elite or to the religious clan. So Luke weaves a second parable into his story, as he often does: "When you give a feast, invite the poor, the maimed, the lame and the blind." But who does that? Nobody — apart from the community of God, the church in its celebration of the eucharist. That is the only table to which not only friends and relatives are invited but also cripples, the blind, the maimed and the oppressed. We can come to it in wheelchairs, with a broken and tormented heart; even our enemies may come. Here we already experience a vision of the future in which all those who are humiliated and discriminated against are exalted; here there is no longer any distinction between Jew and non-Jew, as the reading from Hebrews tells us with the utmost solemnity. Here we come together for the panegyric, the feast, the gathering which the people of the future share with one another. In the game which makes up the liturgy we experience what does not in fact happen in our daily life in the world, even in a monastery. We experience what we cannot fully achieve, much as we would want to. In the liturgy we therefore confess that our love for one another is actually a pure gift of God. Precisely because reconciliation has come near to us in Jesus, in recollection, and in hope, we begin to suffer because the world is not yet redeemed. The liturgy thus provokes us to act outside the liturgy in accordance with this vision of the coming kingdom of God among us, celebrated here symbolically in anticipation, because we cannot make it a reality. At the same time what we do here in the liturgy subjects what we do outside the liturgy to severe criticism. Despite all our good intentions, outside the liturgy we shall fail in our task. And because of our circumstances and because of ourselves we are simply not in a position to succeed. To recognize this in penitence is already to be open to what is possible through grace, through the work of God in us.

So we have moved from the middle-class table to what the gospel calls the eschatological banquet, where without any failure in communications everyone may sit in the place of honor.

Edward Schillebeeckx

R TWENTY-THIRD SUNDAY IN ORDINARY TIME

E PROPER 18

L SIXTEENTH SUNDAY AFTER PENTECOST

When you become aware that you are perceiving and experiencing self and not God, be filled with sincere sorrow and long with all your heart to be entirely absorbed in the experience of God alone. Cease not to desire the loss of that pitiful knowledge and corrupted awareness of your blind being. Long to flee from self as from poison. Forget and disregard your self as ruthlessly as the Lord demands.

Yet do not misunderstand my words. I did not say that you must desire to un-be, for that is madness and blasphemy against God. I said that you must desire to lose the knowledge and experience of self. This is essential if you are to experience God's love as fully as possible in this life. You must realize and experience for yourself that unless you lose self you will never reach your goal. For wherever you are, in whatever you do, or howsoever you try, that elemental sense of your own blind being will remain between you and your God. It is possible, of course, that God may intervene at times and fill you with a transient experience of God's very self. Yet outside these moments this naked awareness of your blind being will continually weigh you down and be as a barrier between you and your God, just as the various details of your being were like a barrier to the direct awareness of your self. It is then that you will realize how heavy and painful is the burden of self. May Jesus help you in that hour, for you will have great need of him.

All the misery in the world taken together will seem as nothing beside this, because then you will be a cross to yourself. See how necessary it is to bear this painful burden, the cross of self. It alone will prepare you for the transcendent experience of God and for union with God in consummate love.

The Book of Privy Counseling

R TWENTY-FOURTH SUNDAY IN ORDINARY TIME

E PROPER 19

L SEVENTEENTH SUNDAY AFTER PENTECOST

But we now follow after the lamp of mother church, and walking in the light of the Lord's countenance we shall come upon the silver piece of Christ; and we shall call together our friends and neighbors, that is, the church of the Gentiles, lest they may not know that our mother has found her silver piece. Behold what we have been seeking through far wide fields and through scattered woods, this let us find in the Lord, this let us find by the lamp of our mother. For this heaven too rejoices, because in one sinner doing penance the multitude of all the Christian people becomes glorious, and the whole character of Christ's divinity shines forth in our silver piece.

Peter Chrysologus

R TWENTY-FIFTH SUNDAY IN ORDINARY TIME

E PROPER 20

L EIGHTEENTH SUNDAY AFTER PENTECOST

The Lord does not praise him for goodness, nor for piety, nor for justice, but he praises the cunning, the artful prudence, of the unjust steward. He praised him because he had prepared his fraud with such subtle evil. He praises him menacingly, and at the same praises him for acting prudently. Menacingly, for by the very word "unjust" he condemns this most wicked prudence of the devil. He praises him as having acted prudently, while at the same time he prepares the minds of his listening disciples against the subtle skill of his schemes, so that they may with all care, with all prudence, oppose this so cunning, this so evilly wise enemy.

Christ bids us be prudent, but not venomous; wise, but not evil; and that putting off, like the snake, our old garment of sin, we are to be formed into a new human person, protecting our head, which is Christ, with every care, and surrendering our members to be torn by the persecutors, that the faith of Christ, the head of our salvation and of our life, may remain sound and unwounded.

Accordingly, let us imitate the prudence of this unjust steward, but not his perfidy. Let us imitate his cunning, but not his wickedness. As he was skilled in injuring others by his evil deeds, so must we be prepared in salutary knowledge, instructed and armed with all prudence; having on us the breastplate of faith, the helmet of salvation, the sword of the Spirit, and the impregnable shield of justice, by means of which we can, as the apostle exhorts us, extinguish the fiery darts of the most wicked one. Otherwise while we are unawares the wicked one may pierce us with the darts of evil promptings; lest being unarmed we may be overcome; lest being asleep we may be slain. For the unclean spirits, whom the Lord calls the children of this world, that is, the children of darkness, are oftentimes more prudent than the children of light, whom God, who is light, has deigned to call to be children by adoption, being born again through the mysteries of heavenly baptism.

Gaudentius

R TWENTY-SIXTH SUNDAY IN ORDINARY TIME

E PROPER 21

L NINETEENTH SUNDAY AFTER PENTECOST

I find a little paragraph in my notebook, "Michael Martin, porter, idle for five years, brought in $2." It was a thanksgiving offering, he explained, and he wanted to give it to some of our children in honor of his daughter in Ireland.

And I remembered how I spoke down in Palm Beach last month before the Four Arts Club, on the invitation of a convert. They told me, when I had finished, "You know we never pay speakers," and another woman said, with a tremor, "Miss Day, I hope you can convey to your readers and listeners that we would give our very souls to help the poor, if we saw any constructive way of doing it." And still another told me, "The workers come to my husband's mill and beg him with tears in their eyes to save them from unions. I hope you don't mind my saying so, but I think you are all wrong when it comes to unions."

They all were deeply moved, they told me, by the picture of conditions in Arkansas and the steel districts and the coal-mining districts, but: "You can't do anything with them, you know, these poor people. It seems to me the best remedy is birth control and sterilization."

We are told always to keep a just attitude toward the rich, and we try. But as I thought of our breakfast line, our crowded house with people sleeping on the floor, when I thought of cold tenement apartments around us, and the lean gaunt faces of the men who come to us for help, desperation in their eyes, it was impossible not to hate, with a hearty hatred and with a strong anger, the injustices of this world.

St. Thomas says that anger is not a sin, provided there is no undue desire for revenge. We want no revolution; we want the brotherhood of men. We want men to love one another. We want all men to have sufficient for their needs. But when we meet people who deny Christ in his poor, we feel, "Here are atheists indeed."

At the same time as I put down these melancholy thoughts, I am thinking of Michael Martin, porter, and the hosts of friends who not only help us to keep the coffee line going, but who on their own account are performing countless works of mercy. And my heart swells with love and gratitude to the great mass of human beings who are one with their fellows, who love our Lord and try to serve him and show their love to his poor.

Our pastor said recently that sixty million of our one hundred and thirty million here in the United States professed no religion, and I thought with grief that it was the fault of those professing Christians who repelled the others. They turned first from Christ crucified because he was a poor worker, buffeted and spat upon and beaten. And now — strange thought — the devil has so maneuvered that the people turn from him because those who profess him are clothed in soft raiment and sit at well-spread tables and deny the poor.

Dorothy Day

R TWENTY-SEVENTH SUNDAY IN ORDINARY TIME

E PROPER 22

L TWENTIETH SUNDAY AFTER PENTECOST

Would you know Christ the seed, Christ the sown? He is the grain
of wheat, because he strengthens the human heart and he is the
grain of mustard seed, because he sets fire to the human heart. And
though either figure may be applied to all things, yet he appears as
the grain of wheat when we speak of his resurrection, in this, that
the word of God and the proof of Christ's resurrection nourish our
minds, whet our hope, and confirm our love. He is the grain of
mustard seed, in that the narrative of the Lord's passion is most bitter and most grievous, most bitter unto tears, most grievous unto
compunction. And so when we hear and when we read that the
Lord fasted, the Lord thirsted, the Lord wept and the Lord cried
out, we justly moderate the more agreeable delights of our body's
pleasures. He therefore who sows the grain of mustard seed sows
the kingdom of heaven.

But Christ is a seed, because he is the seed of Abraham. Not alone is
Christ the seed, but the least of all the seeds, because he came not in
power, nor in wealth, nor in the wisdom of this world. But suddenly he unfolds as a tree the soaring eminence of his might.

Ambrose

R TWENTY-EIGHTH SUNDAY IN ORDINARY TIME

E PROPER 23

L TWENTY-FIRST SUNDAY AFTER PENTECOST

He who had fallen in humble devotion at the Lord's feet is told to
rise and go on his way. For whoever is acutely aware of his own unworthiness and humbles himself before God is told by the comforting divine word to rise and to put his hand to strong things; and
growing daily in merit, to go on his way to the more perfect things.
For if faith made him whole who had hurried back to give thanks
to his Savior and to the one who had made him clean, unfaith has
brought spiritual ruin to those who, receiving favors from God, fail
to return and give him glory.

And so this lesson is joined to the one preceding it in the gospel (that of the unprofitable servants) for this reason that there we learn, through the parable, that faith must grow through humility, while here more clearly we are shown by actual happenings that it is not only confession of faith, but also the doing of the works that follow faith, which makes whole those who believe and give glory to the Father who is in heaven.

Bede

R TWENTY-NINTH SUNDAY IN ORDINARY TIME

E PROPER 24

L TWENTY-SECOND SUNDAY AFTER PENTECOST

Our Lord takes the example of one person's prayer to another that you may learn never to be discouraged, so that when you pray and do not receive the answer to your prayer, you should not cease from praying till you do receive it; provided that, as I said, you ask for what God wishes you to ask.

So henceforth, if a month goes by, or a year, or three years, or four, or many years, do not give up praying till you receive what you ask for; but ask on in faith, and be at the same time steadfast in doing good. It will happen often that some man in his youth strives earnestly for chastity. Then pleasure begins to undermine his resolution, desires awaken his nature, he grows weak in prayer, wine overcomes his youth, modesty perishes, and the man becomes another man. So we change because we have not with high courage of soul stood firm against our passions. It behooves us therefore to resist all things; yet we must cry out to God, to bring us aid.

For if a man through folly gives way to evil desires, and betrays himself to his enemies, God will not aid him, nor hear him, because through sin he has turned away from God. He who hopes to be helped by God should have no part with what is unworthy. But he who does not betray what he owes to God will never be in want of the divine aid. It is just and fitting that in nothing should we be condemned by our own conscience. Only then may we cry out for divine aid and cry earnestly, and not with minds wandering here and there. For one who so prays, not alone shall he continue unheard by

God, but he will also provoke the Lord yet more. For if a man stands in the presence of a king, and speaks with him, he will stand there with great trepidation of mind, careful not to let either his eyes or his mind go wandering. With what greater fear and trembling should we stand in the presence of God, having our whole mind intent on God alone, and on nothing else whatsoever? For God beholds our inward life, not merely the outward one which others see.

Standing then in God's presence, in a manner truly worthy, and laying before God all the desires of your heart, cease not to pray till you receive what you ask for. But should your conscience tell you that you are praying unworthily, and should you stand in prayer while your mind goes wandering when you could well pray with recollection, then venture not to stand thus in the presence of the Lord for fear your prayer becomes an offense. Should it be however that your soul has become weak through sin, and that you are unable to pray without distraction, strive with yourself as best you can, striving earnestly before the Lord, having your mind steadfast on God, and calling out petitions, and God will have compassion on you, since it is not because of indifference but through infirmity that you cannot pray as you ought when you kneel before God. Let those who so strive with themselves in every good work cease not to pray till they obtain what they ask for; but in making their request let them knock patiently at the door: for that which you desire to obtain, what is it but salvation in God?

Basil

R THIRTIETH SUNDAY IN ORDINARY TIME

E PROPER 25

L TWENTY-THIRD SUNDAY AFTER PENTECOST

This is complete and perfect glorying in God, when a man is uplifted, not because of his own justice, but because he knows he is empty of true glory, and made just only through his faith in Christ. In this Paul gloried, that he thought nothing of his own justice; that he sought that justice alone which comes through Christ, which is from God, justice in faith; and that he might know him, and the power of his resurrection, and the sharing of his sufferings, and be made like him in his death, if by any means he might himself attain to the resurrection from the dead. It is here that the whole top-loftiness of arrogance falls down. Nothing is left to you to glory in; your true glorying and hope is in mortifying yourself in all things and in seeking for that future life in Christ, of which we have already a foretaste when we live wholly in the love and in the grace of God.

And it is God who works in you. God has made known to us wisdom, through the Holy Spirit. And in all our efforts it is God who gives us strength. And God has delivered us from danger, and beyond all human expectation.

Why then, I ask you, are you full of pride, because of what you have, when you ought rather to give thanks to the Giver of what you have? You did not come to know God through your own excellence; but God looked upon you out of divine goodness. You have not laid hold of Christ because of your virtue; but it is Christ who through his coming has laid hold of you. And do you pride in this, and make the mercy of God a pretext for arrogance? Recognize yourself for what you are, another Adam cast forth from paradise, another Saul abandoned by the Holy Spirit, another Israel cut off from its holy root. You stand by faith.

Basil

R THIRTY-FIRST SUNDAY IN ORDINARY TIME

E PROPER 26

L TWENTY-FOURTH SUNDAY AFTER PENTECOST

The faithful soul eats its bread, but, alas, in the sweat of its brow. While in the flesh it moves by faith which necessarily acts through charity, for if it does not act, it dies. Moreover, according to our Savior, this work is food. Afterwards, having cast off its flesh, the soul no longer feeds on the bread of sorrow, but, having eaten, it is allowed to drink more deeply of the wine of love, not pure wine but wine mixed with milk. The soul mixes the divine love with the tenderness of that natural affection by which it desires to have its body back, a glorified body. The soul therefore glows already with the warmth of charity's wine, but not to the stage of intoxication, for the milk moderates its strength. Intoxication disturbs the mind and makes it wholly forgetful of itself, but the soul which still thinks of the resurrection of its own body has not forgotten itself completely. For the rest, after finding the only thing needed, what is there to prevent the soul from taking leave of itself and passing into God entirely, ceasing all the more to be like itself as it becomes more and more like God? Then only the soul is allowed to drink wisdom's pure wine. Why wonder if the soul is inebriated by the riches of the Lord's dwelling, when free from worldly cares it can drink pure, fresh wine with Christ in his Father's house?

Wisdom presides over this triple banquet composed of charity which feeds those who labor, gives drink to those who are resting, and inebriates those who reign. As at an earthly banquet, edibles are served before liquid refreshments. Nature has set this order which Wisdom also observes. First, indeed, up to our death, while we are in mortal flesh we eat the work of our hands, laboriously masticating what is to be swallowed. In the spiritual life after death, we drink with ease whatever is offered. Once our bodies come back to life we shall be filled with everlasting life, abounding in a wonderful fullness. Eat before death, drink after death, be inebriated after the resurrection. It is right to call them dearest who are drunk with love; they are rightly inebriated who deserve to be admitted to the nuptials of the Lamb, eating and drinking at his table in his kingdom when he takes his church to him in her glory without a blemish, wrinkle, or any defect of the sort. By all means he will then intoxicate his dearest ones with the torrent of his delight, for in the bridegroom's and bride's most passionate yet most chaste embrace, the force of the river's current gives joy to the city of God.

Here is fullness without disgust; here is insatiable curiosity without restlessness; here is that eternal, inexplicable desire knowing no want. At last, here is that sober intoxication of truth, not from over-drinking, not reeking with wine, but burning for God. From this then that fourth degree of love is possessed forever, when God alone is loved in the highest way, for now we do not love ourselves except for God's sake, that God may be the reward and the eternal recompense of those who love the Lord forever.

Bernard of Clairvaux

R THIRTY-SECOND SUNDAY IN ORDINARY TIME

E PROPER 27

L TWENTY-FIFTH SUNDAY AFTER PENTECOST

And forasmuch as you have, of your bottomless mercy, offered most graciously to me, wretched sinner, to be again my God through Christ, if I would accept of you, I call heaven and earth to record this day that I do here solemnly avouch you for the Lord my God; and with all veneration bowing the neck of my soul under the feet of your most sacred Majesty, I do here take you the Lord Jehovah, Father, Son, and Holy Ghost, for my portion; and do give up myself, body and soul, for your servant; promising and vowing to serve you in holiness and righteousness, all the days of my life. And since you have appointed the Lord Jesus Christ the only means of coming unto you I do here upon the bended knees of my soul accept of him as the only new and living way, by which sinners may have access to you; and do solemnly join myself in a marriage-covenant to him. O blessed Jesus, I come to you unworthy to wash the feet of the servants of my Lord, much more to be solemnly married to the King of Glory; but since such is your unparalleled love, I do here with all my power accept you, and take you for my head and husband, for better, for worse, for richer, for poorer, for all times and conditions, to love, honor, and obey you before all others, and this to the death. I embrace you in all your offices: I renounce my own worthiness, and do here avow you for the Lord my righteousness: I renounce my own wisdom, and do here take you for my only guide; I renounce my own will, and take your will for my law.

And because you have been pleased to give me your holy laws as the rule of my life, and the way in which I should walk to your kingdom, I do here willingly put my neck under your yoke, and set my shoulder to your burden, and subscribing to all your laws as holy, just, and good, I solemnly take them as the rule of my words, thoughts, and actions; promising that though my flesh contradict and rebel, I will endeavor to order and govern my whole life according to your direction, and will not allow myself in the neglect of anything that I know to be my duty.

John Wesley

Let us turn in continual prayer toward our only hope, ever led by it in this corporeal world. O Lord, this mortal world is too weak for your whole gift; but from your fullness, fullness is poured out upon its infirmity. Our afflicted souls, O Lord, thirst for this hope; gladden our souls, Lord, that we may see your grace in your person. Our heart is filled with sadness; we are afflicted without ceasing. Bring joy to our sadness, Lord, and give refreshment to our burning hearts. Day and night sorrow and affliction surround us; cool within us, Lord, the flame of our hearts. For apart from you we have no hope to comfort us in our grief. Place your finger, that gives life to all things, on the pain concealed in our heart. For day and night wars beset us that seek to cut off our hope in you: be our leader in battle! Our mind is invaded without ceasing, with sorrow and with tears; at all times we are in fear of being deprived of the solace of your hope. Let our soul be not robbed of your strengthening, O Savior, that we may not be plunged amid the waves of despair.

Ephraem

L TWENTY-SEVENTH SUNDAY AFTER PENTECOST

I saw a great willow tree that overshadowed plains and mountains, and all who were called by the name of the Lord came under the shelter of the willow. And an angel of the Lord, glorious and very tall, stood beside the willow, with a great sickle, and was cutting branches from the willow, and giving them to the people who were in the shade of the willow; the angel gave them little sticks, about eighteen inches long. After they had all got the sticks, the angel put down the sickle, and the tree was as sound as when I had first seen it. And I wondered and said to myself, How can the tree be sound after so many branches have been cut off? The shepherd said to me, "Do not wonder that the tree has remained sound after so many branches have been cut off; see it all, and it will be made clear to you what it means."

The angel who had given the sticks to the people asked them back again, and in the order in which they had received them, they were recalled and each one of them gave back the sticks. And the angel of the Lord received them and examined them. From some the angel received the sticks dry and apparently moth-eaten. The angel ordered the ones who had given up such sticks to stand by themselves. And others gave them up dry, but they were not moth-eaten. These were ordered also to stand by themselves. And others gave them up half dry and cracked; and these stood by themselves. And others gave the sticks up half dry and cracked; and these stood by themselves. And others gave their sticks up green and cracked, and these stood by themselves. And others gave their sticks up half dry and half green, and these stood by themselves. And others brought their sticks up two-thirds of the stick green and one-third dry, and these stood by themselves. And others gave up their sticks all but a little green, but a very little of their sticks was dry, and the very tip, and they had cracks in them; and these stood by themselves. And of others there was very little green and the rest of each stick was dry, and these stood by themselves. And others came bringing their sticks green, just as they had got them from the angel; most of the people gave up such sticks, and the angel rejoiced exceedingly over them, and they stood by themselves. And others gave up their sticks green and budded, and these stood by themselves; and the angel rejoiced exceedingly over them. And others gave up their sticks green and budded, and their buds seemed to have some fruit. And those people whose sticks were found in this condition were very glad. And the angel rejoiced over them, and the shepherd was very glad about them.

The Shepherd of Hermas

R LAST SUNDAY, CHRIST THE KING

E PROPER 29

L CHRIST THE KING, LAST SUNDAY AFTER
   PENTECOST

The affirmation of faith that "God reigns" is the acknowledgment that God is transcendent. The concept of transcendence does not focus so much on God as on the activity of God in us. Affirming this mystery of God does not diminish our own humanity, but opens the way for our humanity to be fulfilled. The affirmation that God is transcendent requires of us a spontaneous leap into an awareness of that ultimate reality which cannot be comprehended by conventional categories of thought and observation. It is revelation and "divine mystery."

The affirmation that "God reigns" proclaims that God is near. It affirms that in spite of wars, conflict, competition, and all forms of human estrangement, God is near as a unifying force and a witness to the basic oneness of all peoples. Our very nature is mysteriously linked with the fulfillment of the whole human family.

When God's transcendence has been thought of as a source of personal salvation, it has been a constricting influence on our Christian life. In the name of spiritual individualism, it has been misused. We have avoided responsibility, because we have become too self-oriented and inflexible in our understanding of "religious experience." The affirmation of God as transcendent reality, rather than making us rigid in our faith and cutting us off from others, is the very force which joins us together with other human beings and inspires us to reach out. Transcendence is not sectarian; it is borne on the wings of hope, the social transformation of a people, the cosmic transformation of creation, and the renewal of life itself.

To the sleeping and the despairing of spirit, the prophet calls out, "Awake, awake, there is good news, your God reigns!" Like a bird singing before the dawn, announcing the nearness of the break of day, so the prophet cries out, alerting us to the transcendent sources of new life.

Constance F. Parvey

FEASTS AND SOLEMNITIES

CYCLES A, B, C

R MARY, MOTHER OF GOD

E HOLY NAME

L NAME OF JESUS

There will indeed be nothing of evil, nothing impure, in our invoking of the sacred name. If you eat, if you drink, should you marry, if you set out on a journey, do all in the name of Jesus, that is, calling upon him to help you. And having in all that you do invoked him, then apply yourself to the thing in hand. Should you wish to speak concerning any business, do this beforehand. For this reason do we also place the name of the Lord at the head of all our epistles. Wherever there is the Lord's name, everything will be well. For if the names of the consuls are affixed to documents, to insure that they are authentic, how much more the name of Jesus.

Again, the apostle likewise means to say and do everything as is right and fitting in relation to God. Do you eat? Offer thanks to God, both before you eat, and afterwards. Do you sleep? Give thanks to God, both before and after. Are you going out among people? Do the same. Do everything in the name of the Lord, and all that you do will bring you happiness. Wherever the name of the Lord is set up, all things prosper. If it has power to drive away demons, if it can banish illness, much more will it aid your own actions.

Recall how Abraham sent his servant in the name of God. And David in the name of the Lord slew Goliath: great and wonderful is the name of the Lord! They who do this have God for their helper; without whom they can do nothing.

John Chrysostom

R E L THE PRESENTATION OF OUR LORD

See you not that Anna is worthy of praise? She acted as protector of the Lord, and in his presence spoke in his behalf. O new and unheard of thing! She was but a poor widow, and she makes plain that over which the priests and scribes had long pondered, uplifting the hearts of those who heard her with fervent hope. She made manifest to Israel the salvation of its Lord, which she declared by arguments and by signs was now about to be delivered. Anna discerned the infant Lord. She perceived too the gifts and little offerings which were borne with him and for him. Not on that account was she confused, nor by his helpless and tender age. She confessed that this child was both the Lord and the destroyer of sin.

Do not pass lightly over the testimony of Anna, in which she described the power of the Lord to all who were present. See you not, she says to those who stood about her, this little child, nursed at the breast, resting in the bosom of his mother, unable as yet through infancy to press the soles of his feet to the earth, circumcised on the eighth day after the manner of other infants? This child whom you see before you has laid the foundations of the world, he has perfected the heavens; it is he who has shut up the sea with doors when it broke forth; this child has brought the winds from out his stores; in the days of Noah he opened the cataract of heaven; this child covered the earth with clouds, and prepared rain for the earth; he gives snow like wool; by the rod of Moses he freed our forebears from the land of Egypt; he dried up the Red Sea, and led forth the people who trusted in him, and led them with dry feet as through a smiling field; this child rained manna upon them in the desert and gave our forebears a land flowing with milk and honey as their inheritance.

Esteem not lightly this child, because he is a child. He who is a child is coeternal with the Father. His age is measured within a month, yet there were none who went before him. This is but a babbling infant, but the mouth whence wisdom is imparted to others; the one because of birth from the virgin, the other because of the incomprehensible nature of his substance. What is born is seen with the eyes; what is given is known by the mind and the thought alone.

Amphilochius

R E L THE ANNUNCIATION OF OUR LORD

The tender mother of Christ teaches us with her words and by the example of her experience how to know, love, and praise God. For since she boasts, with heart leaping for joy and praising God, that God regarded her despite her low estate and nothingness, we must believe that she came of poor, despised, and lowly parents. Let us make it very plain for the sake of the simple. Doubtless there were in Jerusalem daughters of the chief priests and counselors who were rich, comely, youthful, cultured, and held in high renown by all the people, even as it is today with the daughters of kings, princes, and men of wealth. The same was also true of many another city. Even in her own town of Nazareth she was not the daughter of one of the chief rulers, but a poor and plain citizen's daughter, whom none looked up to or esteemed. To her neighbors and their daughters she was but a simple maiden, tending the cattle and doing the housework, and doubtless esteemed no more than any poor maidservant toady, who does as she is told around the house.

Behold, how completely she traces all to God, lays claim to no works, no honor, no fame. She conducts herself as before, when she still had nothing of all this; she demands no higher honors than before. She is not puffed up, does not vaunt herself or proclaim with a loud voice that she is become the Mother of God. She seeks not any glory, but goes about her usual household duties, milking the cows, cooking the meals, washing pots and kettles, sweeping out the rooms, and performing the work of maidservant or housemother in lowly and despised tasks, as though she cared nothing for such great gifts and graces. She was esteemed among other women and her neighbors no more highly than before, nor desired to be, but remained a poor townswoman, one of the great multitude. Oh, how simple and pure a heart was hers, how strange a soul was this! What great things are hidden here under this lowly exterior! How many came in contact with her, talked, and ate and drank with her, who perhaps despised her and counted her but a common, poor, and simple village maiden, and who, had they known, would have fled from her in terror.

Martin Luther

R E L THE VISITATION

Lord Jesus Christ, Son of the living God, Word of all truth, you are the beginning and ending of our paths. It is with you that we wish to begin our journey. Our road is an old one, which began long ago when you started with us in baptism and when we started with the habits of the children of Adam. Yet it is a new road, because you are he who constantly renews our youth, because in your infinite life and strength you are ever young and you make all things new. Go with us, Lord. Stay with us, even when it is toward evening. Walk with us in the paths of truth, that truth which makes us free. If we are lovers of words, go with us as the word of God; if we are explorers of nature, as the Spirit on which the nature of the world is founded; if we are seekers after what is just, as the Sun of Righteousness; if we are learning to heal, as the saving Healer of the world; if we study the theology of pilgrims, go with us as God incarnate. Go with us on our everyday roads that these too may be paths which lead into your kingdom, for it is sober faithfulness in everyday things that brings us wisdom and maturity. Be with us when we have to bear witness to your truth by acknowledging our faith, when we have to testify to the power of your grace by the purity of our lives, and to your presence in the world by our loyalty to your body which is the church. Go with us on the paths by which we make our pilgrimage to you and find our true selves in you. May there emerge in each one of us faith, hope, and charity, courage in self-discipline and purity in heart, joy in confidence and perseverance in patience. We are still only at the beginning of all these paths, for the goal is in your infinite distance. Yet we are already and always at our end, for you, our goal, live in us in your Holy Spirit. All is contained in you.

Hugo Rahner

R E THE TRANSFIGURATION OF OUR LORD

Wearied of the multitudes Peter had come upon the solitude of the mountain. Here he was close to Christ, the bread of his soul. Why go away, to travail and to suffer, when he could live here in holy love of God, and because of this in holiness also of life?

To this the Lord makes no reply; yet Peter receives an answer. For while he was speaking a bright cloud came and overshadowed them. He wished to make three tabernacles. The heavenly answer shows we have but one, which human understanding would divide. Christ the Word of God, God's word in the law, God's word in the prophets. And why, Peter, do you seek to divide them? Ought you not rather unite them? You prepare for three; know that there is but one.

As the cloud overshadowed them, and in manner formed for them one tabernacle, a voice spoke from out the cloud saying, "This is my beloved Son." Moses was there, and Elijah. The voice did not say, These are my beloved sons. For one only is the son; others are adopted. It is he that is commended to them: he from whom the law and the prophets derive their glory. You have heard him in the prophets; you heard him in the law. And where have you not heard him?

When they hear this they fall to the ground. Here now we are shown that in the church is the kingdom of God. Here is the Lord; here is the law; and here are the prophets. In Moses the law, in Elijah the prophets, but both as servants and ministers. They are as vessels; he is the spring. Moses and the prophets wrote and spoke; but it was from him they were filled when they gave forth.

Augustine

R ASSUMPTION OF THE BLESSED VIRGIN MARY

E ST. MARY THE VIRGIN

L MARY, MOTHER OF OUR LORD

Mary alone, of all the saints, is, in everything, incomparable. She has the sanctity of them all and yet resembles none of them. And still we can talk of being like her. This likeness to her is not only something to desire—it is one human quality most worthy of our desire: but the reason for that is that she, of all creatures, most perfectly recovered the likeness to God that God willed to find, in varying degrees, in us all.

It is necessary, no doubt, to talk about her privileges as if they were something that could be made comprehensible in human language and could be measured by some human standard. It is most fitting to talk about her as a Queen and to act as if you knew what it meant to say she has a throne above all the angels. But this should not make anyone forget that her highest privilege is her poverty and her greatest glory is that she is most hidden, and the source of all her power is that she is as nothing in the presence of Christ, of God.

Thomas Merton

R MICHAEL, GABRIEL, AND RAPHAEL

E L ST. MICHAEL AND ALL ANGELS

Messengers, in the Greek tongue, are called angels, and the chief messengers are called archangels. We must also know that the name angel refers rather to their office, and not to their own nature. For these holy spirits of our heavenly fatherland are indeed always spirits, but cannot always be called angels; for then only are they angels when by means of them certain things are announced.

They who announce things of lesser significance are called angels, and they who announce the greater things are called archangels. Hence it was not any angel that was sent to the virgin Mary, but the archangel Gabriel. It was fitting that for this task the highest order of angel should come, to announce the one who is above all things. That they have proper names is not for the sake of the inhabitants of the holy city, but for our sake; for when they come to us on some mission they take their names from the task they fulfill.

Accordingly Michael is called "Who is like to God?" Gabriel is "The strength of God." Raphael is called "The Medicine of God." And when something of striking power is to be done Michael is said to be sent, so that by Michael's name and action it may be shown that no one can do what God can do.

To Mary was sent Gabriel, who is called "the Strength of God." For Gabriel came to announce him who, that he might cast down the powers of brass, deigned to appear among us as one lowly. Raphael, also who is as we have said "the Medicine of God," is exercising a mission anointed the eyes of Tobias and wiped away the darkness of his blindness. The one therefore who is sent to heal is rightly called the Medicine of God.

Cherubim means the fullness of knowledge. And these sublime spirits are called cherubim for the reason that, contemplating more closely the glory of God, they are filled with a more perfect knowledge of God; so that the closer by reason of their rank they draw near to the vision of their Creator, the more they in due measure as creatures know all things. And the choirs of holy spirits who because of their special closeness to the Creator burn with an incomparable love are called seraphim. For since they are so close to God that no other spirits stand between them and God, the more closely they behold God, the more ardently they love God. And their love is a flame: for the more vivid their perception of the glory of the Divinity, the more ardently do they burn with God's love.

But of what use is it to speak of these angelic spirits unless we seek through fitting reflection upon them to derive some profit from them for ourselves? For since we believe that the heavenly city is made up of both angels and human beings, whither we believe we shall ascend to the number of the chosen angels who remained there, we too should draw something from our earthly contemplation of these different orders of the heavenly citizens for the perfecting of the manner of our own life, and by means of our own zealous devotion excite ourselves to the increase of virtue within us.

Gregory the Great

R E L ALL SAINTS

Then John saw the river, and the multitude was there. And now they had undergone a change; their robes were ragged, and stained with the road they had traveled, and stained with unholy blood; the robes of some barely covered their nakedness; and some indeed were naked. And some stumbled on the smooth stones at the river's edge, for they were blind; and some crawled with a terrible wailing, for they were lame; some did not cease to pluck at their flesh, which was rotten with running sores. All struggled to get to the river, in a dreadful hardness of heart: the strong struck down the weak, the ragged spat on the naked, the naked cursed the blind, the blind crawled over the lame. And someone cried, *"Sinner, do you love my Lord?"*

Then John saw the Lord—for a moment only; and the darkness, for a moment only, was filled with light he could not bear. Then, in a moment, he was set free; his tears sprang as from a fountain; his heart, like a fountain of waters, burst. Then he cried: "Oh, blessed Jesus! Oh, Lord Jesus! Take me through!"

Of tears there was, yes, a very fountain—springing from a depth never sounded before, from depths John had not known were in him. And he wanted to rise up, singing, singing, in that great morning, the morning of his new life. Ah, how his tears ran down, how they blessed his soul!—as he felt himself, out of the darkness, and the fire, and the terrors of death, rising upward to meet the saints.

"Oh, yes!" cried the voice of Elisha. "Bless our God forever!"

And a sweetness filled John as he heard this voice, and heard the sound of singing: the singing was for him. For his drifting soul was anchored in the love of God; in the rock that endured forever. The light and the darkness had kissed each other, and were married now, forever, in the life and the vision of John's soul.

I, John, saw a city, way in the middle of the air,
Waiting, waiting, waiting up there.

He opened his eyes on the morning, and found them, in the light of the morning, rejoicing for him. The trembling he had known in darkness had been the echo of their joyful feet—these feet, blood-stained forever, and washed in many rivers—they moved on the bloody road forever, with no continuing city, but seeking one to come: a city out of time, not made with hands, but eternal in the heavens. No power could hold this army back, no water disperse them, no fire consume them. One day they would compel the earth to heave upward, and surrender the waiting dead. They sang, where the darkness gathered, where the lion waited, where the fire cried, and where blood ran down:

My soul, don't you be uneasy!

They wandered in the valley forever; and they smote the rock, for-ever; and the waters sprang, perpetually, in the perpetual desert. They cried unto the Lord forever, they were cast down forever, and lifted up their eyes forever. No, the fire could not hurt them, and yes, the lion's jaws were stopped; the serpent was not their master, the grave was not their resting-place, the earth was not their home. Job bore them witness, and Abraham was their father, Moses had elected to suffer with them rather than glory in sin for a season. Shadrach, Mechach, and Abednego had gone before them into the fire, their grief had been sung by David, and Jeremiah had wept for them. Ezekiel had prophesied upon them, these scattered bones, these slain, and, in the fullness of time, the prophet, John, had come out of the wilderness, crying that the promise was for them. They were encompassed with a very cloud of witnesses: Judas, who had betrayed the Lord; Thomas, who had doubted Him; Peter, who had trembled at the crowing of a cock; Stephen, who had been stoned; Paul, who had been bound; the blind man crying in the dusty road, the dead man rising from the grave. And they looked unto Jesus, the author and the finisher of their faith, running with patience the race He had set before them; they endured the cross, and they despised the shame, and waited to join Him, one day, in glory, at the right hand of the Father.

My soul, don't you be uneasy!
Jesus going to make up my dying bed!

James Baldwin

R FOR THE UNITY OF ALL CHRISTIANS
E FOR THE UNITY OF THE CHURCH
L UNITY

Unity, then, is a fundamental reality, existing and subsisting in the body of Christ; but Christians must nevertheless pray for their unity—pray that they themselves stay in this unity bestowed by Christ and, when they are divided, pray that the fundamental unity bestowed upon them in Jesus Christ may be rediscovered.

In Christ's prayer, the unity of Christians, founded upon and inspired by the unity of the Father and the Son, is not an end in itself. If Christians are called upon to live in this unity provided for them by God, it is so that the world will believe—so that the world will know that the Father has sent the Son and that the Son has loved as the Father loved him.

Herein we can more plainly see why unity is a reality that expands and is enriched in pace with the advance of history, our closer approach to the kingdom of God, and the development of the world. As the ages pass, the church must answer new questions; and as a rule it will not provide the world repeatedly with the same fixed solution; rather, the Holy Spirit who leads it into all truth causes it to realize progressively the countless riches of the word of God, and the inestimable diversity involved in the unity of the body of Christ.

Thus there is no contradiction between certainty that unity has been given us and prayer for progressively enriched unity. Like Christ's prayer, ours must ask essentially for Christians' discovery of the unity existing among Father, Son, and Holy Spirit, and their radical participation in the life of this unity so that the world may believe. Christians are not obliged to make other requests on this subject; they need not pray that unity be realized in such and such a particular way. Of course, they have the right to believe that there are certain fundamental conditions apart from which unity cannot exist. But when they pray, they are first and foremost bent in adoration before the Father, Son, and Holy Spirit; and their essential prayer is to ask that all Christians receive the grace to live in that divine unity, both actual and becoming.

Max Thurian

Sources

Page number precedes each selection

3 Thomas More, in *Prayer Book of the Saints,* ed. Charles Dollen (Huntington, IN: Our Sunday Visitor, 1984), 121-22.

3 Cyril of Jerusalem, *Lectures on the Christian Sacraments,* tr. F. L. Cross (Crestwood, NY: St. Vladimir's, 1977), 40, 50-51.

5 Hilary, in *The Sunday Sermons of the Great Fathers,* tr. and ed. M. F. Toal (Chicago: Henry Regnery, 1958), I, 35-36.

5 Raymond E. Brown, "The Annunciation to Joseph," *Worship* 61 (1987), 488-89.

7 Martin Luther, *The Martin Luther Christmas Book,* tr. Roland H. Bainton (Philadelphia: Muhlenberg, 1948), 37, 38, 40.

8 Ephraem, in *Sunday Sermons,* II, 49-51.

10 Martin Luther, *The Martin Luther Christmas Book,* 72, 73, 74.

12 Symeon, *Hymns of Divine Love,* tr. George A. Maloney SJ (Denville, NJ: Dimension, n.d.), 233-34.

13 Ambrose, in *Sunday Sermons,* I, 212-23.

14 Tertullian, in *Baptism: Ancient Liturgies and Patristic Texts,* ed. A. Hamman OFM (Staten Island, NY: Alba, 1967), 36-37.

14 inscription, in *Springtime of the Liturgy,* ed. Lucien Deiss, tr. Matthew J. O'Donnell (Collegeville, MN: Liturgical Press, 1979), 264.

15 Margerite d'Oingt, tr. Richard J. Pioli, in *Medieval Women's Visionary Literature,* ed. Elizabeth Alvilda Petroff (NY: Oxford, 1986), 292.

16 Gustavo Gutierrez, *Liberation and Change,* ed. Ronald H. Stone (Atlanta: John Knox, 1977), 90, 92.

17 *Letter of Barnabas,* in *The Apostolic Fathers: An American Translation,* by Edgar J. Goodspeed (NY: Harper & Brothers, 1950), 34-35.

18 Benedict, "The Rule of Benedict," tr. Oswald Hunter Blair OSB, in *The Way to God,* ed. Emmanuel Heufelder OSB (Kalamazoo, MI: Cistercian, 1983), 222.

18 Virginia Ramey Mollenkott, *Godding* (NY: Crossroad, 1987), 1-2.

19 John Chrysostom, in *Sunday Sermons,* IV, 102-03.

20 Ephraem, in *Sunday Sermons,* II, 46-47.

22 Romano Guardini, *Sacred Signs,* tr. Melissa Kay (Wilmington, DE: Michael Glazier, 1979), 53-55.

23 Gregory the Great, in *Sunday Sermons*, II, 34-35.

24 Ephraem, in *Sunday Sermons*, II, 46-47.

24 Zeno, in *Baptism: Ancient Liturgies and Patristic Texts*, 64-66.

25 blessing of the water from the *Liber Ordinum*, in *Documents of the Baptismal Liturgy*, ed. E. C. Whitaker (London: SPCK, 1970), 119-20.

26 Catherine of Siena, *The Prayers of Catherine of Siena*, ed. Suzanne Noffke OP (NY: Paulist, 1983), 121.

27 Martin Niemoeller, in *20 Centuries of Great Preaching*, ed. Clyde E. Fant, Jr., and William M. Pinson, Jr. (Waco, TX: Word, 1971), X, 249-50.

29 Augustine, in *Sunday Sermons*, IV, 119-20.

30 Gregory of Nazianzus, in *Sunday Sermons*, II, 261.

31 Cyril of Alexandria, in *Sunday Sermons*, III, 159-60.

32 Amphilochius, in *Sunday Sermons*, II, 192.

33 "Dayeinu," in *A Passover Haggadah*, ed. Herbert Bronstein (NY: Penguin, 1978), 52-53.

34 Melito, *On Pascha and Fragments*, ed. Stuart George Hall (Oxford: Oxford, 1979), 35-39.

35 Anselm, *Anselm of Canterbury*, ed. Jasper Hopkins and Herbert Richardson (Lewiston, NY: Edwin Mellen, 1974), 93.

36 Evelyn Underhill, *Meditations and Prayers* (London: Longman, Green and Co., 1949), 14, 17, 20.

37 *The Shepherd of Hermas*, in *The Apostolic Fathers: An American Translation*, 183-84.

39 W. H. Auden, "Chorus," *The Collected Poetry of W. H. Auden* (N. Y. : Random House, 1945), 166.

39 Basil, in *Sunday Sermons*, III, 8.

42 Hans Urs von Balthasar, *Heart of the World*, tr. Erasmo S. Leiva (San Francisco: Ignatius, 1979), 76-78.

41 Gregory of Nazianzus, in *Sunday Sermons*, II, 258-59.

42 Basil, in *Sunday Sermons*, II, 386.

43 Gregory the Great, in *Sunday Sermons*, III, 51.

44 Catherine of Siena, *The Prayers of Catherine of Siena*, 16.

45 Augustine, in *The Mass: Ancient Liturgies and Patristic Texts*, ed. A. Hamman OFM (Staten Island, NY: Alba, 1967), 214.

46 *Address to Diognetus*, in *The Apostolic Fathers: An American Translation*, 282-83.

47 John Donne, *The Showing Forth of Christ*, ed. Edmund Fuller (NY: Harper & Row, 1964), 74-75.

48 Ignatius, in *The Apostolic Fathers: An American Translation*, 209-10.

49 Francis of Assisi, *Francis and Clare: The Complete Works*, ed. Regis J. Armstrong OFM CAP and Ignatius C. Brady OFM (NY: Paulist, 1982), 38-39.

50 Dorothy Day, *By Little and By Little*, ed. Robert Ellsberg (NY: Alfred A. Knopf, 1983), 69-70.

51 Ephraem, in *Sunday Sermons*, III, 310-311.

53 Teresa of Avila, in *The Mystics of Spain*, ed. Allison Peers (London: Allen and Unwin, 1951), 81-83.

54 Augustine, in *Sunday Sermons*, I, 337-38.

55 Maximus, in *Sunday Sermons*, I, 357.

56 John Chrysostom, in *The Mass: Ancient Liturgies and Patristic Texts*, 102-04.

57 Umilta of Faenza, tr. Richard J. Pioli, in *Medieval Women's Visionary Literature*, 251.

58 Jean Massillon, in *20 Centuries of Great Preaching*, II, 446-47.

59 Bede, in *Sunday Sermons*, III, 273.

59 Dietrich Bonhoeffer, *The Cost of Discipleship* (NY: Macmillan, 1963), 99-100.

61 Thérèse of Lisieux, *Autobiography of St. Thérèse of Lisieux*, tr. Ronald Knox (NY: P. J. Kenedy and Sons, 1958), 289, 310, 311.

63 John Chrysostom, in *Sunday Sermons*, IV, 289.

64 John Chrysostom, in *A Triduum Sourcebook*, ed. Gabe Huck and Mary Ann Simcoe (Chicago: Liturgy Training Publications, 1983), 11-12.

65 Augustine, in *Sunday Sermons*, III, 101-02.

66 Bonaventure, *The Soul's Journey into God; The Tree of Life; The Life of St. Francis*, ed. Ewert Cousins (NY: Paulist, 1978), 120-22.

67 Augustine, in *Sunday Sermons*, III, 179-80.

68 Desmond Mpilo Tutu, *Hope and Suffering*, ed. John Webster (Grand Rapids, MI: William B. Eerdmans, 1984), 58-59.

69 Augustine, in *Sunday Sermons*, IV, 166.

69 Ephraem, in *Sunday Sermons*, IV, 351.

70 John Ruusbroec, *The Spiritual Espousals and Other Works*, ed. James A. Wiseman OSB (NY: Paulist, 1985), 54-55.

71 Beatrice of Nazareth, tr. Eric Colledge, in *Medieval Women's Visionary Literature*, 204.

72 *Letter of Barnabas*, in *The Apostolic Fathers: An American Translation*, 42.

73 Gregory the Great, in *Sunday Sermons*, III, 354-55.

77 Gertrud Mueller Nelson, *To Dance with God* (NY: Paulist, 1986), 61-62.

78 Edward Schillebeeckx OP, *God Among Us: The Gospel Proclaimed* (NY: Crossroad, 1983), 5-6.

79 Gregory the Great, in *Sunday Sermons*, I, 68-69.

79 Martin Luther, *The Martin Luther Christmas Book* , 22-23.

80 Dorothy Day, *By Little and By Little*, 94, 96.

82 M. Nadine Foley OP, in *Women and the Word: Sermons*, ed. Helen Gray Crotwell (Philadelphia: Fortress, 1978), 50-53.

83 Jacques de Vitry, tr. Margot King, in *Medieval Women's Visionary Literature*, 182.

84 Hildegard of Bingen, tr. Francesca Maria Steele, in *Medieval Women's Visionary Literature*, 152-53.

84 Romanos, *Kontakia of Romanos, Byzantine Melodist*, tr. Marjorie Carpenter (Columbia, MO: University of Missouri, 1970), I, 32-33.

85 anonymous, in *Sunday Sermons*, I, 224.

86 Leo, in *Sunday Sermons*, II, 72.

87 Thomas Merton, *New Seeds of Contemplation* (NY: New Directions, 1961), 155-57.

88 Jerome, in *The Paschal Mystery: Ancient Liturgies and Patristic Texts*, ed. A. Hamman OFM (Staten Island, NY: Alba, 1969), 140-41.

88 exorcism from the Byzantine rite, in *Documents of the Baptismal Liturgy*, 74-75.

89 Alexander Schmemann, *For the Life of the World* (Crestwood, NY: St. Vladimir's, 1973), 102-03.

90 Elisabeth Moltmann-Wendel, *The Women Around Jesus* (NY: Crossroad, 1982), 101-04.

92 Ambrose, in *Sunday Sermons*, IV, 183-84.

93 Mechthild of Magdeburg, tr. Lucy Menzies, in *Medieval Women's Visionary Literature*, 216.

93 John Chrysostom, in *Sunday Sermons*, II, 54-55.

94 confession, *Mahzor for Rosh Hashanah and Yom Kippur*, ed. Rabbi Jules Harlow (NY: Rabbinical Assembly, 1972), 403, 405.

95 Maximus, in *Sunday Sermons*, II, 93-94.

96 Thomas à Kempis, *The Imitation of Christ*, ed. Betty I. Knott (London: Collins, 1963), 103-04.

97 John Chrysostom, in *The Mass: Ancient Liturgies and Patristic Texts*, 162-63.

98 Meister Eckhart, *The Essential Sermons, Commentaries, Treatises, and Defense*, ed. Edmund Colledge OSA and Bernard McGinn (NY: Paulist, 1981), 183-84.

98 Catherine of Siena, *The Prayers of Catherine of Siena*, 78.

99 Teresa of Avila, *The Interior Castle*, tr. Kieran Kavanagh OCD and Otilio Rodriguez OCD (NY: Paulist, 1979), 91-94.

101 Cyprian, in *Sunday Sermons*, II, 349.

101 Justin, in *Sunday Sermons*, III, 110.

102 Umilta of Faenza, tr. Richard J. Pioli, in *Medieval Women's Visionary Literature*, 250.

103 Ambrose, in *Sunday Sermons*, II, 218-19.

104 Nicetas, in *A Treasury of Early Christianity*, ed. Anne Fremantle (NY: Viking, 1953), 401-03.

105 Flannery O'Connor, *The Habit of Being*, ed. Sally Fitzgerald (NY: Vintage, 1980), 353-54.

105 Bonaventure, in *Prayer Book of the Saints*, 88-89.

106 Perpetua, tr. H. R. Musurillo, in *Medieval Women's Visionary Literature*, 71.

107 Catherine of Siena, *The Prayers of Catherine of Siena*, 147, 149, 150, 152.

108 John Wesley, in *John and Charles Wesley: Selected Prayers, Hymns, Journal Notes, Sermons, Letters and Treatises*, ed. Frank Whaling (NY: Paulist, 1981), 372-73.

109 Augustine, in *Sunday Sermons*, II, 415-16.

109 Augustine, in *Sunday Sermons*, II, 195-96.

110 Ambrose, in *Sunday Sermons*, III, 12-13.

111 Catherine of Siena, *The Prayers of Catherine of Siena*, 105.

111 John Chrysostom, in *Sunday Sermons*, III, 138.

112 Reinhold Niebuhr, in *20 Centuries of Great Preaching*, X, 371-72.

113 Margery Kempe, *The Book of Margery Kempe*, tr. B. A. Windeatt (NY: Penguin, 1985), 65-67.

114 Ambrose, in *Sunday Sermons*, I, 349-51.

115 Origen, in *Sunday Sermons*, I, 320.

116 Elizabeth Seton, *Selected Writings*, ed. Ellin Kelly and Annabelle Melville (NY: Paulist, 1987), 228-29.

118 Beatriz Melano Couch, in *Women and the Word: Sermons*, 118, 122.

119 N. F. S. Grundtvig, *Selected Writings*, ed. Johannes Knudsen (Philadelphia: Fortress, 1976), 108-09.

120 *Didache*, in *Springtime of the Liturgy*, 74-76.

121 Hilary, in *Sunday Sermons*, II, 120-21

121 Syncletica, in *Maenads, Martyrs, Matrons, Monastics: A Sourcebook on Women's Religions in the Greco-Roman World*, ed. Ross S. Kraemer (Philadelphia: Fortress, 1988), 119-20, 121-22.

123 Symeon, *Hymns of Divine Love*, 14.

124 Cyril of Alexandria, in *Sunday Sermons*, III, 156.

125 Cyril of Alexandria, in *Sunday Sermons*, III, 155.

126 Caesarius, in *Sunday Sermons*, II, 458.

126 George Whitefield, in *20 Centuries of Great Preaching*, III, 165.

127 Ambrose, in *Sunday Sermons*, IV, 5.

128 *The Little Flowers of St. Francis*, ed. Raphael Brown, (Garden City, NY: Image, 1958), 58-61.

129 Gregory of Nazianzus, in *Baptism: Ancient Liturgies and Patristic Texts*, 110-111.

130 John Chrysostom, in *The Liturgy of the Hours* (NY: Catholic Book Publishing, 1975), IV, 182-83.

131 prayer at Orthodox marriage rite, *Service Book of the Holy Orthodox-Catholic Apostolic Church*, 4th edition, ed. Isabel Florence Hapgood (Brooklyn, NY: Syrian Antiochian Orthodox Archdiocese, 1965), 295, 304.

133 Thomas à Kempis, *The Imitation of Christ*, 203-04, 230.

133 Letty Russell, in *Women and the Word: Sermons*, 87-89.

134 anonymous, in *Sunday Sermons*, I, 415, 417.

135 John Calvin, in *20 Centuries of Great Preaching*, II, 153.

136 Gregory of Nazianzus, in *The Paschal Mystery: Ancient Liturgies and Patristic Texts*, 76-77.

137 *First Clement*, in *The Apostolic Fathers: An American Translation*, 66-67.

138 Karl Barth, in *20 Centuries of Great Preaching*, X, 128.

139 Bridget of Sweden, in Philip Pfatteicher, *Festivals and Commemorations* (Minneapolis: Augsburg, 1980), 297-99.

143 Ambrose, in *Sunday Sermons*, I, 9.

144 John Chrysostom, in *Sunday Sermons*, I, 86.

145 Martin Luther, *Luther's Works*, Vol. 21, 165-66.

146 Julian of Norwich, *Revelations of Divine Love*, ed. M. L. de Mastro (Garden City, NY: Image, 1977), 92, 94.

147 John Chrysostom, in *Sunday Sermons*, I, 110-11.

148 Address to Diognetus, in *The Apostolic Fathers: An American Translation*, 279-80.

149 Aelred, in *Sunday Sermons*, I, 252-53.

150 Ignatius, in *The Apostolic Fathers: An American Translation*, 212-13.

150 Legend of the phoenix, in Pius Parsch, *The Church's Year of Grace* (Collegeville, MN: Liturgical Press, 1959), III, 86-87.

151 Gregory the Great, in *Sunday Sermons*, I, 232-33.

153 Cyril of Jerusalem, *Lectures on the Christian Sacraments*, 60-61.

154 John Chrysostom, in *Sunday Sermons*, I, 264-65.

154 John Chrysostom, in *The Mass: Ancient Liturgies and Patristic Texts*, 114-15.

156 Gregory the Great, in *Sunday Sermons*, I, 383-85.

157 Wilhelm Loehe, *Three Books about the Church*, ed. James L. Schaaf (Philadelphia: Fortress, 1969), 55-57.

158 Edward Schillebeeckx, *God Among Us: The Gospel Proclaimed*, 177-79.

160 Martin Luther King, Jr., *Strength to Love* (Philadelphia: Fortress, 1963), 47-48.

161 John Chrysostom, in *Sunday Sermons*, III, 311-12.

163 Elizabeth of Schoenau, tr. Thalia A. Pandiri, in *Medieval Women's Visionary Literature*, 167.

163 Leo, in *Sunday Sermons*, II, 29-30.

165 Julian of Norwich, *Revelations of Divine Love*, 104-05.

166 Elizabeth of Schoenau, tr. Thalia A. Pandiri, in *Medieval Women's Visionary Literature*, 167.

167 Julian of Norwich, *Revelations of Divine Love*, 191-93.

167 Julian of Norwich, *Revelations of Divine Love*, 123-24.

168 Helmut Thielicke, in *20 Centuries of Great Preaching*, XII, 267-69.

168 Catherine of Genoa, *Purgation and Purgatory, The Spiritual Dialogue*, tr. Serge Hughes (NY: Paulist, 1979), 116-18.

170 *Didascalia of the Apostles*, in *Springtime of the Liturgy*, 169.

170 anonymous, in *The Paschal Mystery: Ancient Liturgies and Patristic Texts*, 64-65.

171 Catherine of Siena, *The Prayers of Catherine of Siena*, 101-02.

172 *The Passion of Sts. Perpetua and Felicitas*, tr. H. R. Musurillo, in *Medieval Women's Visionary Literature*, 75-76.

173 Gregory of Nyssa, in *The Paschal Mystery: Ancient Liturgies and Patristic Texts*, 96-97.

174 Proclus, in *Sunday Sermons*, II, 234.

175 Julian of Norwich, *Revelations of Divine Love*, 172-73.

176 Augustine, in *Sunday Sermons*, II, 277.

177 inscription in consignatorium, in *Springtime of the Liturgy*, 265.

178 Catherine of Siena, *The Dialogue*, ed. Suzanne Noffke OP (NY: Paulist, 1980), 325-26.

178 Julian of Norwich, *Revelations of Divine Love*, 171-72.

180 Augustine, in *Sunday Sermons*, II, 421-22.

181 Symeon, *Hymns of Divine Love*, 28-29.

181 Ambrose, in *Sunday Sermons*, III, 13.

182 Augustine, in *Sunday Sermons*, III, 75-76.

183 Augustine, in *Sunday Sermons*, II, 297-98.

184 Gertrude the Great, in *Medieval Women's Visionary Literature*, 226-27.

186 Augustine, in *Sunday Sermons*, IV, 116.

186 Symeon, *Hymns of Divine Love*, 126, 130, 134.

187 Hadewijch of Brabant, tr. Eric Colledge, in *Medieval Women's Visionary Literature*, 193-94.

189 Roger Schutz, *Parable of Community* (NY: Seabury, 1981), 58-59.

190 John of Damascus, in *Prayer Book of the Saints*, 67.

190 Origen, in *Sunday Sermons*, IV, 34-35.

191 Rosemary Radford Ruether, in *Women and the Word: Sermons*, 94, 98.

193 John Chrysostom, in *Sunday Sermons*, II, 395.

194 Basil, in *Sunday Sermons*, III, 331-32.

195 Lyman Beecher, in *20 Centuries of Great Preaching*, III, 237.

196 Teresa of Calcutta, *Life in the Spirit*, ed. Kathryn Spink (San Francisco: Harper & Row, 1983), 61-63.

198 Augustine, in *Baptism: Ancient Liturgies and Patristic Texts*, 212-13.

199 Edward Schillebeeckx, *God Among Us: The Gospel Proclaimed*, 54-55.

201 *The Book of Privy Counseling*, in *The Cloud of Unknowing and The Book of Privy Counseling*, ed. William Johnston (Garden City, NY: Image, 1973), 172-73.

202 Peter Chrysologos, in *Sunday Sermons*, III, 200.

202 Gaudentius, in *Sunday Sermons*, III, 339-40.

203 Dorothy Day, *By Little and By Little*, 81-82.

205 Ambrose, in *Sunday Sermons*, I, 350-51.

205 Bede, in *Sunday Sermons*, IV, 86.

206 Basil, in *Sunday Sermons*, II, 380-81.

207 Basil, in *Sunday Sermons*, III, 362-63.

208 Bernard of Clairvaux, *The Works of Bernard of Clairvaux* (Washington, D.C.: Cistercian Publications, 1974), V, 123-25.

210 John Wesley, in *John and Charles Wesley: Selected Prayers, Hymns, Jounal Notes, Sermons, Letters and Treatises*, 143-44.

211 Ephraem, in *Sunday Sermons*, IV, 350.

211 *The Shepherd of Hermas*, in *The Apostolic Fathers: An American Translation*, 162-63.

213 Constance F. Parvey, *Come Lord Jesus! Come Quickly!* (Philadelphia: Fortress, 1976), 47.

216 John Chrysostom, in *Sunday Sermons*, I, 190.

216 Amphilochius, in *Sunday Sermons*, I, 176-77.

217 Martin Luther, *Luther's Works*, Vol. 21, 301, 329.

218 Hugo Rahner, in Hugo Rahner and Karl Rahner, *Prayers for Meditation* (NY: Herder & Herder, 1962), 65-67.

219 Augustine, in *Sunday Sermons*, II, 63.

220 Thomas Merton, *New Seeds of Contemplation*, 169.

221 Gregory the Great, in *Sunday Sermons*, III, 205-06.

223 James Baldwin, *Go Tell It on the Mountain* (NY: Dell, 1953), 203-05.

224 Max Thurian, *Visible Unity and Tradition*, tr. W. J. Kerrigan (Baltimore: Helicon, 1962), 115-16.

Acknowledgments

Acknowledgment is gratefully extended for permission to reprint from the following:

Anselm of Canterbury, eds. Jasper Hopkins and Herbert Richardson. Copyright 1974 by The Edwin Mellen Press, Lewiston, N.Y. Used with permission.

The Apostolic Fathers: An American Translation, by Edgar J. Goodspeed. Copyright 1950 by Harper & Bros., Publishers, Inc. Reprinted by permission of the publisher.

The Autobiography of St. Thérèse of Lisieux, tr. Ronald Knox, 1958. Used with permission of Burns & Oates Ltd.

Baptism: Ancient Liturgies and Patristic Texts, ed. A. Hamman. Copyright 1967 by Alba House, Staten Island, N.Y. Used with permission.

Bernard of Clarvaux, Treatises II. Copyright 1974. Used with permission of Cistercian Publications, Kalamazaoo, Mich.

The Book of Margery Kempe, tr. B. A. Windeatt. Copyright © 1985 by B. A. Windeatt. Used with permission of Penguin Books, London.

By Little and By Little: The Selected Writings of Dorothy Day, ed. Robert Ellsberg. Copyright © 1983 by Robert Ellsberg and Tamar Hennessy. Reprinted by permission of Alfred A. Knopf, Inc.

Byzantine Daily Worship. Copyright 1969. Used by permission of Alleluia Press, Allendale, N.J. 07401.

Come Lord Jesus! Come Quickly! by Constance F. Parvey. Copyright 1976 by Fortress Press. Used with permission of Augsburgh Fortress, Minneapolis, Minn.

The Cost of Discipleship, by Dietrich Bonhoeffer. Reprinted with permission of Macmillan Publishing Company. Copyright 1959 by SCM Press, Ltd.

The Church's Year of Grace, by Pius Parsch. Copyright 1959 by The Order of St. Benedict, Inc. Published by The Liturgical Press, Collegeville, Minn. Used with permission.

The Cloud of Unknowing and the Book of Privy Counseling, ed. William Johnston. Copyright © 1973 by William Johnston. Reprinted by permission of Doubleday, a division of Bantam, Doubleday, Dell Publishing Group, Inc.

The Dialogue, by Catherine of Siena, ed. Suzanne Noffke OP. Copyright 1980 by Paulist Press. Used with permission of Paulist Press.

Prayers for Meditation, by Hugo and Karl Rahner. Copyright 1962 by Herder & Herder. Used with permission of The Crossroad Publishing Company, N.Y.

The Prayers of Catherine of Siena, ed. Suzanne Noffke OP. Copyright 1983 by Paulist Press. Used with permission of Paulist Press.

The Pulpit, January 1956, sermon by Reinhold Niebuhr. Used with permission of the Christian Century Foundation.

Purgation and Purgatory, by Catherine of Genoa, ed. Serge Hughes. Copyright 1979 by Paulist Press. Used with permission of Paulist Press.

Revelations of Divine Love, by Juliana of Norwich, ed. M. L. Del Mastro. Copyright © 1977 by M. L. Del Mastro. Reprinted by permission of Doubleday, a division of Bantam, Doubleday, Dell Publishing Group, Inc.

Sacred Signs, by Romano Guardini, tr. Melissa Kay. Copyright 1979 by Michael Glazier, Inc., 1935 West Fourth Street, Wilmington, Del. 19805. Published by permission.

Selected Writings, by N. F. S. Grundtvig, ed. Johannes Knudsen. Copyright 1976 by Fortress Press. Used with permission of Augsburg Fortress, Minneapolis, Minn.

Service Book of the Holy Orthodox—Catholic Apostolic Church, ed. Isabel Florence Hapgood. Copyright 1965 by Syrian Antiochian Orthodox Archdiocese of Brooklyn, N.Y.

The Soul's Journey into God, by Bonaventure, ed. Ewert Cousins. Copyright 1978 by Paulist Press. Used with permission of Paulist Press.

Springtime of the Liturgy, ed. Lucien Deiss, tr. Matthew H. O'Donnell. Copyright 1979 by The Order of St. Benedict, Inc. Published by The Liturgical Press, Collegeville, Minn. Used with permission.

Strength to Love, by Martin Luther King, Jr., Fortress Press. Copyright 1963 by Martin Luther King, Jr. Reprinted by permission of Joan Davis.

The Sunday Sermons of the Great Fathers, tr. and ed. M. F. Toal. Copyright 1958 by Henry Regnery. Used with permission of Regnery Gateway, Inc., Chicago, Ill.

Text for the memorial of St. Bridget from *The Roman Missal.* Copyright © 1973, International Committee on English in the Liturgy, Inc. All rights reserved. Used with permission.

Three Books About the Church, by Wilhelm Loehe, ed. James L Schaaf. Copyright 1969 by Fortress Press. Used with permission of Augsburg Fortress, Minneapolis, Minn.

To Dance with God, Gertrud Mueller Nelson. Copyright 1986 by Paulist Press. Used with permission of Paulist Press.

Visible Unity and Tradition, by Max Thurian, tr. W. J. Kerrigan. Copyright 1962 by Helicon, Baltimore, Md. Used with permission.

W. H. Auden: Collected Poems, ed. Edward Mendelson. Copyright © 1976 by

Edward Mendelson, William Meredith, and Monroe K. Spears, Executors of the Estate of W. H. Auden. Reprinted by permission of Random House, Inc.

The Waiting Father, by Helmut Thielicke, tr. John Doberstein. Copyright 1959. Used with permission of Harper & Row.

The Way to God According to the Rule of Saint Benedict, ed. Emmanuel Heufelder OSB. Copyright 1983 by Cistercian Publications, Kalamazoo, Mich. Used with permission.

Women and the Word: Sermons, ed. Helen Gray Crotwell. Copyright 1978 by Fortress Press. Used with permission of Augsburg Fortress, Minneapolis, Minn.

The Women Around Jesus, by Elisabeth Moltmann-Wendel. Copyright 1982. Used with permission of The Crossroad Publishing Company, N.Y.

Worship. Copyright 1987 by The Order of St. Benedict, Inc. Published by The Liturgical Press, Collegeville, Minn. Used with permission.

Biographical Notes

Address to Diognetus, 3rd century essay and 2nd century homily.
Aelred, 1109-67, Cistercian abbot of Rievaulx.
Ambrose, c. 339-97, bishop of Milan, hymnwriter, and preacher.
Amphilochius, c. 340-95, bishop of Iconium.
Anselm, c. 1033-1109, archbishop of Canterbury and theologian.
Auden, W. H., 1907-73, Anglican, British poet.
Augustine, 354-430, bishop of Hippo and theologian.

Baldwin, James, 1924-87, American author.
von Balthasar, Hans Urs, 1905-88, Swiss Roman Catholic theologian.
Barth, Karl, 1886-1968, Swiss Reformed theologian.
Basil, c. 330-79, bishop of Caesarea, Cappadocian theologian.
Beatrice of Nazareth, c. 1200-68, Flemish Cistercian mystic.
Bede, c. 673-735, English monk and historian.
Beecher, Lyman, 1775-1863, American Congregational preacher.
Benedict, c. 480-550, founder of Benedictine monasticism.
Bernard of Clairvaux, 1090-1153, abbot, founder of Cistercian
    monasticism.
blessing of the water from *Liber Ordinum*, 11th century manuscript.
Bonaventure, 1221-74, Franciscan theologian.
Bonhoeffer, Dietrich, 1906-45, German Lutheran pastor and martyr.
Book of Privy Counseling, 14th century Middle English spiritual classic.
Bridget of Sweden, c. 1303-73, founder of Bridgettine order.
Brown, Raymond E., b. 1928, American Roman Catholic biblical scholar.

Caesarius, c. 470-542, archbishop of Arles.
Calvin, John, 1509-64, French reformer and theologian.
Catherine of Genoa, 1447-1510, lay mystic.
Catherine of Siena, 1347?-80, lay mystic and reformer.
Chrysologos, Peter, c. 400-450, bishop of Ravenna.
Chrysostom, John, c. 347-407, bishop of Constantinople and preacher.
confession from Yom Kippur service.

Couch, Beatriz Melano, contemporary Argentine theologian.
Cyprian, d. 258, bishop of Carthage and martyr.
Cyril of Alexandria, d. 444, bishop and theologian.
Cyril of Jerusalem, c. 315-86, bishop.

Day, Dorothy, 1897-1980, American Roman Catholic lay political activist.
"Dayeinu," medieval chant used in Ashkenazi seder.
Didache, 1st century Syrian manual on church practice.
Didascalia of the Apostles, 3rd century Syrian manual on church practice.
Donne, John, 1572-1631, Anglican preacher, British poet.

Eckhart, Meister, c. 1260-1327, German Dominican mystic.
Elizabeth of Schoenau, 1129-65, Benedictine mystic.
Ephraem, c. 306-73, Syrian theologian and poet.
exorcism from Byzantine rite, 8th century manuscript.

First Clement, c. 95, pastoral letter.
Foley, Nadine, M., b. 1924, American Dominican.
Francis of Assisi, 1181-1226, founder of the Franciscan order.

Gaudentius, d. c. 410, bishop of Brescia.
Gertrude the Great, 1256-c. 1302, German mystic at the convent in
  Helfta.
Gregory of Nazianzus, 329-89, bishop, Cappadocian theologian.
Gregory of Nyssa, c. 330-54, bishop, Cappadocian theologian.
Gregory the Great, c. 540-604, bishop of Rome.
Grundtvig, N. F. S., 1783-1872, Danish Lutheran pastor and hymnwriter.
Guardini, Romano, 1885-1968, German Roman Catholic theologian.
Gutierrez, Gustavo, b. 1928, Peruvian Roman Catholic theologian.

Hadewijch of Brabant, 13th century, Flemish Beguine.
Hermas, 2nd century author of *The Shepherd*.
Hilary, c. 315-67, bishop of Poitiers.
Hildegard of Bingen, 1098-1179, Benedictine abbess of Rupertsberg
  and mystic.

Ignatius, c. 35-c. 107, bishop of Antioch and martyr.
inscription of Roman consignatorium, date unknown.
inscription of Lateran baptistry, 5th century.

Jerome, c. 342-420, biblical scholar and translator of Vulgate.
John of Damascus, c. 675-c. 749, Greek theologian and hymnwriter.
Julian of Norwich, c. 1342-after 1413, English anchorite and mystic.
Justin, c. 100-c. 165, Roman lay apologist and martyr.

Kempe, Margery, c. 1373-after 1433, English lay autobiographer.
à Kempis, Thomas, c. 1380-1471, Augustinian spiritual writer.
King, Martin Luther, Jr., 1929-68, American Baptist preacher and civil rights leader.

legend of the phoenix, ancient Egyptian myth.
Leo, d. 341, bishop of Rome.
Letter of Barnabas, 2nd century manual on church practice.
Little Flowers of St. Francis, legends about Francis of Assisi, compiled c. 1322.
Loehe, Wilhelm, 1808-72, Bavarian Lutheran pastor.
Luther, Martin, 1486-1546, Augustinian biblical scholar, founder of the German Reformation.

Massillon, Jean, 1663-1742, French Oratorian Preacher.
Maximus, c. 380-c. 470, bishop of Turin.
Mechthild of Magdeburg, c. 1210-c. 1280, German mystic and Beguine.
Melito, d. c. 190, bishop of Sardis.
Merton, Thomas, 1915-68, American Cistercian author.
Mollenkott, Virginia Ramey, b. 1932, American Episcopalian theologian.
Moltmann-Wendel, Elisabeth, b. 1926, German Reformed theologian.
More, Thomas, 1478-1535, Lord Chancellor of England and martyr.

Nelson, Gertrud Mueller, contemporary American Roman Catholic graphic artist.
Nicetas, d. c. 414, bishop of Remesiana.
Niebuhr, Reinhold, 1892-1971, American Evangelical theologian.
Niemoeller, Martin, 1892-1984, German Lutheran pastor.

O'Connor, Flannery, 1925-64, Roman Catholic, American author.
d'Oingt, Marguerite, d. 1310, French Carthusian prioress.
Origen, c. 185-c. 254, Alexandrian biblical exegete.
Parvey, Constance F., b. 1931, American Lutheran pastor.
Passion of Sts. Perpetua and Felicitas, c. 203, martyrdom account.

Perpetua, d. 203, African lay martyr.

prayers at contemporary Byzantine marriage rite.

Proclus, d. 446, patriarch of Constantinople.

Rahner, Hugo, 1900-68, Austrian Jesuit theologian.

Romanos, d. 556, Greek hymnwriter.

Ruether, Rosemary Radford, b. 1936, American Roman Catholic
   theologian.

Russell, Letty, b. 1929, American Presbyterian theologian.

Ruvsbroec, John, 1293-1381, Flemish Augustinian prior and mystic.

Schillebeeckx, Edward, b. 1914, Dutch Dominican theologian.

Schmemann, Alexander, 1921-83, American Russian Orthodox
   theologian.

Schutz, Roger, b. 1915, prior of the Reformed Taize Community.

Seton, Elizabeth, 1774-1821, founder of American Sisters of Charity.

Symeon, 949-1022, abbot at Constantinople and mystic.

Syncletica, 5th century, ascetic "Desert Mother."

Teresa of Avila, 1515-82, Spanish Carmelite mystic and reformer.

Teresa of Calcutta, b. 1910, founder of Missionaries of Charity.

Tertullian, c. 160-c. 220, African theologian.

Thérèse of Lisieux, 1873-97, French Carmelite autobiographer.

Thielicke, Helmut, 1908-86, German Lutheran theologian.

Thurian, Max, b. 1921, monk of Taize and theologian.

Tutu, Desmond Mpilo, b. 1931, Anglican archbishop of Cape Town,
   South Africa.

Umilta of Faenza, 1126-1310, Vallombrosan preacher and abbess in
   Tuscany.

Underhill, Evelyn, 1875-1941, British Anglican scholar.

de Vitry, Jacques, biographer and disciple of Marie d'Oignies, 1177-1213.

Wesley, John, 1703-91, British Anglican, founder of Methodist
   movement.

Whitefield, George, 1714-70, British Methodist evangelist.

Zeno, d. c. 375, bishop of Verona.

Index